REQUEST FORM

PRENTICE HALL

World Geography: Building A Global Perspective

COMPUTER TEST BANK

The Computer Test Bank with **Dial-A-Test®** is an easy-to-use software package that allows you to create customized assessment. You can request free customized tests by phone; they come with answers and recording sheets.

How to get your _FREE_ Computer Test Bank package:

1. Complete the information below and mail the postage-paid order form to the address indicated on the reverse side.

OR

2. FAX your request to 1-614-771-7365. If you wish to receive confirmation of your order, please include your fax number.

MAIL THIS CARD FREE   OR   FAX TO 1-614-771-7365

Please send me the following items:

√ *World Geography* CTB Software (Windows & Macintosh) . . . . (ISBN: 0-13-433196-6)

SHIP TO: (PLEASE PRINT CLEARLY)

School: _____

Attention: _____

School address: _____

City: _____ State: _____ Zip: _____

School Phone: (__ __ __) -__ __ __ - __ __ __ __

School Fax: (__ __ __) -__ __ __ - __ __ __ __   (Include fax number for confirmation.)

For office use:	CTS Code 133
Charge to Account HP124	

ATTN: Computer Test Banks

BUSINESS REPLY MAIL
FIRST-CLASS MAIL   PERMIT NO. 1009   COLUMBUS, OH

POSTAGE WILL BE PAID BY ADDRESSEE

PRENTICE HALL
SCHOOL DIVISION OF SIMON & SCHUSTER
4350 EQUITY DRIVE
P.O. BOX 2649
COLUMBUS OH 43272-4480

COMPUTER TEST BANK

PRENTICE HALL

World Geography
Building A Global Perspective

Code 133

Prentice Hall
Upper Saddle River, New Jersey
Needham, Massachusetts

COMPUTER TEST BANK

PRENTICE HALL
World Geography: Building A Global Perspective

Printed in the United States of America.

ISBN 0-13-433197-4

3 4 5 6 7 8 9 10   00 99 98

PRENTICE HALL
Simon & Schuster Education Group
A VIACOM COMPANY

Contents

About the Computer Test Bank

The *Computer Test Bank* for *World Geography: Building A Global Perspective* gives you unparalleled flexibility in creating tests. You can design tests to reflect your particular teaching emphasis. You can use the *Computer Test Bank* to create tests for different classes or to create alternative forms of the same test. You can also create tests for one chapter or for any combination of chapters, as well as for unit, midterm, and final examinations.

QUESTION ORGANIZATION

The *Computer Test Bank* provides printed test questions for all 34 chapters and 10 units, including:
- multiple choice
- matching
- fill-ins
- completion
- graphic study
- short answer / essay

AVAILABLE IN BOTH WINDOWS AND MACINTOSH FORMATS

You may order your easy-to-use software for the *Computer Test Bank* for *World Geography: Building A Global Perspective* in either Windows or Macintosh format. Just complete the order form in the front of the booklet and mail the postage-paid order form to Prentice Hall or fax. You will receive your disks together with complete installation and operating instructions in just a few weeks. For more information, contact your Prentice Hall Sales Representative or call 1-800-848-9500.

FLEXIBLE TEST-MAKING

The *Computer Test Bank* for *World Geography: Building A Global Perspective* allows you to create tests easily and conveniently. You can select or add exactly the questions you want for each test. You can design tests for students of different ability levels, or you can select or add questions based on content you emphasized in class. You can use the *Computer Test Bank* to create different tests for different classes or alternate versions of the same test. The *Computer Test Bank* also allows you to tailor tests to meet your state and local course requirements and to build the appropriate content, skills, and critical thinking into your testing program. And there is no need to cut and paste the map, graph, or chart that students need to answer a test item. When you select a test item linked to an illustration, the Computer Test Bank will automatically print the illustration along with the question.

HELP IS JUST A TELEPHONE CALL AWAY

Stuck at any point? Simply call our toll-free HELP hotline (1-800-237-7136) for continuous and reliable support.

About the Prentice Hall Dial-A-Test® Service

If you do not have access to a computer or would like the convenience of designing your own tests without typing a word, you may want to take advantage of our free Dial-A-Test® Service. Available to all users of *World Geography: Building A Global Perspective*, Dial-A-Test® is simple to use. At the right is an example of a filled-out form.

HERE'S HOW IT WORKS

1. **Choose the questions you want** from the ready-made Chapter Test Questions.

2. **Enter the numbers of the questions** in the order you want on a Dial-A-Test® Order Form (see page viii for a master that you may photocopy). Be sure to include the chapter number on the form. For example, in the case of test question 17, taken from Chapter 1, mark the order form with the designation 1,17.

3. **Use a separate Dial-A-Test® order form** for each original test you request. You may use one form, however, to order multiple versions of the same original test.

4. **If you would like another version** of your original test with the questions scrambled, or put in another sequence, simply check the box labeled *Scramble Questions* on the order form. If you would like more than one scrambled version of your original test, note this on your order form or inform the Dial-A-Test® operator. Please note that Prentice Hall reserves the right to limit the number of tests and versions you can request at any one time, especially during the busier times of the year when midterms and finals are given.

5. **Choose the method** by which you would like to order your original test and/or multiple versions of your original test. To order by telephone, call toll free 1-800-468-8378 between 9:00 A.M. and 4:30 P.M. Eastern Standard Time and read the test question numbers to our Dial-A-Test® operator. Use the Dial-A-Test® Code 133 for *World Geography: Building A Global Perspective*. To order by mail, send your completed Dial-A-Test® order form to the address listed below. Now you may also FAX your order to 1-614-771-7365.

6. **You may order** up to 100 questions per test by telephone on our toll-free 800 number or up to 200 questions per test by mail.

7. **Please allow a minimum of two weeks** for shipping, especially if you are ordering by mail. Although we process your order within 48 hours of your call or the receipt of your form by mail, mailing may take up to two weeks. Thus we ask you to plan accordingly and expect to receive your original test, any alternate test versions that you requested, and complete answer keys within a reasonable amount of time.

8. **Tests are available all year.** You can order tests before the school year begins, during vacation, or as you need them.

9. **For additional order forms** or to ask questions regarding this service, please write to the following address:

Dial-A-Test®
Prentice Hall School Division
4350 Equity Drive
Columbus, OH 43228

-ORDER FORM-
CTS

DIAL-A-TEST®
PRENTICE HALL SCHOOL DIVISION
CUSTOMIZED TESTING SERVICE
TOLL-FREE NUMBER 800-468-8378 (H O-T-T-E-S-T)

-ORDER FORM-
CTS

You may **call** the PH Dial-A-Test® toll-free number during our business hours (9:00 a.m.-4:30 p.m. EST).
Now you may also FAX your order to 1-614-771-7365 anytime.

DIAL-A-TEST®
PRENTICE HALL SCHOOL DIVISION
4350 EQUITY DRIVE
COLUMBUS, OH 43228

FOR PH USE		DATE REC.	DATE SENT
_ PHONE __ MAIL __ FAX		_____	_____

EXACT TEXT TITLE/VOL. _World Geography: Building A Global Perspective_ © DATE _1998_
CODE _133_

CUSTOMER INFORMATION
NAME _____ Ellen Mack _____
SCHOOL _____ Riverside High School _____
ADDRESS _____ 700 River Road _____
CITY _Wells River_ STATE _TN_ ZIP _38578_
PHONE _208-555-2717_ EXT. _34_

DATE BY WHICH TEST IS NEEDED _11/30/97_

TEST USAGE (CHECK ONE)
_ SAMPLE _ QUIZ X CHAPTER TEST
_ UNIT TEST _ SEMESTER TEST _ FINAL EXAM

VERSIONS (SEE REVERSE-INSTR. #4)
(CHECK ONE)
_ 1. ORIGINAL _ 2. SCRAMBLE QUESTIONS

TEST IDENTIFICATION (This information will appear at the top of your test.)

	EXAMPLE:	
Ellen Mack		_Ellen Mack_
World Geography, Period 2		_World Geography, Period 5_
Chapter 1, Test		_Chapter Test_

#		#		#		#		#		#		#		#	
1	_1,3_	26	_1,74_	51		76		101		126		151		176	
2	_1,5_	27	_1,80_	52		77		102		127		152		177	
3	_1,6_	28	_1,81_	53		78		103		128		153		178	
4	_1,9_	29	_1,82_	54		79		104		129		154		179	
5	_1,11_	30	_1,83_	55		80		105		130		155		180	
6	_1,12_	31		56		81		106		131		156		181	
7	_1,14_	32		57		82		107		132		157		182	
8	_1,17_	33		58		83		108		133		158		183	
9	_1,18_	34		59		84		109		134		159		184	
10	_1,21_	35		60		85		110		135		160		185	
11	_1,32_	36		61		86		111		136		161		186	
12	_1,34_	37		62		87		112		137		162		187	
13	_1,35_	38		63		88		113		138		163		188	
14	_1,38_	39		64		89		114		139		164		189	
15	_1,40_	40		65		90		115		140		165		190	
16	_1,41_	41		66		91		116		141		166		191	
17	_1,45_	42		67		92		117		142		167		192	
18	_1,47_	43		68		93		118		143		168		193	
19	_1,55_	44		69		94		119		144		169		194	
20	_1,57_	45		70		95		120		145		170		195	
21	_1,66_	46		71		96		121		146		171		196	
22	_1,67_	47		72		97		122		147		172		197	
23	_1,69_	48		73		98		123		148		173		198	
24	_1,70_	49		74		99		124		149		174		199	
25	_1,71_	50		75		100		125		150		175		200	

DIAL-A-TEST®
PRENTICE HALL SCHOOL DIVISION
CUSTOMIZED TESTING SERVICE
TOLL-FREE NUMBER 800-468-8378 (H O-T-T-E-S-T)

You may **call** the PH Dial-A-Test® toll-free number during our business hours (9:00 A.M.-4:30 P.M. EST).
Now you may also FAX your order to 1-614-771-7365 anytime.

DIAL-A-TEST®
PRENTICE HALL SCHOOL DIVISION
4350 EQUITY DRIVE
COLUMBUS, OH 43228

FOR PH USE   DATE REC.   DATE SENT

__ PHONE __ MAIL __ FAX _____   _____

EXACT TEXT TITLE/VOL. World Geography: Building A Global Perspective © **DATE** 1998
CODE 133

CUSTOMER INFORMATION
NAME _____
SCHOOL _____
ADDRESS _____
CITY _____STATE ____ ZIP _____
PHONE _____ EXT. _____

DATE BY WHICH TEST IS NEEDED _____

TEST USAGE (CHECK ONE)

__ SAMPLE   __ QUIZ   __ CHAPTER TEST
__ UNIT TEST   __ SEMESTER TEST   __ FINAL EXAM

VERSIONS (SEE REVERSE-INSTRUCTION. #4)
(CHECK ONE)

__ 1. ORIGINAL   __ 2. SCRAMBLE QUESTIONS

TEST IDENTIFICATION (This information will appear at the top of your test.)

EXAMPLE: Mr. Hernandez
_____   World Geography, Period 5
_____   Chapter Test
_____
_____

1 ____	26 ____	51 ____	76 ____	101 ____	126 ____	151 ____	176 ____
2 ____	27 ____	52 ____	77 ____	102 ____	127 ____	152 ____	177 ____
3 ____	28 ____	53 ____	78 ____	103 ____	128 ____	153 ____	178 ____
4 ____	29 ____	54 ____	79 ____	104 ____	129 ____	154 ____	179 ____
5 ____	30 ____	55 ____	80 ____	105 ____	130 ____	155 ____	180 ____
6 ____	31 ____	56 ____	81 ____	106 ____	131 ____	156 ____	181 ____
7 ____	32 ____	57 ____	82 ____	107 ____	132 ____	157 ____	182 ____
8 ____	33 ____	58 ____	83 ____	108 ____	133 ____	158 ____	183 ____
9 ____	34 ____	59 ____	84 ____	109 ____	134 ____	159 ____	184 ____
10 ____	35 ____	60 ____	85 ____	110 ____	135 ____	160 ____	185 ____
11 ____	36 ____	61 ____	86 ____	111 ____	136 ____	161 ____	186 ____
12 ____	37 ____	62 ____	87 ____	112 ____	137 ____	162 ____	187 ____
13 ____	38 ____	63 ____	88 ____	113 ____	138 ____	163 ____	188 ____
14 ____	39 ____	64 ____	89 ____	114 ____	139 ____	164 ____	189 ____
15 ____	40 ____	65 ____	90 ____	115 ____	140 ____	165 ____	190 ____
16 ____	41 ____	66 ____	91 ____	116 ____	141 ____	166 ____	191 ____
17 ____	42 ____	67 ____	92 ____	117 ____	142 ____	167 ____	192 ____
18 ____	43 ____	68 ____	93 ____	118 ____	143 ____	168 ____	193 ____
19 ____	44 ____	69 ____	94 ____	119 ____	144 ____	169 ____	194 ____
20 ____	45 ____	70 ____	95 ____	120 ____	145 ____	170 ____	195 ____
21 ____	46 ____	71 ____	96 ____	121 ____	146 ____	171 ____	196 ____
22 ____	47 ____	72 ____	97 ____	122 ____	147 ____	172 ____	197 ____
23 ____	48 ____	73 ____	98 ____	123 ____	148 ____	173 ____	198 ____
24 ____	49 ____	74 ____	99 ____	124 ____	149 ____	174 ____	199 ____
25 ____	50 ____	75 ____	100 ____	125 ____	150 ____	175 ____	200 ____

Chapter 1   Exploring Geography

COMPLETION

A. Vocabulary
Directions: Complete each sentence by underlining the correct term in parentheses.

1. A (formal, functional) region includes one central place and the surrounding areas affected by it.

2. The (Equator, Prime Meridian) is the 0° line of longitude that runs through Greenwich, England.

3. The thick rock layer around the earth's core is the (mantle, crust).

4. Imaginary lines used to measure distance north and south of the Equator are lines of (latitude, longitude).

5. Many caves are formed by (mechanical, chemical) weathering.

6. Half of the globe is called a (hemisphere, great circle).

7. The theory of (plate tectonics, mechanical weathering) says that the earth's outer shell is not solid rock.

8. (Geography, Geology) is the study of where people, places, and things are located, the ways that different things relate to each other at specific places, and the ways that places connect with each other.

9. The (absolute, relative) location of Chicago is 42°N, 88°W.

10. Rock layers that bend and buckle are called (folds, faults).

11. The (absolute, relative) locations on the earth can change.

12. Windblown deposits of mineral-rich dust and silt are called (loess, lava).

13. Lines of (latitude, longitude) are the imaginary lines that run from the North Pole to the South Pole.

14. Acid rain is a kind of (chemical, mechanical) weathering.

15. The (Equator, Prime Meridian) is an imaginary line that circles the globe halfway between the North Pole and the South Pole.

16. The (core, crust) is the outer layer of the earth that has a rocky surface.

17. The (Equator, Prime Meridian) is an imaginary line that runs from the North Pole to the South Pole and passes through Greenwich, England.

18. A (fault, fold) is a break in the earth's crust.

19. (Convection, Volcanism) is the process that most scientists hold responsible for the movements of the earth's plates.

20. When vacationers describe the people, customs, and native dishes of a particular place, they are describing the (physical characteristics, human characteristics) of a place.

MULTIPLE CHOICE

B. Key Geographic Concepts and Skills
Directions: Write the letter of the correct ending in the blank.

21. _____ The physical characteristics of a place include its
a. customs and traditions.
b. growth patterns.
c. landforms and vegetation.
d. systems of government.

22. _____ The movement about which geographers talk usually refers to
a. environmental changes.
b. people, goods, and ideas.
c. relative locations of places on the earth.
d. birth and death rates and family size.

23. _____ The customs, politics, and foods that make a place unique are called its
a. natural features.
b. human characteristics.
c. political characteristics.
d. human-environmental interactions.

24. _____ A region can be defined as
a. a group of places drained by a particular river.
b. a group of places that have similar landform patterns.
c. a group of places ruled by the same government.
d. all of the above.

25. _____ An internal force that helps create new landforms is
a. mechanical weathering.   b. glacial movement.
c. volcanism.   d. wind erosion.

26. _____ Landforms are commonly classified according to differences in
a. weathering.   b. location.
c. geological age.   d. relief.

27. _____ The largest canyons and deepest valleys were created by
a. moving water.   b. chemical weathering.
c. wind erosion.   d. plate tectonics.

28. _____ The force that probably propels the movement of the earth's gigantic rock plates is
a. weathering.   b. frontal precipitation.
c. convection.   d. continental drift.

29. _____ When geographers observe moraines—ridgelike piles of rock and debris—they conclude that
a. a volcano erupted there.
b. a glacier once covered the area.
c. a fault lies nearby.
d. chemical weathering has occurred.

30. _____ The building of dams and canals to irrigate desert regions is an example of the geographic theme of
a. place.
b. location.
c. region.
d. human-environment interaction.

31. _____ The five themes of geography
a. are human-environment interaction, physical characteristics, human characteristics, absolute location, and relative location.
b. form the core of geographic inquiry.
c. relate to absolute and relative location.
d. are based on hypotheses and scientific method.

32. _____ Longitude is measured in degrees east or west of the
a. Prime Meridian.
b. Equator.
c. Tropic of Cancer.
d. Tropic of Capricorn.

33. _____ The dense smog that blankets many cities today is
a. a result of human-environment interaction.
b. a process that shapes the earth's surface.
c. a human characteristic that makes these cities unique.
d. determined by the absolute and relative locations of these cities.

34. _____ Similar climates, vegetation, or landforms can be used to divide the earth into
a. political regions.
b. formal regions.
c. functional regions.
d. census regions.

35. _____ Glaciers that melted and receded sometimes left behind moraine
which are
a. areas of molten rock.
b. ridgelike piles of rocks and debris.
c. breaks in the earth's crust.
d. deep cracks in rocks and soil.

36. _____ The theory of plate tectonics affirms that
a. the earth's outer shell is one solid piece of rock.
b. the basic arrangement of oceans and continents is unchanging.
c. large moving slabs of rock slide slowly over a layer of the mantl
d. the landscape of the ocean is the same as that on earth.

37. _____ The most common type of mechanical weathering takes place when
a. carbon dioxide from the soil combines with water.
b. caves are formed from the action of carbonic acid.
c. rock and soil are moved to another place.
d. frozen water causes frost wedging.

38. _____ The greatest agent of erosion is
a. wind.   b. sediment.
c. running water.   d. acid rain.

39. _____ The circle of volcanoes surrounding the Pacific Ocean is calle
the
a. Ring of Fire.   b. San Andreas Fault.
c. Pacific Plate.   d. Equator.

40. _____ The spread of Christianity throughout Europe best reflects the
geographic theme of
a. location.   b. place.
c. region.   d. movement.

GRAPHIC STUDY

Directions: Use the maps below to answer the following questions. Write
your answers on the lines provided.

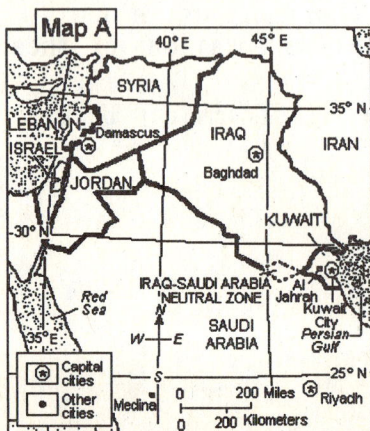

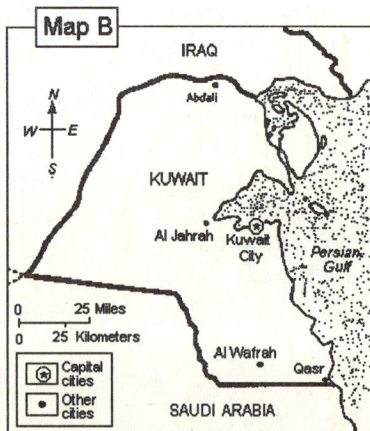

41. Which map shows a greater land area?

_____

42. What are two reference points that appear on both maps?

_____

43. Which map would you use to get a more exact measurement of the distance from Kuwait City to Al Jahrah? Why?

_____

44. What country and body of water appear on both maps?

_____

45. What places labeled on Map B are not labeled on Map A? Why are these places not labeled on Map A?

_____

46. On which map would it be easier to determine the approximate distance across Kuwait from east to west? Why?

_____

SHORT ANSWER

C. Critical Thinking
Directions: Answer the following questions on the back of this paper or on a separate sheet of paper.

47. Drawing Conclusions Explain in what ways the study of geography will help you to better understand the world around you.

48. Identifying Assumptions Identify the assumptions that one geographer was making when he wrote the following: "There . . . are few problems that . . are not in some way geographical."

49. Making Inferences What three factors cause acid rain? What can people do to reduce the problem?

50. Determining Relevance What are three reasons that the study of geography is important to the understanding of current events?

51. Drawing Conclusions If the earth cooled to another ice age, what would happen to coastal cities? Explain why.

52. Formulating Questions What questions might you ask about a place to learn what makes that place unique? List at least four questions.

Answer Key   Chapter 1

COMPLETION

1. functional

2. Prime Meridian

3. mantle   4. latitude

5. chemical   6. hemisphere

7. plate tectonics

8. geography   9. absolute

10. folds   11. relative

12. loess   13. longitude

14. chemical   15. Equator

16. crust   17. Prime Meridian

18. fault   19. convection

20. human characteristics

MULTIPLE CHOICE

21. c   22. b

23. b   24. d

25. c   26. d

27. a   28. c

29. b   30. d

31. b   32. a

33. a   34. b

35. b   36. c

37. d   38. c

39. a   40. d

GRAPHIC STUDY

41. Map A

42. Al Jahrah, Kuwait City, the Persian Gulf

43. Map B. The scale stands for a far smaller distance than does the scale on Map A. Therefore, the distance between two places is more accurately represented on Map B.

44. Kuwait, the Persian Gulf

45. Abdali, Al Wafrah, and Qasr. Because the country of Kuwait is smaller in scale on Map A, there is no room to label all the cities shown on Map B.

46. Map B. Kuwait appears larger on Map B than on Map A because of the different map scales.

SHORT ANSWER

47. The study of geography will help me compare the physical and human features of world regions and better understand how people are affected by their environment and how they in turn affect the environment. It will also help me understand the connections between different places.

48. The geographer was assuming that most problems people have relate to the earth, its people, and the connections between and among them, and can, thus, be linked to one or more of the five themes of geography.

49. Causes are industrial pollution, acid-producing agents in the ocean, and volcanic activity. Humans can reduce acid rain by cutting levels of pollution.

50. The study of geography can help people understand the connections between different places; the background of religious, ethnic, and political conflicts; and the environmental consequences of human activities.

51. In a new ice age, the world's sea levels would lower as more water became trapped in glaciers. Coastal cities would no longer be coastal.

52. What natural resources does this place possess? What are its predominant physical features? What are the ethnic origins of the population? How has the location of this place affected its development?

Chapter 2   Climate and Vegetation

COMPLETION

A. Vocabulary
Directions: Complete each sentence by underlining the correct term in parentheses.

1. Trees that shed their leaves when winter approaches are (deciduous, coniferous).

2. The land in a rain shadow is located on the (leeward, windward) side of a mountain.

3. (Climate, Weather) refers to an area's temperature and level of precipitation over a long period of time.

4. Permafrost is found in a (tundra, savanna) region.

5. The spring and fall (solstices, equinoxes) mark the days when the sun appears directly overhead at the Equator.

6. The mix of interdependent plants that naturally grows in a place is called (a plant community, natural vegetation).

7. The earth's spinning on its axis is called (rotation, revolution).

8. The physical conditions of natural surroundings are a(n) (environment, biome).

9. Tropical grasslands are called (prairies, savannas).

10. (Prairies, Savannas) are temperate grasslands.

11. (Convectional, Orographic) precipitation is common near the Equator.

12. Areas with (continental, Mediterranean) climates have cold, snowy winters and long, hot summers.

13. Tropical grasslands are called (prairies, savannas).

14. The process by which the sun's heat is distributed throughout the world is (convection, precipitation).

15. (Deciduous, Coniferous) trees lose their leaves during one season.

16. (Deciduous, Coniferous) trees carry their seeds in cones.

17. Temperature and precipitation over a long period of time help to determine an area's (climate, weather).

18. The earth completes one (revolution, rotation) in approximately 24 hours.

19. Low, scrubby trees that grow in Mediterranean climates mark (chaparra tundra).

20. The water that falls to earth from the atmosphere is called (humidity precipitation).

21. Day and night are nearly the same length at a(n) (solstice, equinox).

22. The typical plant life of a region is its (environment, natural vegetation).

23. Temperatures are always cold in (tundra, biome) regions.

24. The (leeward, windward) slopes of mountains are those on the opposite side from the rain shadow.

MULTIPLE CHOICE

B. Key Geographic Concepts and Skills
Directions: Write the letter of the correct ending in the blank.

25. _____ Regions of light winds near the Equator are called
   a. the horse latitudes.
   b. the doldrums.
   c. the trade winds.
   d. the Coriolis effect.

26. _____ The process that transfers heat from wind or water from one pla to another is called
   a. revolution.
   b. convection.
   c. permafrost.
   d. orographic precipitation.

27. _____ Small evergreens and low, scrubby vegetation grow in
   a. chaparrals.   b. tropical grasslands.
   c. rain forests.   d. tundra.

28. _____ The climate of Mount Kilimanjaro demonstrates the effect of
   a. wind patterns on climate.   b. latitude on climate.
   c. rainfall on climate.   d. elevation on climate.

29. _____ The most common type of precipitation is
   a. orographic.   b. dew.
   c. frontal.   d. convectional.

30. _____ Climate regions are classified mainly on the basis of
a. distance from the Equator.
b. elevation.
c. seasonal temperatures and precipitation.
d. rainfall and location.

31. _____ Winds and ocean currents do not move in straight lines because of
a. the Coriolis effect.   b. orographic precipitation.
c. the greenhouse effect.   d. the process of convection.

32. _____ Most geographers accept the division of world climate regions into
a. three latitude zones.
b. six broad climate regions.
c. three precipitation regions.
d. basically two temperature regions.

33. _____ All of the following statements are correct except:
a. Ocean waters and winds help to distribute the sun's heat.
b. Precipitation depends on air temperature and winds.
c. Coastal areas usually have milder climates than do areas at the same latitude inland.
d. Most areas with continental climates have a mild, humid climate all year long.

34. _____ All of the following statements are correct except:
a. The plants in a plant community depend upon one another for shade, support, and food.
b. The same types of plants grow in similar environments around the world.
c. The plants and animals in a biome frequently are not suited to one another.
d. Climate, sunlight, temperature, precipitation, elevation, soil, and landforms make up the plant environment.

35. _____ Broadleaf deciduous forests grow best in regions with a
a. temperate climate and adequate rainfall.
b. Mediterranean climate.
c. tropical climate and heavy seasonal rainfall.
d. cool and dry climate.

36. _____ The central regions of several continents are covered by
a. forests.   b. deserts.
c. grasslands.   d. tundra.

37. _____ Climate depends on such factors as an area's
a. elevation and longitude.   b. latitude and solstice.
c. elevation and latitude.   d. elevation and equinox.

38. _____ All of the following statements are true except:
    a. Winds around the Equator are light.
    b. Winds at about 30° North and South are heavy.
    c. The trade winds blow steadily toward the Equator.
    d. Wind direction is affected by the earth's rotation.

39. _____ In a humid continental climate region, you would find plants and animals adapted to
    a. hot summers and winters.
    b. mild summers and winters.
    c. warm summers and cold winters.
    d. hot summers and cold winters.

40. _____ Dry seasons of natural wildfires are common to
    a. prairies.   b. tundras.
    c. chaparrals.   d. savannas.

41. _____ The type of precipitation common on seacoasts is
    a. orographic.   b. convectional.
    c. snow.   d. dew.

42. _____ Hot summers and cool winters mark the
    a. Mediterranean climate.   b. arid climate.
    c. subarctic climate.   d. highland climate.

43. The six climate regions into which geographers have divided the earth were defined mainly by
    a. latitude and elevation.
    b. temperature and precipitation.
    c. atmospheric pressure.
    d. location and landforms.

44. _____ The countries of Western Europe have a mild marine climate because they are located
    a. in low latitudes.   b. near the Atlantic Ocean.
    c. in highland areas.   d. in a rain shadow.

45. _____ All of the following statements are true except:
    a. The greenhouse effect assures that all places on earth get roughly the same heat and light from the sun.
    b. Much of the United States has a continental climate.
    c. Human actions are causing the climate to change.
    d. Whether precipitation falls as rain, snow, sleet, or hail depends air temperature and wind conditions.

46. _____ Because of warm temperatures and plentiful rainfall, the natural vegetation in areas nearest to the Equator consists of
    a. an abundance of chaparral plants.
    b. thick tropical rain forests.
    c. relatively few plants.
    d. evergreen trees and low bushes.

47. _____ The vegetation within a vegetation region
    a. is determined primarily by climate and soil.
    b. seldom remains unchanged for many years.
    c. is not suited to the animal life in the region.
    d. is determined primarily by landforms and longitude.

48. _____ Both warm air and warm water flow generally
    a. from the Equator to the poles.
    b. from the poles toward the Equator.
    c. straight because of the Coriolis effect.
    d. from high-pressure areas to low-pressure areas.

GRAPHIC STUDY

Directions: Use the three climate graphs below to answer the following
questions. Write your answers on the lines provided.

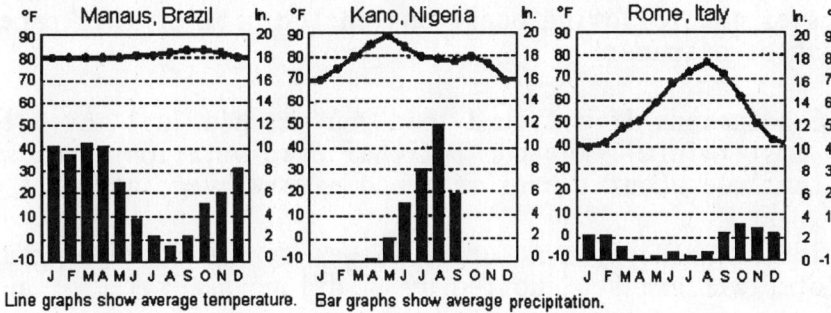

Line graphs show average temperature.   Bar graphs show average precipitation.

49. In which month does Kano, Nigeria, receive the most rainfall?

   _____

50. How do the average August temperatures in all three cities compare?

   _____

51. How would you describe the year-round temperatures in Manaus, Brazil?

   _____

52. How would you describe Rome's climate?

   _____

53. (a) In which month does Manaus, Brazil, receive the most rainfall?
    (b) About how many inches of rain fall during that month?

   _____

54. (a) In which city is precipitation most even throughout the year?
(b) Which city shows the greatest annual variation of average temperatures?

_____

55. What are the three coolest months in Rome?

_____

56. How would you describe the climate of Kano, Nigeria?

_____

SHORT ANSWER

C. Critical Thinking
Directions: Answer the following questions on the back of this paper or on a separate sheet of paper.

57. Drawing Conclusions If a friend told you she had just moved to a regi in which most rainfall was convectional precipitation, what would you able to conclude about the climate and natural vegetation of the regi

58. Distinguishing False from Accurate Images Is the image of grasslands regions of "tall grasses" dotted by wildflowers a false or an accurat image? Give reasons to support your answer.

59. Perceiving Cause-and-Effect Relationships If the earth began rotating the opposite direction, how would the prevailing winds in each latitu zone be affected?

60. Synthesizing Information The terms doldrums, horse latitudes, and tra winds are used to identify certain portions of the earth. Explain how each nickname is appropriate for the area it designates.

61. Predicting Consequences Some scientists believe that the greenhouse effect is increasing. What consequences would such an increase have f climate and vegetation?

62. Checking Consistency Explain how you would prove this statement: Plan grow everywhere on earth.

Answer Key   Chapter 2

COMPLETION

1. deciduous

2. leeward   3. climate

4. tundra   5. equinoxes

6. a plant community

7. rotation   8. environment

9. savannas   10. prairies

11. convectional

12. continental

13. savannas   14. convection

15. deciduous

16. coniferous

17. climate   18. rotation

19. chaparrals

20. precipitation

21. equinox   22. natural vegetation

23. tundra   24. windward

MULTIPLE CHOICE

25. b   26. b

27. a   28. d

29. c   30. c

31. a   32. b

33. d   34. c

35. a   36. c

37. c	38. b
39. c	40. d
41. a	42. a
43. b	44. b
45. a	46. b
47. a	48. a

GRAPHIC STUDY

49. August

50. They are all approximately 80°F.

51. They average about 80°F.

52. Possible answer: Temperatures in Rome show pronounced seasonal variations. Rainfall is moderate all year, although it is heavier in fall and winter than in spring and summer.

53. (a) March
    (b) about 10.5 inches

54. (a) Rome
    (b) Rome

55. December, January, and February

56. Kano is warm all year long, with temperatures ranging from approximately 70°F to 90°F. Summers are wet and winters are dry.

SHORT ANSWER

57. Since convectional precipitation is common near the Equator and in the tropics, I would conclude that the climate was tropical and that natural vegetation of the region would be that of the rain forest.

58. Inaccurate. Different kinds of grassland regions contain grasses of different lengths and kinds, depending on rainfall and soil. The characteristics of a grassland are also influenced by latitude. The low-latitude zones of year-round warm temperatures produce huge tropical grasslands, or savannas, dotted with trees that can survive the dry season. In temperate zones with cool and dry climates, the grasses are shorter; in general, the less rainfall an area receives, the shorter and sparser are the grasses. In many of the cool, temperate grasslands, trees and shrubs grow along rivers and streams.

59. In the Northern Hemisphere, the Coriolis effect "curves" the normal paths that winds take between the Equator and the poles to the right; in the Southern Hemisphere, the Coriolis effect causes winds to curve to the left. If the direction of rotation were reversed, the Coriolis effect would be reversed. This would mean, for example, that the "prevailing westerlies" that dominate the middle latitudes of the Northern Hemisphere would blow from the east as the "prevailing easterlies."

60. The term doldrums, meaning "slow and dull," was applied in the days of sailing ships to the low-pressure area near the Equator that has very light winds. The so-called horse latitudes are the high-pressure regions of light and unpredictable winds at about 30° North and South latitude. The nickname supposedly originated with Spanish sailors who threw their horses overboard in order to make their ships lighter and, thus, faster. The term trade winds was first used to describe the "northeast trades" that blow from the horse latitudes toward the Equator. Because these winds were dependable, they were useful to merchant trading ships.

61. As the greenhouse effect increased, the
atmosphere would slowly warm, melting the
polar ice caps, raising water levels, and
flooding low-lying areas all over the world.
In turn, climates would generally get warmer
and wetter. The pattern of ocean currents
and probably of prevailing winds would change,
affecting temperatures and precipitation
patterns. This would in turn create major
changes in vegetation patterns and regions.

62. I would research the areas of the world that
are remote and inhospitable to life, such as
polar and tundra regions. Even in these regions
considered to be bare of vegetation I would
find scattered small and simple plants.
Similarly, above the tree line in highland
regions I would encounter little shrubs and
wildflowers growing in sheltered spots and
lichens on rocks.

Chapter 3   Population and Culture

MATCHING

A. Vocabulary
Directions: Match the definitions with the terms. Write the correct
letter in each blank. You will not use all the terms.

a. authoritarian government
b. demography
c. communism
d. acculturation
e. democracy
f. culture hearth
g. socialism
h. capitalist system
i. immigrant
j. urbanization
k. death rate
l. birthrate
m. federal system
n. sovereignty
o. diffusion
p. confederation
q. population density

1. _____ study of human populations

2. _____ number of deaths per year per 1,000 people

3. _____ a country's freedom from outside control

4. _____ growth of city populations

5. _____ process by which cultural traits move from one culture to another

6. _____ area where cultural ideas begin and from which they spread

7. _____ average number of people in a square mile or a square kilometer

8. _____ political system in which power is shared by the national
government and smaller political units

9. _____ type of government in which the leaders hold most of the political
power

10. _____ economic system in which decisions to buy and sell are made in a
free market

11. _____ type of government in which the people choose their leaders and
determine government policy

12. _____ person who moves into a country

13. _____ number of live births each year per 1,000 people

Directions: Match the definitions with the terms. Write the correct letter in each blank. You will not use all the terms.

a. diffusion
b. socialism
c. population density
d. constitutional monarchy
e. communism
f. unitary system
g. dictatorship
h. democracy
i. capitalism
j. acculturation
k. demography
l. monarchy
m. cultural hearth
n. confederation
o. sovereignty
p. totalitarianism
q. federal system

14. _____ the average number of people living in a given area

15. _____ authoritarian government in which people inherit their position

16. _____ place where important ideas began

17. _____ type of government in which rulers often gain and keep power by military force

18. _____ process of adapting traits from other cultures

19. _____ political system in which a central government makes laws for entire nation

20. _____ type of government in which smaller political units hold nearly all the power

21. _____ economic system based on the state making all economic decisions

22. _____ type of government in which a ruler plays a symbolic role and elected lawmaking body holds the political power

23. _____ economic system in which means of production and distribution privately owned and operated for profit

24. _____ economic system in which the free market and the government jointly make decisions

25. _____ a country's freedom from outside control

26. _____ extreme type of government in which rulers control every part of society and aspect of a person's life

MULTIPLE CHOICE

B. Key Geographic Concepts and Skills
Directions: Write the letter of the correct answer in the blank.

27. _____ Which of the following has been responsible for the declining death rate in many of the world's less industrialized nations?
   a. a declining birthrate
   b. migration to rural areas, where living conditions are better
   c. absence of diseases prevalent in industrialized nations
   d. improved health

28. _____ Where do most people in Europe and the United States live?
   a. Both Europeans and Americans live mainly in urban areas.
   b. Europeans live on farms, while most Americans live in cities.
   c. The populations in both Europe and the United States are spread evenly throughout the two regions.
   d. Most people in Europe and the United States live in the west, where climates are milder.

29. _____ Which of the following are part of a country's nonmaterial culture?
   a. arts and technology
   b. religion and language
   c. styles of food and clothing
   d. food and architecture

30. _____ What would you expect to find in a country with zero population growth?
   a. a high birthrate and a low death rate
   b. more or less equal birth and death rates
   c. a low birthrate and a high death rate
   d. low birth and death rates

31. _____ In which region did the cultures of Teotihuacán and the Maya form the first culture hearth?
   a. the Americas
   b. Europe
   c. Africa
   d. China

32. _____ What region was the culture hearth for most of East Asia?
a. the United States
b. modern Japan
c. Teotihuacán
d. ancient China

33. _____ What kind of government structure do Japan and Great Britain ha
a. confederation   b. federal
c. unitary   d. republic

34. _____ Which of the following statements refers to a mixed economy?
a. Industry and agriculture are both important to the economy.
b. All decisions to buy and sell are made in a free market.
c. Government owns and operates all major farms and factories.
d. Free market and government jointly make economic decisions.

35. _____ Which of the following statements describes the general trend i
world population since 1950?
a. World population has grown slowly over the past 50 years.
b. There are fewer people in the world today than there were before
1950.
c. Most countries have reached zero population growth since 1950.
d. World population has grown rapidly since 1950.

36. _____ Why are people unevenly distributed throughout the world?
a. People prefer to live in warm areas near the Equator.
b. People tend to cluster in places that have rich soil, fresh water,
and mild climates.
c. Most people live in regions that have coal and iron ore deposits.
d. People generally live in cultural regions that value individual
achievement.

37. _____ How do people survive living in harsh environments such as the
desert?
a. by adapting and making changes to their environments
b. by moving to more hospitable areas
c. by not altering the natural landscape of their environments
d. none of the above

38. _____ Which of the following is not part of a country's material
culture?
a. food   b. language
c. architecture   d. technology

39. _____ How do social scientists define a country?
a. a political unit whose population shares a common language
b. a political unit with a sovereign government and a sound economy
c. a political unit with a clearly defined territory, population,
sovereignty, and a government
d. a political unit with clearly defined water and land boundaries

40. _____ What kind of government structure does the United States have?
a. confederation
b. federal system
c. unitary system
d. capitalist system

41. _____ By which of the following are modern economic systems distinguished from one another?
a. means of production
b. kinds of goods and services produced
c. amount of investment capital
d. degree of government involvement

42. _____ Which of the following statements refers to a pure capitalist economy?
a. The government provides goods and services needed by the public.
b. The government takes no part in the economy.
c. The government regulates businesses to ensure efficiency.
d. The government and the free market jointly make economic decisions.

GRAPHIC STUDY

Directions: Use the population density map of China to answer the following questions. Write your answers on the lines provided.

43. How many categories of population density does this map include?

_____

44. What is the population density around the cities of Beijing and Shanghai?

_____

45. What region of China has the greatest concentration of people? What might explain the high population density of this region?

_____

46. What is the lowest population density shown on this map?

_____

47. What is the general pattern of population density in China?

_____

48. What part of China is the least heavily populated? What factors might explain why this is so?

_____

SHORT ANSWER

C. Critical Thinking
Directions: Answer the following questions on the back of this paper or on a separate sheet of paper.

49. Predicting Consequences Explain the possible consequences that a continued dramatic increase in the earth's population over the next [years would have for both the developing and the industrialized natic of the world.

50. Identifying Assumptions Explain how the values held by leaders of a democratic society might differ from those held by leaders of an authoritarian society.

51. Demonstrating Reasoned Judgment Some people believe that it is impor to erase the differences between world cultures in order to create a global culture. Explain why you agree or disagree with this idea.

52. Perceiving Cause-and-Effect Relationships How has physical landscape influenced human settlement?

53. Drawing Conclusions How is the United States a large-scale example o acculturation?

54. Demonstrating Reasoned Judgment Under which political system would y prefer to live, a democratic or a totalitarian system? Give reasons your answer.

Answer Key   Chapter 3

1. b	2. k
3. n	4. j
5. o	6. f
7. q	8. m
9. a	10. h
11. e	12. i
13. l	14. c
15. l	16. m
17. g	18. j
19. f	20. n
21. e	22. d
23. i	24. b
25. o	26. p

MULTIPLE CHOICE

27. d	28. a
29. b	30. b
31. a	32. d
33. c	34. d
35. d	36. b
37. a	38. b
39. c	40. b
41. d	42. b

GRAPHIC STUDY

43. 5

44. more than 250 people per sq. mi. (more than 100 per sq. km.)

45. Possible answer: The east. This region probably has fertile soil, an adequate supply of fresh water, a mild climate, natural resources, rivers, and other physical characteristics that make it an attractive place to live.

46. uninhabited

47. Population is densest on the east coast and thins out toward the west.

48. Possible answer: The western part is the least heavily populated. The region probably lacks the physical characteristics that would make it habitable, such as fertile soil, an adequate supply of fresh water, nearness to rivers, and mild climates.

SHORT ANSWER

49. Continued population growth would result in an increased demand on the world's supply of food, water, and other resources. While these conditions would present a challenge to all nations, their impact would be greatest on the developing nations of the world, which tend to be poorer and have fewer resources.

50. Democratic leaders might believe that individual freedom, human rights, and equal opportunities for all people are the most important values for a society. Authoritarian leaders might believe that the interests and goals of the state are more important than individual freedom or rights.

51. Agree—Erasing cultural differences to create a global culture is a good idea because it would make understanding and cooperation among people easier.
Disagree—Creating a global culture is a bad idea because it would erase the richness and diversity of human culture.

52. Most people live in places where the soil is reasonably fertile, the water supply sufficient, and the climate mild enough to grow crops. They avoid harsh environments.

53. The culture of the United States came about because of acculturation. It is a mix of the cultural traits of the Native Americans and of the Europeans, Africans, Asians, and others who migrated to the United States.

54. I would prefer to live under a democratic system of government because in such a system all eligible adult citizens have the right to choose who will represent them in making the country's laws. Also, democratic governments stress values such as individual freedom, human rights, and equal opportunities for all people.

Chapter 4   Resources and Land Use

MATCHING

A. Vocabulary
Directions: Match the definitions with the terms. Write the correct letter in each blank. You will not use all the terms.

a. manufacturing
b. per capita GNP
c. developed country
d. commercial farming
e. geothermal energy
f. natural resources
g. fossil fuels
h. gross national product
i. nuclear energy
j. solar energy
k. subsistence farming
l. developing country

1. _____ material people take from the environment to meet their needs

2. _____ energy produced from the earth's internal heat

3. _____ agriculture with the goal of raising crops or livestock to sell

4. _____ energy source formed from the remains of ancient plants and animals

5. _____ process of turning raw materials into finished products

6. _____ energy produced by the sun

7. _____ all of the goods and services a country produces in a year

8. _____ country that lacks industries and modern technology

9. _____ agriculture whose goal is to grow only enough food to feed a family or a village

10. _____ modern industrial society with a well-developed economy

FILL-IN-THE-BLANK

Directions: Complete each sentence by writing the correct term in the blank. You will not use all the terms.

manufacturing
per capita GNP
developed country
geothermal energy
commercial farming
fossil fuels
gross national product
nuclear energy
renewable resources
subsistence farming
developing country
nonrenewable resources

11. The power produced by splitting uranium atoms to release their stored energy is called _____.

12. Resources that cannot be replaced when they are used are called _____.

13. Agriculture in which people grow only enough food to satisfy the needs of their family or village is called _____.

14. The _____ is the total value of goods and services produced by a country in a year divided by the total population.

15. A country with little industry and a lack of technology is considered _____.

16. _____ were formed from the remains of ancient plants and animals.

17. Resources that the environment continues to supply or replace are called _____.

18. A modern industrial society is considered a _____.

19. Iceland, Italy, Japan, and New Zealand make use of _____, energy that comes from the earth's internal heat.

20. The process of turning raw materials into finished products is called _____.

MULTIPLE CHOICE

B. Key Geographic Concepts and Skills
Directions: Write the letter of the correct answer in the blank.

21. _____ Which of the following statements about nonrenewable resources is not true?
   a. Nonrenewable resources are minerals formed in the earth's crust by geologic forces over millions of years.
   b. Nonrenewable resources can be replaced when they are used.
   c. Supplies of nonrenewable resources vary greatly.
   d. Coal, oil, and natural gas are among the most important nonrenewable mineral resources.

22. _____ How long is the world's known supply of oil expected to last at the present rate of use?
   a. less than a century
   b. more than 200 years
   c. forever
   d. between 400 and 500 years

23. _____ Which statement explains why water, forests, and wildlife are renewable resources?
   a. They can be continually replenished by nature.
   b. They are not replaced by nature after being used.
   c. They are essential for life.
   d. They are not being used up as quickly as nonrenewable resources.

24. _____ What is the earth's most important renewable energy source?
   a. soil
   b. fossil fuels
   c. coal
   d. the sun

25. _____ Why is it important to conserve renewable resources?
   a. The sun's energy will keep the earth warm for only two million more years.
   b. The environment does not continue to supply or replenish renewable resources after they are used.
   c. Since natural growth takes time, it is possible to use up renewable resources before they can be renewed.
   d. It takes millions of years for the earth to replenish its supply of minerals.

26. _____ Where are more than half of the world's known oil reserves located?
   a. in Alaska
   b. in Siberia
   c. in Southwest Asia
   d. in Iceland

27. _____ Which of the following is a primary economic activity?
   a. subsistence farming
   b. food processing
   c. manufacturing
   d. government

28. _____ Which of the following is not a secondary activity?
a. processing food
b. forestry
c. making paper from wood
d. making cloth from cotton plants

29. _____ What information would be least helpful in measuring the econom
development of a country?
a. how people in the country earn a living
b. the country's climate
c. the gross national product of the country
d. the per capita GNP of the country

30. _____ How do about half the people in developing countries make their
living?
a. in forestry   b. in fishing
c. in farming   d. in manufacturing

31. _____ How were nonrenewable resources formed?
a. by intense human labor
b. by volcanic eruptions along the tectonic plates
c. by geologic forces in the earth's crust over millions of years
d. by the power of running water

32. _____ How long is the earth's supply of coal likely to last?
a. millions of years   b. less than 50 years
c. more than 500 years   d. at least 200 years

33. _____ Burning which source of energy produces acid rain?
a. wood   b. coal
c. geothermal   d. nuclear

34. _____ Which of the following statements is not true?
a. One advantage of nuclear energy is its use of uranium, one of the
earth's renewable resources.
b. The refining of uranium contributes to global warming.
c. Nuclear energy involves the danger of leaks or explosions and the
disposal of long-lasting radioactive waste and contaminated water
d. Many countries supply part of their energy needs through electric
generated by nuclear power.

35. _____ Over half of the world's supply of which natural resource is f
in Southwest Asia?
a. coal   b. oil
c. uranium   d. iron ore

36. _____ In what areas of the world is geothermal energy a possible
alternative to fossil fuels?
a. in areas near large rivers or the ocean
b. in areas of intense solar radiation
c. in areas with volcanic activity
d. in areas with rich uranium deposits

37. _____ How are natural resources distributed throughout the world?
   a. Most natural resources are found in developed nations.
   b. Most natural resources lie beneath the ocean floor.
   c. Natural resources are distributed evenly among all nations.
   d. Natural resources are spread out unevenly around the earth.

38. _____ Which of the following economic activities is most influenced by
   the land and climate of a region?
   a. farming   b. industry
   c. mining   d. fishing

39. _____ Which of the following is not a primary or a secondary activity?
   a. manufacturing   b. food processing
   c. farming   d. tourism

40. _____ What factor has helped make commercial farming in developed
   countries more successful than subsistence farming in developing
   countries?
   a. longer growing seasons
   b. better climates
   c. greater numbers of farmers
   d. modern techniques and equipment

GRAPHIC STUDY

Directions: Use the map of China below to answer the following
questions. Write your answers on the lines provided.

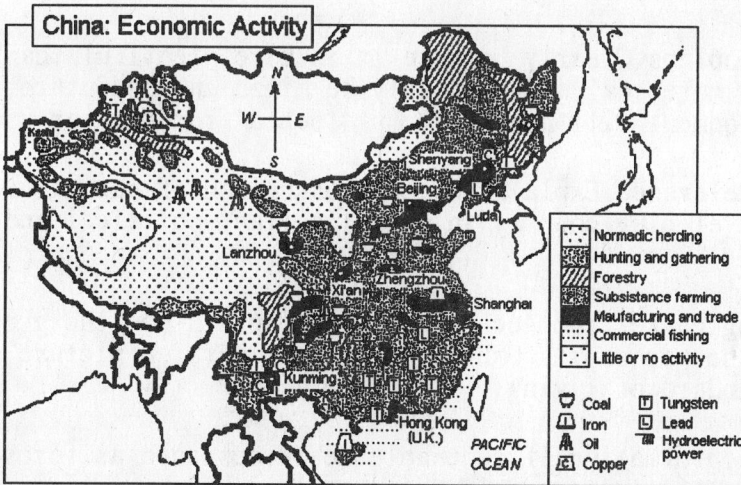

41. What is China's greatest source of energy?

_____

42. Around which cities are China's three large manufacturing centers located?

_____

43. In which part of the country are China's major oil fields located?

_____

44. What metal is mined in southeastern China in the area around Hong Kon

_____

45. What is the greatest land use in eastern China?

_____

46. What natural resources in the areas around Shenyang, Beijing, and Shanghai have contributed to the growth of industry and manufacturing there?

_____

SHORT ANSWER

C. Critical Thinking
Directions: Answer the following questions on the back of this paper or on a separate sheet of paper.

47. Expressing Problems Clearly Because it is more plentiful than other fossil fuels, more coal will probably be mined in the future. Explair how the environment will need to be protected from heavier use of coa

48. Determining Relevance Explain how the possession of natural resource can turn a developing country into an important political and econom world force.

49. Distinguishing False from Accurate Images Explain how the gross natic product and the per capita GNP might present a false picture of a country's standard of living.

50. Synthesizing Information If renewable resources such as forests, soi and fish are continually supplied and replenished by nature, why is important to conserve them?

51. Analyzing Information Why do people need to develop alternative sour of renewable energy and become less dependent on fossil fuels?

52. Determining Relevance How do resources and climate influence the cul of a region?

Answer Key   Chapter 4

MATCHING

1. f   2. e

3. d   4. g

5. a   6. j

7. h   8. l

9. k   10. c

FILL-IN-THE-BLANK

11. nuclear energy

12. nonrenewable resources

13. subsistence farming

14. per capita GNP

15. developing country

16. fossil fuels

17. renewable resources

18. developed country

19. geothermal energy

20. manufacturing

MULTIPLE CHOICE

21. b   22. a

23. a   24. d

25. c   26. c

27. a   28. b

29. b   30. c

31. c   32. d

33. b	34. a
35. b	36. c
37. d	38. a
39. d	40. d

GRAPHIC STUDY

| 41. coal | 42. Shenyang, Beijing, and Shanghai |

43. in the northwest

| 44. tungsten | 45. subsistence farming |

46. Possible answer: oil, coal, iron (ore)

SHORT ANSWER

47. The environment will need to be protected from the acid rain that coal smoke produces.

48. The possession of resources that are in world demand can turn a developing country into an important political and economic force. Oil is one such resource. As the world continues to search for untapped sources of oil, competition for the known supplies remains high among the developed nations that depend on oil as their main energy source.

49. The GNP and the per capita GNP measure the wealth of a country, not necessarily the wealth of individual people. In countries where the government controls industry and profits, the country's GNP may be high, while the standard of living for the citizens is low.

50. Though these resources are renewable, people need to use them wisely. Natural growth takes time, and nature cannot always replenish forests that are cut down, fishing grounds that are overfished, and soil that is overused. When natural resources are not replenished, people will eventually run out of them.

51. There is a limited supply of fossil fuels (about 100 years for oil). Also, fossil fuels are a major cause of pollution and environmental damage.

52. Resources and climate determine the economic
    activities of a region, which, in turn, influence
    how people live and what cultures they develop.

Chapter 5   Regional Atlas: The United States and Canada

MATCHING

A. Vocabulary
Directions: Match the definitions with the terms. Write the correct
letter in each blank. You will not use all the terms.

a. tundra
b. hydroelectricity
c. St. Lawrence River
d. prairie
e. literacy
f. standard of living
g. cordillera
h. continental divide
i. tributaries
j. highlands
k. life expectancy
l. drainage basin
m. Atlantic Ocean

1. _____ boundary separating rivers flowing west from rivers flowing east

2. _____ ability to read and write

3. _____ cold region that supports only a few types of plants

4. _____ rivers and streams that flow into a river

5. _____ type of power generated by moving water

6. _____ related set of mountain ranges

7. _____ entire area of land whose runoff is collected by a major river and
its tributaries

8. _____ measurement of a person's or a group's education, housing, health
care, and nutrition

9. _____ body of water that is a source of power for major industrial areas
in both Canada and the United States

10. _____ temperate grassland characterized by a great variety of grasses

FILL-IN-THE-BLANK

Directions: Complete each sentence by writing the correct term in the blank. You will not use all the terms.

standard of living
literacy
prairie
tundra
glaciers
St. Lawrence River
continental divide
highlands
cordillera
drainage basin
hydroelectricity
tributaries
Atlantic Ocean

11. Much of the area above the Arctic Circle is _____, which suppor lichens, mosses, and a few other plants.

12. The entire area of land drained by a major river and its tributaries called a _____.

13. The Rocky Mountains are a _____, a related set of mountain rang

14. Electric power generated by moving water is called _____.

15. A country's _____ is a measurement of its education, housing, health care, and nutrition.

16. The _____ provides power for major industrial areas in the Unit States and Canada.

17. In a country with a high _____ rate, a large percentage of the population can read and write.

18. A _____ is the boundary on a large landmass that separates rive flowing toward opposite sides of a continent.

19. Rivers and streams carrying water to a river are called _____.

20. A temperate grassland characterized by a great variety of grasses is called a _____.

MULTIPLE CHOICE

B. Key Geographic Concepts and Skills
Directions: Write the letter of the correct ending in the blank.

21. _____ All of the following landforms are located in both the United States and Canada except the
a. Rocky Mountains.
b. Great Plains.
c. Laurentian Highlands.
d. Atlantic Coastal Plain.

22. _____ The peaks of the Rocky Mountains are higher and more jagged than the peaks of the Appalachian Mountains because
a. glaciers moved across the Rockies during the last ice age.
b. the tectonic forces that created the Rockies were very strong.
c. volcanoes formed the peaks of the Appalachians.
d. the Appalachians have been worn down by rain, ice, and wind over time.

23. _____ Canada's climates are generally colder than those of the United States because
a. there are no coastal ranges in Canada.
b. Canada is located farther north of the Equator than is the United States.
c. Canada does not lie near any warm bodies of water.
d. the Canadian Shield blocks ocean winds from blowing onto the land.

24. _____ Only lichens, mosses, and tiny plants can live in
a. the prairie.
b. the desert.
c. bedrock.
d. the tundra.

25. _____ The Canadian Shield, a vast expanse of ancient rock, is located
a. along the Pacific coast of Canada.
b. along the banks of the St. Lawrence River.
c. around Hudson Bay.
d. in the far northern regions of Canada.

26. _____ All of the following refer to the natural vegetation in the United States and Canada except
a. forest.
b. permafrost.
c. grassland.
d. desert scrub.

27. _____ All of the following features are shared by the populations of the United States and Canada except
a. a high per capita income.
b. cultural diversity.
c. a predominantly rural lifestyle.
d. a long life expectancy.

28. _____ The majority of the people in the United States and Canada live
a. on the coastal plains.
b. in or near industrial centers.
c. in the Great Plains region.
d. in or near regions with rich mineral deposits.

29. _____ For most of their histories, the United States and Canada have
been
a. closely tied economically and culturally.
b. distrustful neighbors of each other.
c. economic competitors.
d. linked only by a common landmass.

30. _____ The major landforms of North America generally extend
a. from east to west.   b. along the coasts.
c. from north to south.   d. in all directions.

31. _____ Two major landforms stretching across both the United States and
Canada are the
a. Appalachian Mountains and the Laurentian Highlands.
b. Rocky Mountains and the Great Plains.
c. Canadian Shield and the Interior Plains.
d. Atlantic Coastal Plain and the Sierra Nevada.

32. _____ Four major vegetation regions common to both the United States a
Canada are
a. tundra, rain forest, ice cap, and desert scrub.
b. forest, desert scrub, savanna, and continental.
c. tundra, forest, grassland, and desert scrub.
d. ice cap, grassland, forest, and savanna.

33. _____ Because Canada is located farther north than the United States,
a. interior regions in Canada have a continental climate.
b. the climates of the two countries differ greatly.
c. coastal cities in Canada have a more moderate climate than do coas
cities in the United States.
d. eastern Canada is drier than the eastern United States.

34. _____ Cold temperatures, strong winds, and permafrost characterize th
a. deciduous forest.
b. Arctic tundra.
c. grassland.
d. desert scrub.

35. _____ The people of the United States and Canada share all of the
following traits except
a. a long life expectancy.   b. a high standard of living.
c. a high literacy rate.   d. little cultural diversity.

36. _____ Which of the following is a true statement about the population distribution of Canada?
   a. Most Canadians live in the northern two thirds of the country.
   b. The Canadian population is evenly distributed throughout the country.
   c. Nearly four fifths of all Canadians live within two hundred miles (322 km) of the United States.
   d. About half of all Canadians live in the province of Nova Scotia.

37. _____ Which of the following pairs of cities is located on the Great Lakes?
   a. New York City and Ottawa
   b. Chicago and Toronto
   c. Buffalo and Quebec
   d. Boston and Vancouver

38. _____ The most densely populated region of Canada lies along the St. Lawrence River and in the
   a. Canadian Shield.   b. Interior Plains.
   c. Northwest Territories.   d. Great Lakes region.

GRAPHIC STUDY

Directions: Use the cross-sectional diagram below to answer the following questions. Write your answers on the lines provided.

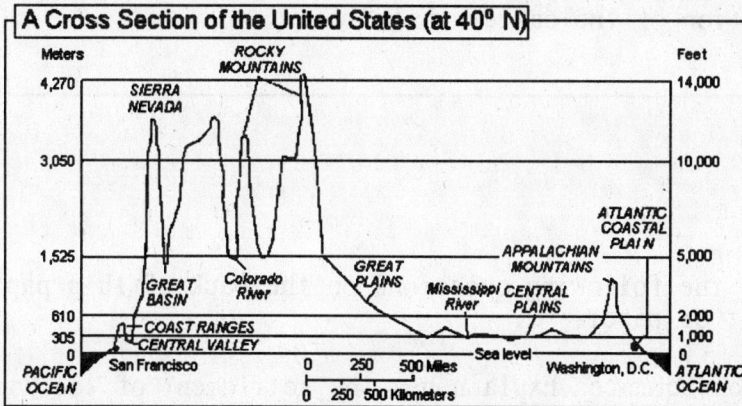

A Cross Section of the United States (at 40° N)

39. What units of measurement are shown in the vertical scale?

_____

40. Which is located farther west, the Central Valley or the Coast Ranges?

_____

41. What is the approximate elevation of the Appalachian Mountains at the highest point shown on this diagram?

_____

42. Is there a greater difference in elevation between the Rocky Mountains and the Great Basin or between the Appalachian Mountains and the Central Plains?

_____

43. In what units is the distance along the earth's surface measured on this diagram?

_____

44. How does the elevation of the Central Plains compare to the elevation the Central Valley?

_____

45. What is the approximate elevation of the Coast Ranges?

_____

46. How does the elevation of the western half of the United States compare to the elevation of the eastern half?

_____

SHORT ANSWER

C. Critical Thinking
Directions: Answer the following questions on the back of this paper or on a separate sheet of paper.

47. Predicting Consequences Explain how the settlement of the United States might have been affected if the colonists had landed on the west coast rather than on the east coast of North America.

48. Perceiving Cause-and-Effect Relationships Explain how physical geography has affected the population density of the United States and Canada.

49. Expressing Problems Clearly Why is it sometimes difficult to make decisions involving economic development and the environment?

50. Analyzing Information What factors contribute to the high standard of living in both the United States and Canada?

51. Perceiving Cause-and-Effect Relationships How do the similar cultural and economic environments of the United States and Canada help to keep people and goods passing easily from one country to the other?

52. Making Comparisons For what geographic reasons is the western half of the United States much more sparsely populated than the eastern half?

Answer Key   Chapter 5

MATCHING

1. h   2. e

3. a   4. i

5. b   6. g

7. l   8. f

9. c   10. d

FILL-IN-THE-BLANK

11. tundra   12. drainage basin

13. cordillera

14. hydroelectricity

15. standard of living

16. St. Lawrence River

17. literacy   18. continental divide

19. tributaries

20. prairie

MULTIPLE CHOICE

21. c   22. d

23. b   24. d

25. c   26. b

27. c   28. b

29. a   30. c

31. b   32. c

33. b   34. b

35. d   36. c

37. b   38. d

GRAPHIC STUDY

39. meters and feet

40. the Coast Ranges

41. about 3,500 feet (1,067 m)

42. between the Rocky Mountains and the Great Basin

43. miles and kilometers

44. the Central Plains are slightly higher

45. about 1,700 feet (518 m)

46. Land in the western half is generally at
    a much higher elevation than is land in
    the eastern half.

SHORT ANSWER

47. The settlement of the United States would
    have taken place over a longer period of
    time because of the difficulty of crossing
    the jagged Rockies once pioneers ventured
    eastward in search of new farmlands.

48. Northern Canada and the arid desert and
    mountain regions of the western United States
    are thinly populated because of the severe
    climate and rugged landscape. Densely
    populated industrial centers have developed
    in regions on or near water.

49. Decisions about economic development and the
    environment are difficult because the same
    activity can have both economic or social
    benefits (providing jobs, improving the local
    economy) and environmental or health
    drawbacks (air pollution, depletion of
    resources). Weighing advantages and
    disadvantages can be difficult.

50. Factors such as abundant natural resources,
    large and diverse populations, and access to
    major waterways allow both countries to
    develop effective transportation and
    communication systems and to experience
    continued economic development.

51. Since both countries have abundant natural resources and are industrial giants, they have no reason to be economic rivals. Instead, they share close economic ties. Because of similar cultures and histories, they are allies in foreign affairs. The physical geography of the border makes communication convenient and economically profitable.

52. The eastern half of the United States has the resources needed for trade and industry. Densely populated areas are generally located in and around manufacturing centers. The western half of the country is more sparsely populated because it is a region of mountains and deserts with harsh climates, rugged landscapes, and limited water resources.

Chapter 6   A Profile of the United States

FILL-IN-THE-BLANK

A. Vocabulary
Directions: Complete each sentence by writing the correct term in the blank. You will not use all the terms.

hierarchy
free enterprise
hinterland
rugged individualism
gross national product
service industries
reforestation
suburbs
telecommunications
metropolis
transportation

1. The _____ system is also known as capitalism.

2. The total value of all the goods and services produced by a country in a year is its _____ .

3. Cities can be placed in a _____, or rank, according to their function.

4. Fax machines and e-mail are both examples of _____ .

5. The area served by a city is called its _____ .

6. People who are willing to struggle long and hard for something on the basis of their own personal beliefs, resources, or opinions support the quality of _____ .

7. Banking and health-care companies are examples of _____ .

8. Better transportation systems caused many people to move from the cities to the _____ after World War II.

MATCHING

Directions: Match the definitions with the terms. Write the correct letter in each blank. You will not use all the terms.

a. hierarchy
b. free enterprise
c. hinterland
d. rugged individualism
e. gross national product
f. service industries
g. reforestation
h. suburbs
i. telecommunications
j. metropolis
k. transportation

9. _____ an area served by a city

10. _____ the total value of all the goods and services produced by a country in a year

11. _____ communications by electronic means

12. _____ rank

13. _____ system that allows individuals to own, operate, and profit from their own businesses

14. _____ the mostly residential areas on the outer edges of a city

15. _____ the willingness of individuals to stand alone and struggle long and hard to survive and prosper, relying on their own personal resources, opinions, or beliefs

16. _____ businesses that are not directly related to manufacturing or gathering raw materials

MULTIPLE CHOICE

B. Key Geographic Concepts and Skills
Directions: Write the letter of the correct ending in the blank.

17. _____ All of the following factors influenced the economic development of the United States except
a. an abundance of land.
b. a belief in rugged individualism.
c. strict immigration laws.
d. an economic system based on capitalism.

18. _____ After the Erie Canal was built,
a. New Orleans flourished as a center of trade.
b. Buffalo, Cleveland, and Detroit became important centers of trade.
c. Chicago declined in importance.
d. Boston and Philadelphia became busy port cities.

19. _____ All of the following are nonrenewable resources vital to the energy supply and economy of the United States except
a. coal.
b. oil.
c. natural gas.
d. forests.

20. _____ After the Civil War, which ended in 1865, Chicago grew to become the largest city in the Midwest because
a. many people from the South and the West migrated to the area.
b. the construction of the Erie Canal made the city an important center of trade.
c. most of the agricultural industries were located near the city.
d. Chicago had the best location along the railroad network, located centrally between the coasts.

21. _____ After World War II, many businesses and people moved to
a. the hinterlands from rural areas.
b. the suburbs from the cities.
c. small towns and villages from the metropolises.
d. East Coast cities from cities in the South and the West.

22. _____ In recent years, more and more Americans have been finding jobs in
a. agriculture and food processing.
b. manufacturing and trade.
c. service industries.
d. mining and lumbering.

23. _____ The entire United States and the rest of the world serve as the hinterland for all of the following cities except
a. New York.
b. Chicago.
c. Tucson.
d. Los Angeles.

24. _____ Cities in the South and the West have flourished in recent years because of popular preferences to live in cities that
a. have mild year-round climates.
b. offer a variety of jobs and activities.
c. are the site of large industrial centers.
d. provide easy access to important waterways.

25. _____ Today the majority of the American population lives
a. in metropolitan areas.
b. in rural areas.
c. on the East Coast.
d. in the Southwest.

26. _____ All of the following contributed to the economic success of the United States except
a. transportation technology.
b. the hard work of the people.
c. economic freedom and opportunity.
d. strict trade regulations.

27. _____ The steam engine was important because it
a. gave boats the power to travel against both wind and current.
b. made possible the building of canals.
c. made farming more profitable.
d. created a need for fossil fuels.

28. _____ One of the most abundant resources in the United States, which contributed to its economic success, was
a. iron.
b. land.
c. uranium.
d. diamonds.

29. _____ The construction of the Erie Canal was important because it
a. linked the Hudson River in New York and the Great Lakes in the Midwest, greatly increasing the trade between the two regions.
b. helped eastern cities such as Boston and Philadelphia become important port cities.
c. allowed eastern crops to be transported faster and more efficientl to cities in the South and the West.
d. provided the best access to the Pacific Ocean.

30. _____ Changes in all of the following areas have had an important imp on the growth of cities in the United States except changes in
a. transportation.
b. economic activities.
c. climate.
d. popular preferences.

31. _____ As the availability of cars and public transportation increase many people moved from
a. the cities to the suburbs.
b. rural areas to the cities.
c. the cities to hinterlands.
d. hinterlands to metropolitan areas.

32. _____ A regional metropolis such as Atlanta differs from a city such Tucson in that a regional metropolis
a. has a larger hinterland and a wider range of activities than a ci
b. has a smaller hinterland and a narrower range of activities than a city.
c. is generally the same size as a city but with fewer activities.
d. is generally twice as large as a city and has twice as many activities.

33. _____ By 1900, people and goods in nearly every settled part of the United States were connected by
a. steamboats.
b. railroads.
c. airplanes.
d. cars and trucks.

34. _____ Because they functioned largely as centers of trade between the United States and Europe, all major American cities during the first 50 years of independence were located
a. near the Great Lakes.
b. along the Erie Canal.
c. along the Mississippi River.
d. along the Atlantic Coast.

GRAPHIC STUDY

Directions: Use the models of urban structure below to answer the following questions. Write your answers on the lines provided.

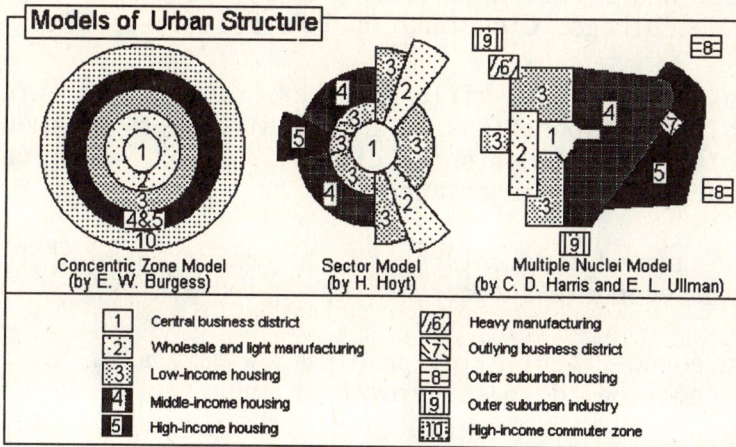

Models of Urban Structure

Concentric Zone Model (by E. W. Burgess)
Sector Model (by H. Hoyt)
Multiple Nuclei Model (by C. D. Harris and E. L. Ullman)

1	Central business district	6	Heavy manufacturing
2	Wholesale and light manufacturing	7	Outlying business district
3	Low-income housing	8	Outer suburban housing
4	Middle-income housing	9	Outer suburban industry
5	High-income housing	10	High-income commuter zone

35. Which two models depict cities as having a single core, the CBD?

_____

36. Which model emphasizes the importance of transportation routes?

_____

37. What type of housing pattern does the multiple nuclei model depict?

_____

38. Which model emphasizes that cities have more than one business district?

_____

39. Which model shows industry running outward from the CBD along transportation routes?

_____

40. What type of housing pattern does the concentric zone model depict?

_____

SHORT ANSWER

C. Critical Thinking
Directions: Answer the following questions on the back of this paper or on a separate sheet of paper.

41. Checking Consistency In what way is the belief in rugged individualis[m] consistent with an economic system based on the principle of free enterprise?

42. Perceiving Cause-and-Effect Relationships Why did the completion of t[he] Erie Canal cause Chicago, Cleveland, and Detroit to grow?

43. Drawing Conclusions Why have cities such as New York and Chicago been able to maintain their positions as important centers of industry and trade, while other once-flourishing cities, such as New Orleans and Buffalo, have declined in importance?

44. Demonstrating Reasoned Judgment Why is the conservation of fossil fue[l] important to the economic success of the United States?

45. Perceiving Cause-and-Effect Relationships How have advances in communication contributed to the growth of industry in the United States?

46. Synthesizing Information What factors have enabled American farmers [to] grow huge amounts of crops for sale in cities throughout this countr[y] and in foreign countries?

Answer Key Chapter 6

FILL-IN-THE-BLANK

1. free enterprise

2. gross national product

3. hierarchy   4. telecommunications

5. hinterland

6. rugged individualism

7. service industries

8. suburbs

MATCHING

9. c   10. e

11. i   12. a

13. b   14. h

15. d   16. f

MULTIPLE CHOICE

17. c   18. b

19. d   20. d

21. b   22. c

23. c   24. a

25. a   26. d

27. a   28. b

29. a   30. c

31. a   32. a

33. b   34. d

GRAPHIC STUDY

35. the concentric zone and sector models

36. the sector model

37. low-income housing located near the CBD
    and industrial areas, middle-income
    housing extending outward from one side
    of the CBD and low-income housing areas,
    followed by high-income housing with an
    outlying business district between

38. the multiple nuclei model

39. the sector model

40. low-income housing encircling the industrial
    zone, and a mixed zone of middle- and
    high-income housing encircling the low-income
    zone

SHORT ANSWER

41. Both reflect a belief in the value
    of the individual. The free enterprise
    system supports the concept of rugged
    individualism by providing individuals
    with an opportunity to use their own
    resources to succeed in business.

42. The canal provided the best water
    connection between the East Coast and
    the Great Lakes, greatly increasing the
    trade between the two regions. Cleveland,
    Detroit, and Chicago, cities located
    along this trade route, flourished and
    began to rival the older cities of the
    East in importance and size.

43. Chicago and New York continue to thrive
    because of their location along rail lines
    and waterways and because they offer jobs
    in a variety of economic activities. New
    Orleans and Buffalo declined when the single
    industry or trade route on which they
    depended economically declined in importance.

44. These fossil fuels are nonrenewable and are
    vital to the energy supply and thus to the
    economy of the United States.

45. Advances in communication have helped
    businesses to communicate faster and more
    efficiently with people who supply raw
    materials and parts for their machines as
    well as with their customers.

46. Transportation technologies link farms to
    cities thousands of miles away and to foreign
    countries, thus creating a global market for
    American farm products. Continuing improvements
    in farming methods and technologies have
    resulted in large-scale harvesting and the
    production of surplus crops for trade.

Chapter 7 Regions of the United States

MATCHING

A. Vocabulary
Directions: Match the definitions with the terms. Write the correct
letter in each blank. You will not use all the terms.

a. mangrove
b. grain elevator
c. Alaskan tundra
d. Sunbelt
e. aqueduct
f. growing season
g. silo
h. megalopolis
i. grain exchange
j. bayou
k. temperate grasslands

1. _____ marshy inlet of a lake or a river

2. _____ average number of days between the last spring frost and the first fall frost

3. _____ name for the area stretching from Boston to Washington, D.C.

4. _____ place where buyers and sellers deal for grain

5. _____ band of southern states from the Carolinas to southern California

6. _____ tall, round, airtight building in which grain is stored

7. _____ tropical swampland tree

8. _____ large pipe built to carry water over a long distance

9. _____ tall building equipped with machinery for loading, cleaning, mixing, and storing grain

FILL-IN-THE-BLANK

Directions: Complete each sentence by writing the correct term in the blank. You will not use all the terms.

silos
mangrove
Sunbelt
megalopolis
grain exchange
aqueducts
bayou
grain elevators
Alaskan tundra
growing season
temperate grassland

10. The _____ region of Louisiana is often pictured in movies as mysterious, mossy swampland.

11. Tropical _____ trees grow in the swampy ground along riverbanks the South.

12. The southern states stretching from southern California to the Caroli are known as the _____.

13. The area of high population density that stretches from Boston to Washington, D.C., is a(n) _____.

14. A region's _____ is the average number of days between the last spring frost and the first fall frost.

15. In many Midwestern cities, business activities center on dairies or _____, where grain is loaded, cleaned, mixed, and stored.

16. Large pipes built to carry water to arid regions are called _____

17. Across the Midwest, common sights include farmhouses, barns, and _____, which are tall, round, airtight buildings.

18. At the _____, dealers trade products such as wheat, barley, and oats.

MULTIPLE CHOICE

B. Key Geographic Concepts and Skills
Directions: Write the letter of the correct ending in the blank.

19. _____ In this text, the United States has been divided into regions based on
    a. vegetation and physical features.
    b. land use and population density.
    c. cultural and historical factors.
    d. the U.S. government's regional classifications.

20. _____ The most valuable natural resource of the Northeast is its
    a. forests.   b. rich farmlands.
    c. waters.   d. minerals.

21. _____ Industry and trade grew rapidly in the Northeast during the nineteenth century because
    a. the region is rich in mineral resources.
    b. people were eager to move from the farm to the suburbs.
    c. a well-planned system of roads connected the major cities.
    d. rivers provided transportation routes and water power for factories.

22. _____ The climate of most areas of the South is
    a. humid subtropical.
    b. warm and semiarid.
    c. humid continental.
    d. temperate.

23. _____ The 1970s and the 1980s in the Sunbelt were characterized by
    a. the beginning of development of the oil and natural gas industries.
    b. rapid population growth and business expansion.
    c. the development of farm-related industries.
    d. the immigration of Asian Americans.

24. _____ Many industries moved south from northern cities for all of the following reasons except that
    a. land was cheaper in the South.
    b. industrial plants were often newer, in better condition, and more efficient than those in the North.
    c. labor unions were less popular in the South.
    d. the South had a more diverse population.

25. _____ The Midwest is called "the nation's breadbasket" because
    a. millions of loaves of bread are produced there every day.
    b. it is the crossroads of the United States.
    c. it is the nation's largest producer region of grain, dairy products, and hogs.
    d. most of the nation's fruit and vegetables are grown there.

26. _____ Cleveland, Chicago, Minneapolis, St. Louis, Detroit, and Omaha a
all
a. steel-producing centers.
b. located on major rivers or on the Great Lakes.
c. located on the Mississippi River system.
d. capital cities in the Midwest.

27. _____ Because of variations in climate and soil, Midwestern farmers
a. grow various crops.
b. can raise only dairy cattle.
c. use special irrigation techniques.
d. have been forced to sell their land to farming corporations.

28. _____ The natural factor limiting development of the West is the
availability of
a. water.   b. land.
c. mineral deposits.   d. natural vegetation.

29. _____ Residents of the West have adapted to their environment in all c
the following ways except by
a. building aqueducts.
b. working in forestry and commercial fishing.
c. surmounting distances by traveling by boat and airplane.
d. moving from the cities to the countryside.

30. _____ The jagged shoreline of the Northeast
a. has hindered farming in the region.
b. makes fishing nearly impossible.
c. provides many excellent harbors.
d. contains few sandy beaches.

31. _____ By the early 1900s, the Northeast had become the dominant cente
of
a. agriculture.   b. government.
c. tourism.   d. industry.

32. _____ The Northeast became a leader in commerce because of its
a. abundant mineral resources.
b. many rivers.
c. rolling farmlands and lush forests.
d. agricultural diversity.

33. _____ The Northeast remains a world leader in
a. commercial fishing.
b. shipbuilding.
c. business and industry.
d. agriculture.

34. _____ The most common type of vegetation found in the South is
a. tropical rain forest.
b. swampland covered with tall grasses.
c. grassland.
d. mixed forest.

35. _____ The South is attractive to businesses because
a. labor unions are popular in the South.
b. land and labor are less expensive than in the Northeast.
c. its population is diverse.
d. the region receives ample precipitation.

36. _____ During the 1970s, the population of the South increased greatly because of
a. the discovery of oil in eastern Texas.
b. increased farm productivity.
c. job opportunities in industries that had moved south.
d. the migration of many Europeans to the region.

37. _____ One characteristic common to all the states in the Midwest is
a. productive farmland.
b. a mild, predictable climate.
c. heavy industry.
d. a lush, wooded, hilly landscape.

38. _____ All of the following statements about the Great Lakes and the Mississippi River system are true except
a. They aided the growth of industry in the Midwest.
b. They are still important trade routes today.
c. Cities connected by this transportation network are home to heavy manufacturing.
d. They have helped the region become the nation's center of business and finance.

39. _____ Because of the West's natural resources, two important economic activities in the region are
a. heavy manufacturing and commerce.
b. shipbuilding and trade.
c. forestry and fishing.
d. oil refining and agriculture.

40. _____ The major factor shaping population density in the West is
a. the natural landscape.
b. economic activities.
c. the abundance or scarcity of water.
d. the climate.

GRAPHIC STUDY

Directions: Use the weather map below to answer the following questions. Write your answers on the back of this paper or on a separate sheet of paper.

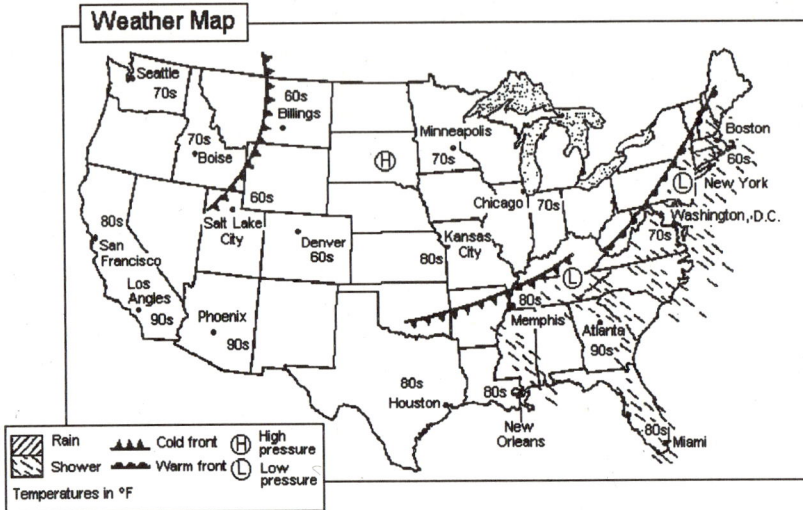

Weather Map

41. (a) Which cities shown on the map are the hottest?
    (b) Is it hotter in Seattle or in Memphis?

42. How is the weather in Memphis, New Orleans, and Atlanta likely to cha
    in the next few days?

43. What regions of the United States are experiencing precipitation?

44. What is the weather like in New York City?

45. (a) Which city shown on the map is colder, Minneapolis or Billings?
    (b) Is it hotter in Phoenix or in Atlanta?

46. What is the weather like in Houston, Texas?

47. How is the weather likely to change in Washington, D.C., New York, an
    Boston over the next few days?

48. What is the relationship between the areas of precipitation and of
    pressure systems?

SHORT ANSWER

C. Critical Thinking
Directions: Answer the following questions on the back of this paper or
on a separate sheet of paper.

49. Making Comparisons Compare the region of the country where you live with
   another region. Compare the regions in terms of climate, natural
   landscape, economic activities, and population.

50. Identifying Alternatives Describe two possible ways in which cities such
   as Los Angeles might obtain adequate freshwater supplies in the future.

51. Synthesizing Information Explain the relationship between water
   resources and economic activity in the United States. Give examples to
   illustrate the relationship.

52. Predicting Consequences Name some problems that may arise in cities
   where there is a significant rise in population.

53. Distinguishing Facts from Opinion In 1981, a newspaper editor wrote that
   "change has become [the South's] most identifiable characteristic."
   Support this editor's opinion with at least two facts from the chapter.

54. Demonstrating Reasoned Judgment The nickname of the Midwest is "the
   nation's breadbasket." Give nicknames that would be appropriate for the
   West, the South, and the Northeast. Cite reasons for each of your
   choices.

Answer Key   Chapter 7

MATCHING

1. j   2. f

3. h   4. i

5. d   6. g

7. a   8. e

9. b

FILL-IN-THE-BLANK

10. bayou   11. mangrove

12. Sunbelt   13. megalopolis

14. growing season

15. grain elevators

16. aqueducts

17. silos   18. grain exchange

MULTIPLE CHOICE

19. d   20. c

21. d   22. a

23. b   24. d

25. c   26. b

27. a   28. a

29. d   30. c

31. d   32. b

33. c   34. d

35. b   36. c

37. a   38. d

39. c   40. c

GRAPHIC STUDY

41. (a) Los Angeles and Phoenix
    (b) Memphis

42. It will probably get colder, since the front is a cold front.

43. the South and the Northeast

44. It is cool and rainy.

45. (a) Billings (b) Phoenix

46. It is warm and dry.

47. It will probably get warmer, since the front is a warm front.

48. Areas of precipitation appear to be within low-pressure systems.

SHORT ANSWER

49. Students' answers will vary.

50. More aqueducts could be built to bring water to the region from untapped water bodies many thousands of miles away. A second option would be to devise methods to convert ocean water into fresh water.

51. Areas on or near rivers and lakes have developed into centers of industry and trade. In the Northeast, the growth of commercial fishing, manufacturing, and trade was aided by the region's jagged coastline with its excellent harbors. Throughout the 1800s, water-powered factories were built near waterfalls along the Northeast's many rivers. In the Midwest, trade routes on the Great Lakes or on the Mississippi River aided the growth of commerce and manufacturing centers. In the South, entrepreneurs built textile mills along the fall line in the Piedmont region. In the West, commercial fishing thrives in the Pacific Coast states.

52. The safety, health, and general welfare
    of city residents may be threatened as
    basic services are overloaded. Incidents
    of violence may increase if people are
    crowded or living in poor conditions.

53. New industries such as the space industry
    mushroomed in Florida, Alabama, and Texas;
    older industries migrated to the region;
    and the South became a retirement and
    tourism center. Consequently, by the 1970s
    the Sunbelt's population was growing faster
    than that of any other region. The population
    of the South is also changing. African
    Americans are moving back into the region;
    older Americans are settling there; and the
    number of Hispanic residents is increasing.

54. Because of its natural landscape, the West
    could be nicknamed "The Region of Natural
    Wonders"; the new industrial South, "The
    Region of Change"; the Northeast, still a
    center of commerce and trade, "A Capital Region."

Chapter 8   Canada

MATCHING

A. Vocabulary
Directions: Match the definitions with the terms. Write the correct letter in each blank. You will not use all the terms.

a. lock
b. transcontinental
c. bedrock
d. separatism
e. tundra
f. maritime
g. customs
h. province
i. secede

1. _____ bordering on or related to the sea

2. _____ to withdraw

3. _____ solid rock that is usually covered by soil, gravel, and sand

4. _____ political division

5. _____ favoring the making of a region into a separate country

6. _____ an enclosed area on a canal that raises or lowers ships from one water level to another

7. _____ tariffs or fees

FILL-IN-THE-BLANK

Directions: Complete each sentence by writing the correct terms in the blank. You will not use all the terms.

maritime
bedrock
locks
tundras
transcontinental
secede
customs
separatism
provinces

8. Solid rock that is usually covered by soil, gravel, and sand is called _____.

9. Canada includes 2 territories and 10 _____.

10. Travelers between Canada and the United States must pay _____ on goods brought in from the other country.

11. Many Quebecois favor _____, or making Quebec an independent country.

12. Because the Atlantic provinces all border the sea, they are sometimes called the _____ provinces.

13. To make up for the differences in water levels between the ocean and t Great Lakes, the St. Lawrence Seaway includes a series of _____.

14. In 1995, a referendum held to decide whether the residents of Quebec should _____, or withdraw, from the rest of Canada failed by a narrow margin.

MULTIPLE CHOICE

B. Key Geographic Concepts and Skills
Directions: Write the letter of the correct ending in the blank.

15. _____ The smallest and poorest of Canada's regions comprises
    a. the Atlantic provinces.
    b. the northern territories.
    c. the Prairie provinces.
    d. British Columbia.

16. _____ The provinces of Quebec and Ontario contain parts of all of the following except the
    a. Canadian Shield.
    b. Hudson Bay Lowlands.
    c. Rocky Mountains.
    d. St. Lawrence Lowlands.

17. _____ The economic development of Ontario and Quebec was greatly influenced by their location
    a. bordering the United States.
    b. bordering the Great Lakes and the St. Lawrence River.
    c. along the Grand Banks.
    d. in the Canadian Shield.

18. _____ Many of the mineral deposits and oil reserves in the Yukon and Northwest Territories have not been developed because
    a. environmental laws prohibit the mining of land in these territorie
    b. native Inuit refuse to give up their lands.
    c. the area is sparsely settled.
    d. harsh climate and rugged terrain make mining difficult.

19. _____ Two important economic activities in the Prairie provinces are
a. forestry and fishing.
b. petroleum processing and farming.
c. manufacturing and trade.
d. transportation and banking.

20. _____ Warfare between British and French colonists in North America between 1689 and 1763 ended with
a. the British defeat in the Battle of Quebec.
b. France surrendering most of its lands to Britain.
c. independence for Canada.
d. France gaining control of Canada.

21. _____ Many French Canadians feel that they are victims of discrimination because
a. English is the official language in Canada.
b. the majority of French-speaking Canadians live in Quebec.
c. they cannot get jobs in government or industry due to their French ancestry.
d. Quebec has seceded from Canada.

22. In an effort to preserve cultural diversity, the Canadian national government has adopted a policy of
a. separatism.
b. multiculturalism.
c. ethnic unity.
d. nationalism.

23. _____ Building a pipeline above ground to transport Canada's oil and mineral resources
a. creates barriers to the migration of Arctic animals.
b. causes acid rain.
c. disrupts the permafrost of the fragile environment.
d. permanently damages the natural vegetation.

24. _____ Links with developing countries as well as the European Community are provided by Canada's membership in
a. the British Empire.
b. the North American Free Trade Agreement.
c. the Commonwealth of Nations.
d. the Highland Games.

25. _____ The most important natural resource of the Atlantic provinces is
a. wildlife.   b. rich soil.
c. the sea.   d. petroleum.

26. _____ Quebec and Ontario developed as Canada's economic heart because of the provinces' location
a. on the major waterway linking the Canadian interior and the Atlantic Ocean.
b. along Canada's major railroad lines.
c. bordering the Hudson Bay.
d. in the southeastern corner of Canada near the United States.

27. _____ The large cities of the Prairie provinces developed in the late 1800s
   a. along the newly built railroads.
   b. along major waterways.
   c. around mining centers.
   d. around oil fields.

28. _____ The rich mineral deposits and large reserves of petroleum in the northern territories are
   a. being exploited at the expense of the environment.
   b. causing a population boom in the region.
   c. largely undeveloped because of the harsh climate and terrain.
   d. forcing the native Inuit to radically alter their lifestyle.

29. _____ All of the following factors have contributed to making national unity difficult to achieve except
   a. many Canadians' strong ties to regional and ethnic groups.
   b. rivalry between Canadians of English and French heritage.
   c. great differences among the provinces and territories.
   d. immigration of central and eastern Europeans to Canada.

30. _____ The province of Quebec has its strongest ties to the customs and culture of
   a. Britain.   b. the United States.
   c. France.   d. Native Americans.

31. _____ When Canada became an independent nation in 1931, the government
   a. continued to protect the rights of French-speaking citizens.
   b. made English the official language of Canada.
   c. passed laws to end the influence of French culture.
   d. established Quebec as a distinct society within the nation.

32. _____ Today Canada must balance the opportunities of developing its northern resources with the challenge of
   a. competing for markets with the United States.
   b. protecting the fragile environment of the tundra.
   c. building transportation and communication facilities in the region.
   d. supplying a labor force large enough to mine the area.

33. _____ In the very important economic link between the United States and Canada, the United States buys
   a. almost 75 percent of all Canadian exports.
   b. almost 25 percent of all Canadian exports.
   c. all of Canada's petroleum and natural gas.
   d. manufactured goods only.

34. _____ Which of the following statements about Canada is false?
   a. It has a stable government.
   b. It has attracted millions of immigrants in recent decades.
   c. It has few economic links with the United States.
   d. It has links with members of the European Community.

GRAPHIC STUDY

Directions: Use the map below to match Canada's regions with the correct descriptions. Write the letter of the correct region in the blank.

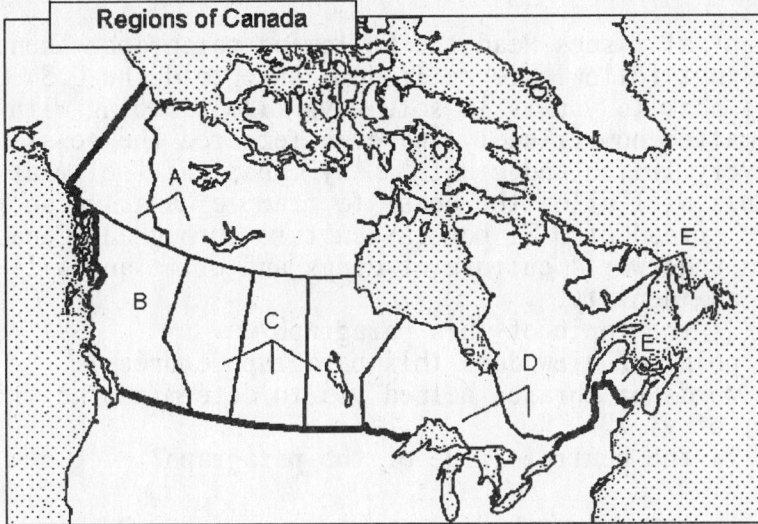

Regions of Canada

35. _____ Mountains cover nearly all of this region, one of Canada's wealthiest.

36. _____ This region is the center of Canada's population and economic activity.

37. _____ These cold lands are sparsely settled.

38. _____ This region includes some of the world's richest fishing areas.

39. _____ This region provides most of Canada's grain and cattle.

40. _____ This largely treeless region is home to the Inuit.

SHORT ANSWER

C. Critical Thinking
Directions: Answer the following questions on the back of this paper or on a separate sheet of paper.

41. Identifying Central Issues Read the following paragraph. Then, answer the questions that follow. Pierre Trudeau once told the U.S. Congress that "(l)iving next to you is in some ways like sleeping with an elephant: No matter how friendly and even-tempered the beast, one is affected by every twitch and grunt." Many Canadians feel that recent trade agreements will allow the beast to trample Canadian society. The worry that the spread of U.S. popular culture throughout Canada will be followed by an underworld culture of drugs and crime and will lead to loss of Canadian identity.
  (a) What is the topic of this paragraph?
  (b) What point of view does this paragraph express?
  (c) What words or phrases helped you to determine the writer's point of view?
  (d) What is the central issue of the paragraph?

42. Making Comparisons Compare the points of view of the Quebecois separatists and of Canadian government leaders toward the province of Quebec.

43. Identifying Central Issues Read the following comments that a radio talk show host in Toronto made to a writer for National Geographic. Then, answer the questions that follow. "People of my age grew up British—a part of the British Empire. And now we have to figure out whether we're part of the `American Empire' or not. [W]hat grates on us is that we know everything about American facts, and Americans know nothing about our facts. I can talk American politics, tell [American political] jokes. You and I have the same vocabulary. But if we start talking Ottawa politics, there's no conversation. Because I have to explain everything to you. That's a nuisance."
  (a) What is the general topic of the paragraph?
  (b) What is the speaker's point of view?
  (c) What example does the speaker offer as evidence to support his point of view? Do you think he is correct?
  (d) What is the central issue of this passage?

44. Expressing Problems Clearly Explain why it is difficult for Canada's people to think of themselves as "Canadians."

Answer Key   Chapter 8

MATCHING

1. f
2. i
3. c
4. h
5. d
6. a
7. g

FILL-IN-THE-BLANK

8. bedrock
9. provinces
10. customs
11. separatism
12. maritime
13. locks
14. secede

MULTIPLE CHOICE

15. a
16. c
17. b
18. d
19. b
20. b
21. c
22. b
23. a
24. c
25. c
26. a
27. a
28. c
29. d
30. c
31. a
32. b
33. a
34. c

GRAPHIC STUDY

35. B
36. D
37. A
38. E

39. C   40. A

SHORT ANSWER

41. (a) the relationship between the United States and Canada
(b) Canada will be adversely affected by cultural and economic ties with the United States.
(c) "the beast," "to trample Canadian society," "be followed by an underworld culture of drugs and crime"
(d) Some Canadians worry that the integration of American and Canadian societies endangers the Canadian identity.

42. The separatists believe that Quebec should secede from Canada to assure the preservation of its French language and culture. The Canadian government views the diversity of the nation's cultures as a strength and has developed legal measures that it hopes will satisfy both French speakers and others in an effort to keep Quebec as a province of Canada.

43. (a) Canada's identity
(b) Although Canadians know much about the United States, Americans know little about Canada.
(c) He says he can talk and joke about U.S. politics, but an American knows nothing of Canadian politics. I believe he is probably correct.
(d) Canada must develop its own identity.

44. Many Canadians identify more with regional and ethnic groups than with the nation as a whole. A long history of conflict between French and English cultures within the country and differences among regions have made national unity difficult to achieve. No one has been able to formulate a precise definition of a "Canadian" that is acceptable to all the diverse groups that make up the Canadian population.

Chapter 9   Regional Atlas: Latin America

MATCHING

A. Vocabulary
Directions: Match the definitions with the terms. Write the correct
letter in each blank. You will not use all the terms.

a. savanna
b. cay
c. canopy
d. tropical storm
e. mestizo
f. coral
g. El Niño
h. basin
i. hurricane
j. plateau

1. _____ storm with winds of at least 39 miles (63 km) per hour

2. _____ area drained by a river

3. _____ person of mixed European and Indian ancestry

4. _____ rocklike skeletons of tiny sea animals

5. _____ tropical storm with winds of or exceeding 74 miles (119 km) per
hour

6. _____ warm ocean current that alters weather patterns

7. _____ low coral island

8. _____ top layer of a forest

FILL-IN-THE-BLANK

B. Key Geographic Concepts and Skills

Directions: Complete each sentence by writing the correct term in the blank.

hurricanes
coral
El Niño
cays
basin
tropical storms
savanna
canopy
pampas
mestizo

9. Tropical grasslands, or _____, appear in the northern plains of South America.

10. The _____ drained by the Amazon River is a huge area.

11. The warm current called _____ changes world weather patterns.

12. The temperate grasslands, called the _____ range over much of Argentina and Uruguay.

13. A _____ has both European and Indian ancestors.

14. A spreading _____ often prevents sunlight from reaching the floor of the rain forest.

15. The rocklike skeletons of tiny sea animals are called _____.

16. In late summer and early fall, Caribbean islands are often hit by _____, which have winds of at least 39 miles (63 km) per hour.

17. Some Caribbean islands are volcanic mountains. Others—low-lying islands made of coral—are called _____.

18. Each year, an average of six Atlantic Ocean tropical storms develop i _____ with winds of at least 74 miles (119 km) per hour.

MULTIPLE CHOICE

B. Key Geographic Concepts and Skills
Directions: Write the letter of the correct ending in the blank.

19. _____ The Yucatán Peninsula helps separate the Gulf of Mexico from
    a. Lake Nicaragua.
    b. the Pacific Ocean.
    c. the Atlantic Ocean.
    d. the Caribbean Sea.

20. _____ All of the following constitute the Caribbean islands except the
    a. Greater Antilles.
    b. Lesser Antilles.
    c. Sierra Madres.
    d. Bahamas.

21. _____ Separating the mountain ranges of Mexico is the
    a. Sierra Madre del Sur.
    b. central plateau.
    c. Sierra Madre Occidental.
    d. Sierra Madre Oriental.

22. _____ Although most of South America lies within the tropical latitudes,
    a. climate and vegetation differ greatly in the region.
    b. cold ocean currents keep the air cool and dry.
    c. there is little tropical vegetation on the continent.
    d. the abundance of highlands and mountains keeps growing seasons short.

23. _____ The world's single largest mass of vegetation is found in the
    a. Andes Mountains.
    b. Amazon rain forests.
    c. Gran Chaco grasslands.
    d. Brazilian Highlands.

24. _____ The culture of Latin America reflects all of the following except
    a. Roman Catholicism.
    b. Chinese cultures.
    c. Aztec and Incan cultures.
    d. Spanish and Portuguese influences.

25. _____ Tenochtitlán, the ancient Aztec capital, stood on the site of modern
    a. Rio de Janeiro.   b. Buenos Aires.
    c. Havana.   d. Mexico City.

26. _____ The chief crop grown on the colonial plantations in the Caribbean was
    a. coffee.   b. sugar.
    c. bananas.   d. tea.

27. _____ An important economic activity in the Caribbean islands today is
a. coffee growing.   b. iron mining.
c. manufacturing.   d. tourism.

28. _____ Latin American society is marked by
a. large gaps between rich and poor.
b. great equality of income.
c. declining population growth.
d. a growing middle class.

29. _____ All of the following are regions of South America except
a. the pampas.
b. the Amazon Basin.
c. the Andes Mountains.
d. the central plateau.

30. _____ The only region of Mexico in which mountains do not dominate the
landscape is
a. Baja California.
b. the Pacific coast.
c. central Mexico.
d. the Yucatán Peninsula.

31. _____ Well over half of all Latin Americans today live in
a. Bolivia and Ecuador.
b. rural areas.
c. the Amazon Basin.
d. urban areas.

32. _____ The largest country in Central America is
a. Panama.   b. Mexico.
c. Brazil.   d. Nicaragua.

33. _____ The three island groups of the Caribbean are the Greater Antilles
the Lesser Antilles, and the
a. Andes.   b. Bahamas.
c. Guianas.   d. Windward Islands.

34. _____ All of the following groups made major contributions to Latin
American culture except
a. Europeans.   b. Asians.
c. Africans.   d. Indians.

35. _____ Two great Indian civilizations of the Latin American region were
a. the Portuguese and the Incan.
b. the Aztec and the Mayan.
c. the Mayan and the Inuit.
d. the Spanish and the Portuguese.

36. _____ South America's largest lowland is the
   a. Sierra Madre Occidental.
   b. Llanos.
   c. pampas.
   d. Amazon Basin.

37. _____ Spanish and Portuguese colonization made a lasting impression on Latin American culture in all of the following ways except by introducing
   a. Roman Catholicism to the region.
   b. the Spanish language to the region.
   c. silver and gold to the region.
   d. the Portuguese language to the region.

38. _____ Over half of Central America's income from exports comes from
   a. mining of silver and gold.
   b. crops such as wheat and corn.
   c. crops such as coffee, bananas, and cotton.
   d. manufacturing of heavy machinery.

39. _____ The main landforms of Mexico are the Sierra Madres and the
   a. central plateau.
   b. isthmus of Panama.
   c. Amazon Basin.
   d. Andes.

GRAPHIC STUDY

Directions: Use the map below to answer the following questions. Write your answers on the lines provided.

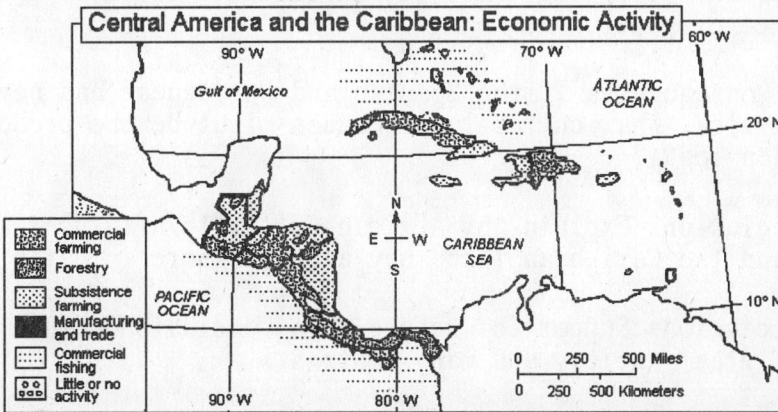

Central America and the Caribbean: Economic Activity

40. Where does most commercial farming take place in Central America?

   _____

41. How many manufacturing centers does each country tend to have?

   _____

42. What is the major economic activity in the northernmost Caribbean islands?

_____

43. On which coast of Central America does most commercial fishing take place?

_____

44. Where does most of Central America's subsistence farming take place?

_____

45. What is the greatest land use on the Caribbean islands?

_____

46. What is the greatest land use in the southernmost part of Central America?

_____

47. In which areas is commercial fishing an important activity?

_____

SHORT ANSWER

C. Critical Thinking
Directions: Answer the following questions on the back of this paper or on a separate sheet of paper.

48. Predicting Consequences If the Spanish and Portuguese had never settl
in Latin America, what cultural influences might be the predominant c
in the region today?

49. Drawing Conclusions Explain why African cultural influences are stror
in Brazil and the Caribbean than they are elsewhere in Latin America.

50. Testing Conclusions Support or refute this conclusion: South America
a region of great variety and many contrasts.

51. Identifying Assumptions Think about the locations of densely populate
areas throughout Latin America. Identify several geographic features
that may have drawn people to these areas

Answer Key   Chapter 9

MATCHING

1. d	2. h
3. e	4. f
5. i	6. g
7. b	8. c

FILL-IN-THE-BLANK

9. savanna	10. basin
11. El Niño	12. pampas
13. mestizo	14. canopy
15. coral	16. tropical storms
17. Cays	18. hurricanes

MULTIPLE CHOICE

19. d	20. c
21. b	22. a
23. b	24. b
25. d	26. b
27. d	28. a
29. d	30. d
31. d	32. b
33. b	34. b
35. b	36. d
37. c	38. c
39. a	

GRAPHIC STUDY

40. along the Pacific coast

41. one   42. commercial fishing

43. the Pacific coast

44. on the Caribbean coast

45. commercial farming

46. forestry

47. in the Bahamas and along the Pacific coast of Central America

SHORT ANSWER

48. The influences of other European countries would be greater. If Europeans had never colonized Latin America, Aztec and other Indian cultures might have had a greater influence.

49. Because the Caribbean islands and Brazil had large sugar plantations, the colonial powers brought many people from Africa to work as slaves. Their descendants are major elements of the populations of those regions.

50. Support—The variety and contrast in South America encompass landscape and climate. Some of the world's highest mountains and the world's largest rain forest share the continent with vast grasslands. Refute—South America is not a region of contrasts in terms of its population. Most of its inhabitants share a similar ancestry and history.

51. Geographic factors include water sources, natural ports along coasts or rivers, mild climate, land suitable for agriculture, and location of resources needed for manufacturing.

Chapter 10   Mexico

SHORT ANSWER

A. Vocabulary
Directions: Use each term below in a sentence that shows the meaning of
the term. Write your sentences on the lines provided.

1. irrigation

_____

_____

2. hacienda

_____

_____

3. ejido

_____

_____

4. latifundio

_____

_____

MULTIPLE CHOICE

B. Key Geographic Concepts and Skills
Directions: Write the letter of the correct ending in the blank.

5. _____ Mexico's physical setting is dominated by
   a. lowlands.
   b. coastal plains.
   c. high and rugged mountains.
   d. an elevated plateau.

6. _____ Most of Mexico's people live
   a. between the Sierra Madre Oriental and the Gulf coast.
   b. south of the central plateau on the Pacific coast.
   c. in the country's major cities located on the central plateau.
   d. between the Pacific coast and the Sierra Madre Occidental.

7. _____ Because it lies at the crossroads of four tectonic plates, Mexico's central plateau
   a. experiences a variety of climates ranging from arid and semiarid to tropical wet and dry.
   b. is under a constant threat of earthquakes and volcanic activity.
   c. experiences numerous tropical storms and hurricanes.
   d. is an attractive place to live.

8. _____ One of the world's major oil-producing regions is located along Mexico's
   a. central plateau.
   b. northern Pacific coast.
   c. Yucatán Peninsula.
   d. Gulf coastal plain.

9. _____ The major economic activity along Mexico's southern Pacific coast is
   a. manufacturing.
   b. farming.
   c. petroleum mining.
   d. tourism.

10. _____ There are underground caverns in the Yucatán Peninsula because
    a. water seeps through the ground and dissolves the limestone bedrock
    b. inactive volcanoes have formed large holes underground.
    c. earthquakes have opened caverns under the mountains.
    d. mining has carved these holes in the earth.

11. _____ The highest-ranking social class that emerged after the Spanish conquest of Mexico in the 1500s was the
    a. mestizos.   b. criollos.
    c. Indians.   d. peninsulares.

12. _____ Under the encomienda system established in the colony of New Spain,
    a. the Spanish were forced to work on Indian farms and cattle ranches
    b. low wages and constant debt forced most Indians to live like slave
    c. large estates were divided up among landless peasants.
    d. the Spanish king granted criollo labor and haciendas to the native Indians.

13. _____ Mexico's struggle for democracy lasted for more than 100 years because
    a. the country was torn between democratic leaders and dictators.
    b. Spain regained control of its former colony.
    c. few Mexicans were in favor of a democratic society.
    d. the Aztecs were furious warriors.

14. _____ As a result of the Mexican Revolution, which lasted from 1910
until 1920,
a. Mexico won its independence from Spain.
b. the peninsulares gained more political power.
c. the Mexican president and constitution remained unchanged.
d. Mexico became a democratic republic.

15. _____ The heart of Mexican culture today is its
a. urban areas.
b. countryside.
c. older neighborhoods.
d. mountainous regions.

16. _____ Of Mexico's five regions, the largest and most important is the
a. Yucatán Peninsula.
b. central plateau.
c. northern Pacific coast.
d. Gulf coastal plain.

17. _____ Although the southern part of the central plateau lies in the
tropics, the region
a. receives little precipitation.
b. has mild temperatures because of high elevation.
c. is dominated by arid and semiarid conditions.
d. is relatively dry because the mountains block moist ocean air.

18. _____ Mexico's northern Pacific coast is described as
a. a mountainous desert.
b. a resort area with wave-washed beaches.
c. a dry, hot, and thinly populated region.
d. an area of flat plains and poor farmland.

19. _____ The major economic activity in the Gulf coastal plain is
a. farming.
b. tourism.
c. manufacturing.
d. petroleum and natural gas extraction.

20. _____ Mexico today has roots in all of the following cultures except
a. ancient Indian.   b. modern Mexican.
c. colonial British.   d. colonial Spanish.

21. _____ The Aztec capital of Tenochtitlán occupied the area that is today
a. Mexico City.   b. Acapulco.
c. Guadalajara.   d. the Yucatán Peninsula.

22. _____ Which of the following statements is not true?
    a. The Aztecs had a small, weak empire before the Spanish conquest in the 1500s.
    b. Four social classes based on race emerged as the Spanish settled Ne Spain.
    c. The encomienda system set up by the Spanish forced the Indians to live in slave-like conditions.
    d. The social order established by the Spanish colonizers remained in force until the 1800s.

23. _____ The Mexican war for independence began in 1810 when
    a. Miguel Hidalgo, a criollo priest, called for a rebellion against Spanish rule.
    b. the encomienda system was put into force.
    c. peasants and middle-class Mexicans stood up to the military dictato and wealthy landowners.
    d. Hernán Cortés defeated the Indians in the Aztec capital of Tenochtitlán.

24. _____ After Mexico's efforts to modernize the country in the late 180C
    a. the gap between the rich and poor narrowed.
    b. a large middle class was created.
    c. the gap between the rich and the poor continued unchanged.
    d. the Spanish became colonial rulers once again.

25. _____ A basic difference between the democratic republic of Mexico and that of the United States is that in Mexico
    a. two political parties dominate the nation.
    b. the president and congress are appointed.
    c. the president is elected, but the congress is appointed.
    d. one political party has held power continuously.

26. _____ Tourism is an important industry for Mexico because
    a. the country has no large industrial centers.
    b. petroleum mining is expensive.
    c. Mexicans view tourism as a cleaner alternative to pollution-produc industries.
    d. tourism is Mexico's only source of income.

Name _____ Class _____ Date _____

GRAPHIC STUDY

Directions: Use the population pyramid below to answer the following questions. Write your answers on the lines provided.

Brazil

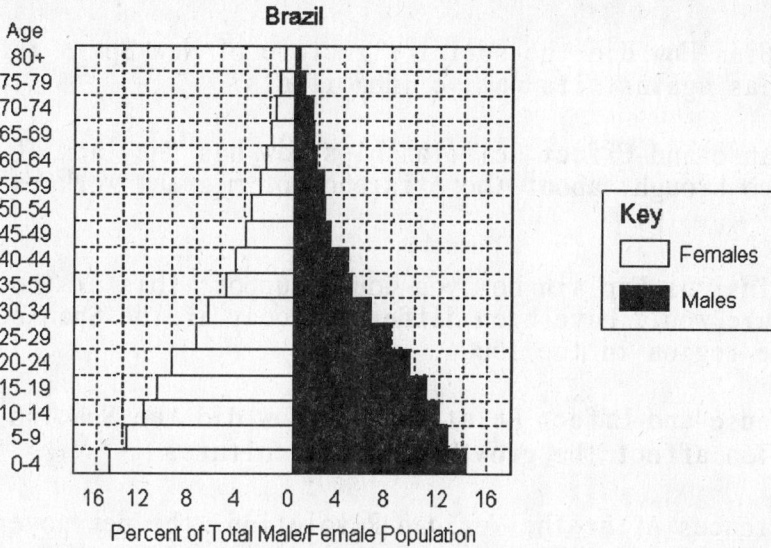

Percent of Total Male/Female Population

Key
Females
Males

27. Approximately what percentage of Brazil's population is between ages 5 and 9?

_____

28. Are there more males or females in Brazil?

_____

29. Is the population of Brazil growing or declining?

_____

30. Approximately what percentage of Brazil's population is between ages 20 and 24?

_____

31. Are the majority of people in Brazil over or under age 30?

_____

32. Will Brazil have a greater or lesser demand in the future for housing, food, and health care?

_____

SHORT ANSWER

C. Critical Thinking
Directions: Answer the following questions on the back of this paper or on a separate sheet of paper.

33. **Recognizing Bias** How did the social structure of New Spain reflect the Spaniards' bias against its native inhabitants?

34. **Perceiving Cause-and-Effect Relationships** How has the lack of arable land in Mexico brought about the existence of migrant workers in the country?

35. **Testing Conclusions** Explain how you would support this statement: Mexican culture would have been different today if the Spanish had not conquered the region in the 1500s.

36. **Perceiving Cause-and-Effect Relationships** How did the Spanish conquest of Tenochtitlán affect the growth of Aztec culture?

37. **Drawing Inferences** After the Mexican Revolution, the new government promised "land, bread, and justice for all." What does this slogan tell you about the living conditions of the people before the revolution?

38. **Demonstrating Reasoned Judgment** What events in Mexico's history might explain why the country continues to have difficulty improving social justice and economic opportunities for all people?

Answer Key   Chapter 10

SHORT ANSWER

1. Irrigation enables farmers to raise crops in arid regions.

2. In colonial Mexico, a large estate operated as a farm or a cattle ranch was called a hacienda.

3. An ejido is a farm owned collectively by members of a rural community.

4. A Mexican commercial farm is called a latifundio.

MULTIPLE CHOICE

5. c	6. c
7. b	8. d
9. d	10. a
11. d	12. b
13. a	14. d
15. a	16. b
17. b	18. c
19. d	20. c
21. a	22. a
23. a	24. c
25. d	26. c

GRAPHIC STUDY

27. about 13 percent

28. slightly more females

29. growing   30. almost 10 percent

31. under   32. greater

SHORT ANSWER

33. The Spanish established a social structure
    in which the peninsulares, the Spanish who
    came from Spain, held the highest social
    rank. Below them were the criollos, people
    of Spanish descent born in the colony.
    Below these groups were the mestizos, people
    of mixed Spanish and Indian ancestry.
    Indians had the lowest social standing.

34. Because of a lack of arable land, millions
    of rural families have no land or jobs.
    Unable to support themselves or their
    families by farming, they become migrant
    workers, traveling from place to place in
    search of a day's work.

35. Mexico's language, religion, and social
    structure reflect Spanish influence. If
    the Spanish had not conquered the region,
    these cultural aspects might have been
    different. The Aztec civilization might have
    continued to flourish and become the dominant
    culture, or the region might have been
    colonized by a different European

36. The Spanish destroyed the Aztec civilization
    and forced the Indians into the lowest rank
    of New Spain's social hierarchy. More than
    300 years of slave-like conditions prevented
    the Indians from further developing their
    culture.

37. Living conditions were difficult and unfair
    for the lower social classes. Only the wealthy
    owned land, and many people were hungry.
    Political equality among the four social
    classes did not exist.

38. After the Spanish conquest in 1521, Mexico was
    divided into strict social classes in which the
    highest social rank controlled the country's
    wealth and political power. This social structure
    lasted hundreds of years. Independence in 1821
    and democracy in 1920 modified, but did not
    totally change, the situation.

Chapter 11   Central America and the Caribbean

MATCHING

A. Vocabulary
Directions: Match the definitions with the terms. Write the correct
letter in each blank. You will not use all the terms.

a. isthmus
b. mestizo
c. caudillo
d. guerrilla
e. windward
f. leeward
g. archipelago

1. _____ side of an island away from the wind

2. _____ armed force not part of a nation's army

3. _____ narrow strip of land connecting two larger masses

4. _____ group of islands

5. _____ military dictator

Directions: Match the definitions with the terms. Write the correct
letter in each blank. You will not use all the terms.

a. isthmus
b. mestizo
c. caudillo
d. guerrillas
e. windward
f. leeward
g. archipelago

6. _____ group of islands

7. _____ side of an island facing the wind

8. _____ members of a military force that is not part of a nation's regular
army

9. _____ narrow stretch of land connecting two larger land masses

10. _____ military dictator

MULTIPLE CHOICE

B. Key Geographic Concepts and Skills
Directions: Write the letter of the correct ending in the blank.

11. _____ The basic landform pattern of Central America consists of
    a. mountains in the north, a high plateau in the center, and lowlands along the southern border.
    b. a core of mountains, with lowlands along the Caribbean and plains o the Pacific coast.
    c. rugged mountains along both coasts, with plains in the center.
    d. mountains edging the northern border, with plains in both the east and the west.

12. _____ A major difference between the climate of the Pacific coastal plain and the Caribbean lowlands is that the Pacific coastal plain
    a. is drier.
    b. is rainier.
    c. has higher year-round temperatures.
    d. has denser rain forest vegetation.

13. _____ All of the following statements are true of Central America's population except:
    a. Most of the people of African American descent live on the Pacific coast.
    b. Central American Indians make up more than half of the population i Guatemala.
    c. Mestizos are a large part of El Salvador's population.
    d. Ninety percent of the people living in Costa Rica are of European—mostly Spanish—descent.

14. _____ Central America's major exports include all of the following except
    a. coffee.   b. rice.
    c. cotton.   d. bananas.

15. _____ All of the following factors have been responsible for the arme conflicts troubling Central America since the 1960s except
    a. a lack of available farmland.
    b. governments that serve the interests of the wealthy.
    c. a growing middle class.
    d. an unequal distribution of farmland.

16. _____ Central America's wealthy citizens
    a. are mostly subsistence farmers.
    b. make up a large percentage of the population.
    c. are mainly of mestizo or European descent.
    d. have little influence on the politics of their countries.

17. _____ The Bahamas were created by
   a. tectonic activity that thrust mountains up from the ocean floor.
   b. repeated volcanic eruptions.
   c. built-up remains of once-living creatures called coral polyps.
   d. built-up layers of volcanic soil.

18. _____ Temperatures in the Caribbean are moderate because of the islands'
   a. nearness to water.
   b. high mountains.
   c. location in the tropics.
   d. elevation.

19. _____ Little mixing of ethnic groups took place throughout Central America's history because
   a. no one group wanted to be dominated by any other.
   b. ethnic pride was too strong for mixing to take place.
   c. mountains blocked travel between areas.
   d. repressive governments kept ethnic groups from mixing.

20. _____ Widespread unemployment in the Caribbean islands has forced many islanders to
   a. seek work in rural areas.
   b. migrate to other countries.
   c. develop their own businesses.
   d. work in the sugar industries.

21. _____ Central America consists of all of the following landform regions except
   a. a mountainous core.
   b. Caribbean lowlands.
   c. Pacific coastal plains.
   d. an elevated central plateau.

22. _____ The climate on the Caribbean coast of Central America is rainier than the climate on the Pacific coast because the Caribbean coast
   a. receives moisture throughout the year from the northeasterly winds blowing toward Central America.
   b. has no high mountains to prevent moisture from reaching the area.
   c. lies at a higher elevation.
   d. has many inlets and lakes.

23. _____ The population of Central America is made up of all of the following ethnic groups except
   a. people of African descent.
   b. Europeans and mestizos.
   c. Portuguese.
   d. Indians.

24. _____ The majority of the people in Central America earn their living from
   a. farming.   b. industry.
   c. fishing.   d. forestry.

25. _____ More than a decade of Sandinista rule in Nicaragua ended in 1990 with the
   a. election of a Communist president.
   b. inauguration of a democratically elected president.
   c. defeat of the democratic government.
   d. election of a socialist president.

26. _____ At least two thirds of all Central Americans
   a. own huge plantations.
   b. belong to the middle class.
   c. are poor and have little political power.
   d. are wealthy.

27. _____ The islands of the Greater Antilles were created by
   a. repeated volcanic eruptions that built up layers of volcanic soil.
   b. tectonic activity that pushed up mountains from the ocean floor.
   c. built-up remains of once-living creatures called coral polyps.
   d. calcium carbonate, or limestone.

28. _____ All of the islands of the Bahamas are
   a. flat, sandy islands that support little vegetation.
   b. made up of rugged, mountainous terrain.
   c. made up of active volcanoes.
   d. covered with dense rain forest vegetation.

29. _____ There are few Indians living on the Caribbean islands today because
   a. they migrated to Central America after the arrival of Columbus.
   b. the mestizos forced them off the land.
   c. European cruelty and diseases killed most of them.
   d. they moved to the United States in search of work.

30. _____ The economies of the Caribbean islands depend mainly upon
   a. mining.
   b. tourism.
   c. commercial fishing.
   d. agriculture.

Name _____ Class _____ Date _____

GRAPHIC STUDY

Directions: Use the table to answer the following questions. Write your answers on the lines provided.

Population, Wealth, and Literacy for Four Countries				
	Costa Rica	Cuba	Honduras	Panama
Population	3,300,000	11,200,000	5,500,000	2,600,000
Infant Mortality Rate (per 1,000 births)	13.7	9.4	50	28
Per Capita GNP*	$2,160	$1,250	$580	$2,580
Literacy Rate	93%	96%	73%	88%

Source: *World Population Data Sheet*, 1995; *World Almanac*, 1996.
*Gross National Product

31. Which nation has the lowest literacy rate and the highest infant mortality rate?

_____

32. List the nations in order from lowest to highest infant mortality rate.

_____

33. What is the general relationship between literacy rate and per capita GNP?

_____

34. Which nation has the highest infant mortality rate?

_____

35. List the nations in order from lowest to highest per capita GNP.

_____

36. Generally speaking, higher literacy rates are associated with a higher per capita GNP. What country is an exception to this relationship?

_____

SHORT ANSWER

C. Critical Thinking
Directions: Answer the following questions on the back of this paper or on a separate sheet of paper.

37. Perceiving Cause-and-Effect Relationships Discuss how location influences temperatures and rainfall on the Caribbean Islands.

38. Making Comparisons Compare the two types of farming that take place in Central America.

39. Drawing Conclusions What problem has been at the heart of the intense political struggles in Central America? Explain.

40. Perceiving Cause-and-Effect Relationships How does location influence the climate of Central America's coastal lowlands?

Answer Key   Chapter 11

MATCHING

1. f   2. d

3. a   4. g

5. c   6. g

7. e   8. d

9. a   10. c

MULTIPLE CHOICE

11. b   12. a

13. a   14. b

15. c   16. c

17. c   18. a

19. c   20. b

21. d   22. a

23. c   24. a

25. b   26. c

27. b   28. a

29. c   30. d

GRAPHIC STUDY

31. ~~Guatemala~~ Honduras

32. Costa Rica, Panama, Belize, ~~Guatemala~~ Honduras

33. Higher literacy rates correlate with higher per capita GNPs.

34. Honduras   35. Honduras, Cuba, Costa Rica, Panama

36. Cuba

SHORT ANSWER

37. Because the islands lie in the tropics and are surrounded by large bodies of water, the temperatures are warm all year. Heavy rain falls on the windward side of mountains in the region.

38. The two types of farming in Central America are subsistence farming and plantation farming. Subsistence farmers use only a few basic tools to grow enough food to stay alive. Most of the rural population of Central America lives on subsistence farms. The large plantations are owned by wealthy families or corporations. Plantation owners hire laborers at very low wages and bring in the newest machines, fertilizers, and pesticides to produce huge crops for export.

39. Rural poverty has been the cause of the intense political struggles in Central America. Most people in Central America are poor and powerless. Land, money, and political power are controlled by a small percentage of people. Many groups have risen up in armed rebellion in attempts to change governments that have traditionally served the interests of the elite.

40. Winds that sweep from the northeast across the Caribbean toward Central America drop heavy rain on the Caribbean coast year-round because of the mountainous core of the region. The Pacific coast falls in the rain shadow of these winds and can depend on rain only in the summer.

Chapter 12   Brazil

TRUE/FALSE

A. Vocabulary
Directions: Read the statements below. If a statement is true, write T in the blank. If it is false, write F.

1. _____ A steep escarpment that divides Brazil's interior from its coastal plain formed a barrier to transportation for many years.

2. _____ Many poor people in Brazil live in the urban communities called sertaos.

3. _____ Reliance on gasohol, an alcohol-based fuel, has cut Brazil's need to import foreign oil.

FILL-IN-THE-BLANK

Directions: Complete each sentence by writing the correct term in the blank. You will not use all the terms.

sertao
escarpment
basin
favelas
gasohol

4. Brazil's huge interior plateau drops steeply to the lowlands beyond to form a(n) _____.

5. Many urban poor in Brazil live in communities called _____.

6. Brazilians cut their need for imported oil by using sugar cane to make _____, an alcohol-based fuel.

MULTIPLE CHOICE

B. Key Geographic Concepts and Skills
Directions: Write the letter of the correct ending or answer in the blank.

7. _____ The basic pattern of Brazil's landscape consists of
   a. low coastal plains in the east rising to plateaus and mountains in the west.
   b. coastal plains rising to a huge interior plateau that includes the Amazon River basin.
   c. high mountain ranges stretching across the entire region.
   d. a raised central plateau surrounded on all sides by lowland plains.

8. _____ Brazil's northeast region reflects much African influence becaus
   a. many Africans migrated to Brazil in the last 50 years in search of jobs.
   b. the Portuguese colonists brought more than three million enslaved Africans to work on the sugar plantations.
   c. many Africans escaped to Brazil from the Caribbean plantations in t 1700s and the 1800s.
   d. Brazil has traded mostly with Africa since the 1700s.

9. _____ More than 40 percent of Brazil's population lives
   a. in the country's interior.
   b. in the northeast.
   c. in the southeast.
   d. along the Amazon River basin.

10. _____ A major difference between Brasília and other major cities in Brazil is that Brasília is
   a. located along the southeastern coast of the country.
   b. not accessible by a major system of roads.
   c. located in the interior of the country on the Brazilian Highlands.
   d. populated by fewer than one million people.

11. _____ Few Indians still live in the Amazon Basin today because
   a. over the years many were killed or died from diseases brought by th settlers.
   b. the Amazon's entire Indian population was forced into slavery.
   c. millions of Indians migrated to the other regions of South America.
   d. many Indians were assimilated into the Portuguese culture.

12. _____ Although Brazil is rich in natural resources,
   a. the country lacks the necessary technology to use them.
   b. its people do not receive equal shares of the nation's wealth.
   c. the country has not yet begun to industrialize.
   d. the government has not been able to boost economic development.

13. _____ The Brazilian government did all of the following to promote industrial growth except
   a. build a steel mill and oil refinery.
   b. build a series of huge dams for electricity.
   c. encourage Brazilians to move to coastal cities.
   d. establish a bank for lending money to new businesses.

14. _____ Land cleared from the rain forest for farming
   a. will remain fertile for decades and yield large crops.
   b. becomes overgrown with heavy vegetation soon after being cleared.
   c. is productive for about 10 years before turning into rain forest again.
   d. becomes exhausted by both rains and planting, and turns into hard, barren red clay.

15. _____ All of the following are reasons that Brazil can look forward to a bright future except
   a. Brazil has millions of acres of fertile land outside the Amazon regions capable of producing more food and a better living for its people.
   b. Brazil has a rich culture and good climate that can draw increasing numbers of tourists from other countries.
   c. A growing Indian population in the Amazon region will help in developing the interior.
   d. The growth of industry and manufacturing in Brazil has helped to create a middle class.

16. _____ The two major types of landforms in Brazil are
   a. plains and mountains.
   b. mountains and valleys.
   c. plateaus and plains.
   d. canyons and plateaus.

17. _____ Because of its tropical wet and dry climate, Brazil's interior plateau
   a. has highly productive farmland.
   b. is the country's most densely populated region.
   c. is the country's most attractive tourist site.
   d. experiences long periods of drought.

18. _____ Most of the people in the southeast live
   a. in rural areas where agriculture is healthy and economic opportunities are plentiful.
   b. in or near Rio de Janeiro and São Paulo.
   c. in favelas scattered throughout the region.
   d. away from the coast, where large mining sites are located.

19. _____ In the mid-1950s, Brazil's capital was moved from Rio de Janeiro to Brasília because
   a. the government wanted to draw people away from the coastal cities and develop the interior of the country.
   b. many people had already moved to Brasília in search of better job opportunities.
   c. Brasília's climate is more appealing than that of Rio de Janeiro.
   d. Brasília is more centrally located than Rio de Janeiro.

20. _____ Because of their impoverished lives and chronic malnutrition,
   a. most people in the southeast have migrated to other areas.
   b. many people in Brazil's Amazon Basin have moved to urban areas.
   c. most of Brazil's Indians have migrated to other countries in South America.
   d. the people in the northeast have an average life expectancy at birth well below that of the rest of Brazil.

21. _____ The sertao, Brazil's interior land, is best described as a region with
a. poor soil, scarce grazing lands, and uncertain rainfall.
b. enough wealth to buy the machines necessary to boost farm productivity.
c. fertile lands capable of producing enough food for its people.
d. a favorable climate that can draw large numbers of tourists.

22. _____ After clearing the rain forest for farming, many settlers have discovered that rain forest soil
a. becomes quickly exhausted by constant rains and planting.
b. is the most fertile soil in Brazil.
c. needs little irrigation to produce large crop yields every year.
d. turns to red, barren clay only after many years of planting.

23. _____ The most important crop grown in the southeast is
a. sugar.   b. coffee.
c. cotton.   d. cacao.

24. _____ All of the following statements about Brazil's economy are true except:
a. Because of the development of gasohol, Brazil no longer has to import expensive foreign oil.
b. Industrial developments have destroyed the middle class.
c. Jobs in service industries usually pay more than jobs in agriculture.
d. Despite industrial development, poverty remains in the cities and the agricultural northeast.

GRAPHIC STUDY

Directions: Use the map to answer the following questions. Write your answers on the lines provided.

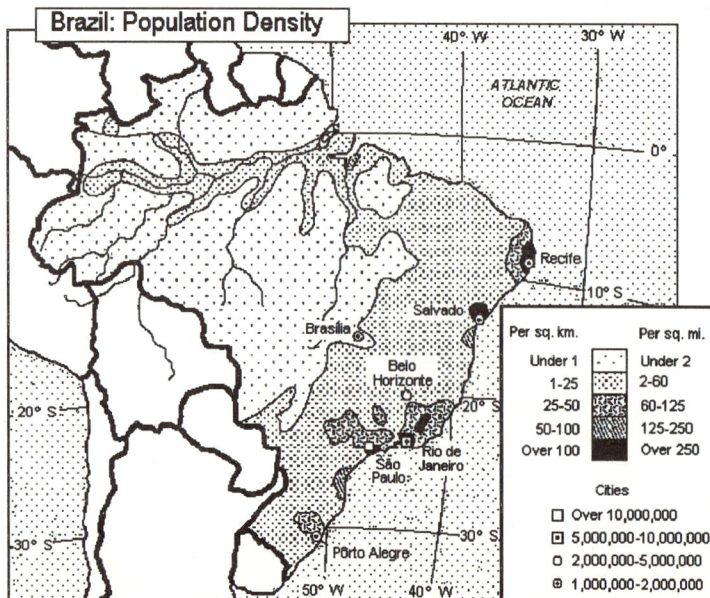

Brazil: Population Density

25. What is the population of Rio de Janeiro?

_____

26. What is the overall pattern of population density in Brazil?

_____

27. How do the populations of Brasília and São Paulo compare?

_____

28. Estimate the distance from Pôrto Alegre to Brasília using latitude.

_____

29. Estimate the distance from Brasília to Salvador using longitude.

_____

30. What is the population density of the land around the Amazon River?

_____

31. Where is Brazil's highest population density?

_____

32. What region of Brazil would you expect to be the most industrialized? Why?

_____

33. Estimate the distance from Rio de Janeiro to Salvador using latitude.

_____

34. Estimate the distance from Brasília to Recife using longitude.

_____

SHORT ANSWER

C. Critical Thinking
Directions: Answer the following questions on the back of this paper or on a separate sheet of paper.

35. Determining Relevance How has Brazil's physical geography influenced the development of the country?

36. Synthesizing Information What was the Brazilian government hoping to achieve with its construction of Brasília as the nation's new capital?

37. Perceiving Cause-and-Effect Relationships Why did Brazil develop gasohol? What effect has its development had on Brazil's economy?

38. Perceiving Cause-and-Effect Relationships Why did Brazil's Indian population decline from between two million and five million in the 1500s to about 200,000 today?

39. Checking Consistency You have read that Brazilian agriculture is productive and highly profitable, and that many farmers live in poverty. How can these statements be consistent?

40. Determining Relevance How did the Brazilian government in the 1940s and the 1950s help to make Brazil the highly industrialized country it is today?

Answer Key Chapter 12

TRUE/FALSE

1. T

2. F

3. T

FILL-IN-THE-BLANK

4. escarpment

5. favelas

6. gasohol

MULTIPLE CHOICE

7. b

8. b

9. c

10. c

11. a

12. b

13. c

14. d

15. c

16. c

17. d

18. b

19. a

20. d

21. a

22. a

23. b

24. b

GRAPHIC STUDY

25. between 5 and 10 million people

26. Brazil is most densely populated along the southeastern coast and becomes less densely populated as you move toward the northwest.

27. With one to two million people, Brasília's population is much smaller than São Paulo's. São Paulo has a population of more than 10 million.

28. about 1,000 miles (1,609 km)

29. about 690 miles (1,110 km)

30. 2-60 people per square mile (1-25 per sq km)

31. along the southeast coast around São Paulo and Rio de Janeiro

32. the southeast coast, because it has the highest population densities and the largest cities to provide labor

33. about 690 miles (1,110 km)

34. about 895 miles (1,440 km)

SHORT ANSWER

35. An escarpment forms a natural barrier between Brazil's huge interior plateau and the coastal plains. As a result, much of Brazil's interior is still undeveloped. The coastal plains are heavily populated, contain productive farms, have a few large ports, and are the site of all but one of Brazil's major cities.

36. Government leaders hoped that by moving the capital from Rio de Janeiro on the coast to Brasília, a site 600 miles inland, they would be able to boost the development of the country's interior and draw the population away from the overcrowded coastal areas.

37. The high cost of imported oil in the 1970s led Brazil to develop gasohol. Because the fuel is made from Brazil's own sugar cane, the country no longer depends upon foreign oil.

38. Millions of Indians lived in Brazil when the Portuguese arrived in the 1500s. Over the years, many Indians were killed by these and later settlers, and by diseases the settlers brought.

39. While Brazil's agriculture is a productive
    and highly profitable industry, the large
    plantations are owned by a handful of families;
    the rest of the rural population owns tiny
    farms or no land at all. Farmers who do not own
    land usually work on the plantations and
    receive very low wages. Thus, many plantation
    workers live in poverty. Many farmers who do
    not work on large plantations live in the
    sertao, where the soil is poor, grazing lands
    scarce, and rainfall uncertain. Few of these
    small farmers can afford the farm machines that
    can boost productivity.

40. During the 1940s and the 1950s, the Brazilian
    government built the country's first steel mill
    and oil refinery and built many huge dams that
    would produce the electricity on which industry
    could run. It encouraged the growth of industry
    by establishing a bank that granted loans to
    people to start new businesses.

Name _____ Class _____ Date _____

Chapter 13   Countries of South America

MATCHING

A. Vocabulary
Directions: Match the descriptions with the terms. Write the correct
letter in each blank. You will not use all the terms.

a. mulattoes
b. hacienda
c. páramos
d. altiplano
e. selva
f. campesinos
g. favela
h. guerrillas
i. gauchos
j. latifundio

1. _____ persons of mixed African and other ancestry

2. _____ small farmers in Colombia

3. _____ Andean Highlands in Ecuador

4. _____ Andean Highlands in Peru and Bolivia

5. _____ forested regions of Ecuador, Peru, and Bolivia

6. _____ cowboys who herded cattle on the pampas of Argentina and Uruguay

FILL-IN-THE-BLANK

Directions: Complete each sentence by writing the correct term in the
blank. You will not use all the terms.

latifundio
campesinos
páramos
mulattoes
altiplano
selva
guerrillas
gauchos
hacienda
favela

7. About 30 percent of the population in Suriname is made up of _____,
   people of mixed ancestry.

8. Because Colombia's _____, or small farmers, focus their efforts on
   a cash crop, they often cannot grow enough food to feed their families.

9. The Andean Highlands in Ecuador are known as the _____.

10. The Andean Highlands in Peru and Bolivia are known as the _____.

11. The forested regions to the east of the Andes are known as _____ i
    Ecuador, Peru, and Bolivia.

12. Argentina's _____, or cowboys, lived on the pampas where they
    herded cattle.

MULTIPLE CHOICE

B. Key Geographic Concepts and Skills
Directions: Write the letter of the correct answer in the blank.

13. _____ Which of the following explains why the human geographics of the
    three Guianas are different?
    a. different types of government
    b. distinct patterns of colonization
    c. varying landscape patterns
    d. different natural resources

14. _____ Which of the following statements about the Guianas is true?
    a. None of the countries has a population of African descent.
    b. The three countries have similar economies because of their shared
       natural resources.
    c. Manufacturing is an important industry in all three countries.
    d. All three countries have a hot and dry climate.

15. _____ Venezuela's economy is based on which of the following?
    a. oil   b. coffee
    c. sugar   d. copper

16. _____ Why is it difficult for small farmers in Colombia to produce
    enough to feed their families?
    a. There is very little fertile land in the country.
    b. The climate of the country is too dry to be productive.
    c. The agricultural economy has never been developed.
    d. They focus their efforts on cash crops instead of crops for food.

17. _____ Which of the following statements about the Andes is true?
    a. The Andes is a region of rich soil and abundant mineral resources.
    b. High elevations make the Andes too dry and rugged for farming.
    c. Although the region lacks fertile soil, it is rich in fossil fuels
       and other mineral resources.
    d. The mountains have not affected trade among the Andean nations very
       greatly.

18. _____ Which of the following is not true of the people in Ecuador and Peru?
   a. Indians make up about 25 to 45 percent of the population and generally make their living in the highlands as subsistence farmers.
   b. Asians make up about 10 percent of the population and generally own most of the large plantations and means of industrial production.
   c. Mestizos make up from 25 to 50 percent of the population and are usually factory workers or tenant farmers on lowland plantations.
   d. Europeans make up a small percent of the population and generally control most of the countries' wealth and political power.

19. _____ Which of the following is not a physical region in southern South America?
   a. temperate grasslands of the pampas
   b. cold desert of the Patagonia
   c. tropical lowlands of the Gran Chaco
   d. tropical grassland of the Llanos

20. _____ Uruguay's economy is based on which of the following?
   a. oil and the oil-refining industry
   b. meat and meat-processing industries
   c. mining and mineral processing
   d. coffee beans and sugar

21. _____ Where do most of the people in Argentina live?
   a. in cities
   b. in Patagonia
   c. in rural areas
   d. on the Gran Chaco

22. _____ What element of physical geography binds the countries of southern South America together?
   a. the Andes Mountains
   b. a tropical rain forest
   c. a highland plateau
   d. the Plata River system

23. _____ Which of the following will best help you to determine whether the facts given in a particular passage are relevant to the main idea of the passage?
   a. distinguishing between facts and opinions
   b. identifying the background of the author
   c. looking for connections among ideas
   d. identifying bias in the passage

24. _____ Which of the following is not shared by the countries of Guyana, Suriname, and French Guiana?
   a. a tropical wet climate   b. narrow coastal plains
   c. French heritage   d. vast areas of rain forest

25. _____ On which of the following do Venezuela's varied climates depend the most?
a. distance from the Equator b. elevation
c. nearness to the ocean d. natural vegetation

26. _____ Where do most of the people in Venezuela and Colombia live?
a. in fertile mountain valleys
b. along the coastal lowlands
c. in the tropical rain forest
d. on the grassy plains of the Llanos

27. _____ Colombia's economy is based on which of the following?
a. oil b. coffee
c. sugar d. minerals

28. _____ What vegetation region lies east of the Andes in the Andean nations of Ecuador, Peru, and Bolivia?
a. tropical rain forest b. chaparral
c. desert scrub d. savanna

29. _____ What factor influences the way most people in the Andean nations make a living?
a. religion b. climate
c. land elevation d. ethnic background

30. _____ What is a major difference between Bolivia and the countries of Ecuador and Peru?
a. Bolivia does not have the profitable coastal ports and factories th. Ecuador and Peru have.
b. Unlike the people of Ecuador and Peru, most of the people of Bolivi are of European descent.
c. Bolivia's annual per capita income is higher than that of either Ecuador or Peru.
d. Unlike Ecuador and Peru, Bolivia has practically no mineral resources.

31. _____ Which of the following statements is true?
a. A handful of Indians controls most of the wealth and political powe in Peru.
b. Ecuador has a large Asian population.
c. Chile has an almost nonexistent Indian population.
d. The majority of Bolivia's people are mestizos.

32. _____ What is Patagonia?
a. a river system that binds together southern South America
b. a hot, lowland region of savanna and dense shrub
c. a region of temperate grasslands that stretches for hundreds of mil
d. a desolate, dry, cold, and sometimes foggy windswept plateau

33. _____ Why were the 1970s in Argentina known as the period of the "dirty wars"?
   a. Argentina was engaged in a war with Great Britain over the Falkland Islands.
   b. Juan Perón fought hard during these years to keep the labor unions in the country weak.
   c. Many people were kidnapped by the military in the 1970s and never seen again.
   d. The government sponsored a long-term project to clean up Argentina's major cities.

34. _____ Which of the following will best help you to determine whether the facts given in a particular passage are relevant to the main idea of the passage?
   a. looking for connections among ideas
   b. identifying unstated assumptions
   c. distinguishing between facts and opinions
   d. identifying the author's point of view

GRAPHIC STUDY

Directions: Use the population pyramids below to answer the following questions. Write your answers on the lines provided.

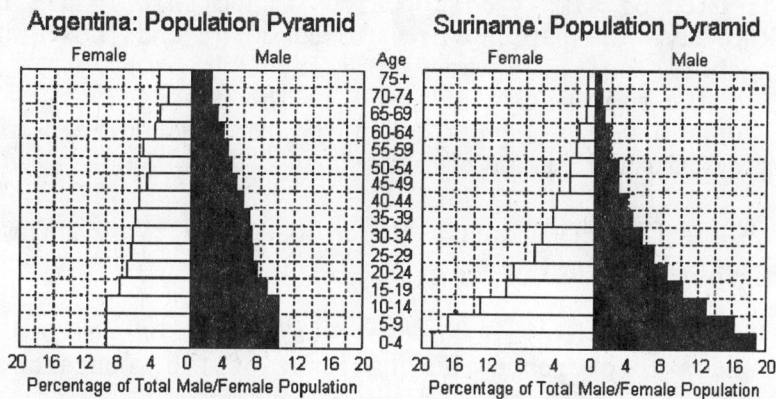

Argentina: Population Pyramid

Suriname: Population Pyramid

35. What percentage of Argentina's population is between the ages of 5 and 9?

   _____

36. Are most people in Suriname over or under age 30?

   _____

37. In general, how do the populations of Argentina and Suriname compare?

   _____

38. How does the number of males in Argentina compare with the number of females?

_____

39. What percentage of Suriname's population is between ages 5 and 9?

_____

40. How might Suriname's population growth affect demands for housing, foo and health care?

_____

SHORT ANSWER

C. Critical Thinking
Directions: Answer the following questions on the back of this paper or on a separate sheet of paper.

41. Determining Relevance Read the following passage. Then, answer the questions below. Augusto Pinochet led a harsh military dictatorship in Chile from 1973 to 1983. Thousands of dissidents—people who opposed the government—died or simply disappeared. Censorship in all forms wa the order of the day. Newspapers were closed down, and those who criticized Pinochet's policies were imprisoned.
    (a) What is the main idea expressed in the passage?
    (b) What connection is suggested in the passage between military dictatorship and human rights?

42. Expressing Problems Clearly Discuss the problem that Venezuela might face if the country does not diversify its economy.

43. Synthesizing Information Explain how vertical trade has helped the people in the Andes to overcome the challenge of the mountains.

44. Determining Relevance Read the following passage. Then, answer the questions below. Chile's long tradition of democracy ended in 1970 wi the election of Marxist president Salvador Allende. In the process of changing to a Marxist economy, Allende's government took over several American-owned copper mines and many large Chilean-owned farms and factories. Chile's elite, angered by these policies, eventually helped to topple the government in 1973.
    (a) What are two main ideas expressed in the passage?
    (b) How are Chile's elite and Allende's Marxist government linked in the passage?

45. Synthesizing Information Explain how the pyramidal social structure t exists in the Andean countries has influenced the way in which the people of the region make a living.

46. Predicting Consequences Explain how Colombia's economy would be affected if the price of coffee on the world market were to drop.

Answer Key   Chapter 13

MATCHING

1. a	2. f
3. c	4. d
5. e	6. i

FILL-IN-THE-BLANK

7. mulattoes	8. campesinos
9. páramos	10. altiplano
11. selva	12. gauchos

MULTIPLE CHOICE

13. b	14. b
15. a	16. d
17. a	18. b
19. d	20. b
21. a	22. d
23. c	24. b
25. a	26. b
27. a	28. d
29. a	30. c
31. d	32. c
33. a	34. c

GRAPHIC STUDY

35. about 10 percent

36. under age 30

37. While Argentina's population is more
or less evenly distributed between
young and old, Suriname has a very
large young population.

38. There are approximately the same number
of males and females.

39. about 18 percent

40. Suriname's growing population will put
demands on housing, food, and health care
for the country.

SHORT ANSWER

41. (a) Chile was ruled by a harsh dictatorship
from 1973 until 1983.
(b) Human rights are not respected in
military dictatorships.

42. Venezuela's economy, based on oil, is
susceptible to the world's demand for
the fuel. If the price of oil falls,
Venezuela's economy will be hurt. Also,
the country's oil reserves will not
last forever; when they are depleted,
Venezuela must have something to replace
this source of income.

43. The mountains have often served as
economic barriers, making trade in the
Andean countries extremely difficult.
People from different villages meet to
trade the crops that they are able to
grow. Because villages at different
elevations grow crops specific to that
climate zone, people trade "up" and
"down," or vertically.

44. (a) Chile's tradition of democratic rule
ended in 1970 with the election of a
Marxist president. Chile's wealthy helped
to topple the Allende government.
(b) The policies of Allende's government
were incompatible with the economic interest
of Chile's elite.

45. The particular group into which a person is born determines how that person will make a living. For example, Indians are mostly subsistence farmers, and mestizos are mostly small farmers and factory workers. The European minority controls the wealth and political power in the region.

46. Colombia's economy is dependent upon coffee. If the price of coffee were to fall, Colombia's economy would be affected negatively.

Chapter 14   Regional Atlas: Western Europe

SHORT ANSWER

A. Vocabulary
Directions: Use each term below in a sentence that shows the meaning of the term. Write your sentences on the lines provided.

1. summit

   _____

   _____

2. prevailing westerlies

   _____

   _____

3. multilingual

   _____

   _____

4. European Union

   _____

   _____

MULTIPLE CHOICE

B. Key Geographic Concepts and Skills
Directions: Write the letter of the correct answer in the blank.

5. _____ Which of the following best describes the continent of Europe?
   a. a huge isthmus connecting the continents of Asia and Africa
   b. a giant peninsula of peninsulas jutting out from the huge landmass of Eurasia
   c. a large continent equal in land size to Eurasia
   d. a continent consisting mostly of large islands

6. _____ How do the northern mountains differ from the southern mountains in Western Europe?
   a. The mountains in southern Europe are higher and younger than those the north.
   b. The mountains in southern Europe run north and south while those in northern Europe run east and west.
   c. The mountains in northern Europe run only along the coasts, and tho in southern Europe all are far inland.
   d. Northern Europe is very mountainous, but southern Europe has few mountains.

7. _____ What are the two major language groups in Western Europe?
   a. Romance and Germanic   b. Celtic and Hellenic
   c. Basque and Slavic   d. French and Germanic

8. _____ Which of the following is a true statement about Western Europe?
   a. Few Western European countries have a coastline.
   b. Most of Western Europe's people live in Spain and Italy.
   c. There are few large metropolitan areas in the United Kingdom and Germany.
   d. Shipping and trade have traditionally been an important part of Western Europe's economy.

9. _____ What kind of climate does Mediterranean Europe have?
   a. warm, moist climate year-round
   b. hot, dry summers with mild, moist winters
   c. hot, wet climate year-round
   d. hot, wet summers with cool, dry winters

10. _____ How has human settlement affected the natural vegetation of Western Europe?
    a. People have carefully protected all of the scenic areas in Western Europe.
    b. Most of the natural forests in Western Europe have been cleared to make way for farms and to provide timber for field and building materials.
    c. Human settlement has ensured the survival of Germany's Black Forest and other forest regions in Western Europe.
    d. Forests have been planted to replace pastures, orchards, vineyards, and gardens.

11. _____ What kind of climate does the North European Plain have?
    a. continental   b. Mediterranean
    c. marine west coast   d. highlands

12. _____ What is the European Union?
    a. a cooperative banking and transportation organization
    b. a region-wide trade organization
    c. a European defense organization
    d. a proposed political alliance that has never been realized

13. _____ Which of the following describes the basic landform pattern of Western Europe?
   a. mountains in the east and west with an elevated plateau in the center
   b. elevated mountains spreading across the entire region
   c. mountains in the north and south bordering a broad plain in the center
   d. broad coastal plains in the west, a central plain in the center, and high mountains in the east

14. _____ What two elements together produce the marine west coast climate in Western Europe?
   a. the North Atlantic Drift and the prevailing westerlies
   b. mountain ranges and the prevailing westerlies
   c. the Gulf Stream and the North Atlantic Drift
   d. mountain ranges and moist Mediterranean winds

15. _____ What are two densely populated countries of Western Europe?
   a. Norway and Sweden
   b. Germany and Italy
   c. Norway and Portugal
   d. Greece and Spain

16. _____ How is Western Europe able to provide enough food for its dense population?
   a. The region imports most of its food supply.
   b. Large, densely populated agricultural regions harvest crops year-round.
   c. Sophisticated farming methods are used to produce high crop yields.
   d. Most of the region's labor force works in agriculture.

17. _____ "A peninsula of peninsulas" describes
   a. the United Kingdom
   b. Northern Eurasia
   c. Western Europe
   d. Germany

18. _____ Human beings changed the environment of Western Europe by
   a. introducing tropical plants to the area.
   b. using the vegetation of the tundra.
   c. clearing most of the natural forests for farmland and pastures.
   d. planting broadleaf forests around the Mediterranean Sea.

19. _____ Which of the following conditions is characteristic of Western Europe?
   a. uneven population density
   b. lack of seaports
   c. severe winter climate
   d. poor farmland

20. _____ Which of the following is not true of the rivers of Western Europe?
   a. They have carried much of the region's commerce.
   b. The rivers of Western Europe empty into the Black Sea.
   c. Many rivers crisscross Western Europe.
   d. Many Western European cities are located on the banks of rivers.

GRAPHIC STUDY

Directions: Use the map to answer the following questions. Write your answers on the lines provided.

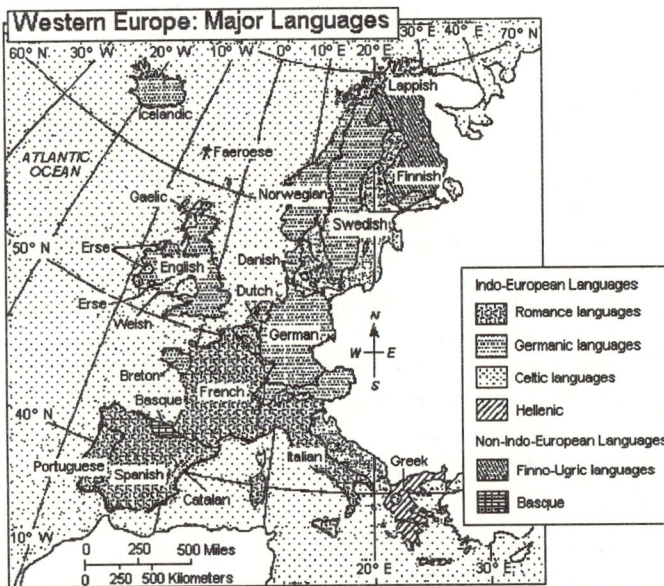

Western Europe: Major Languages

21. What is the purpose of this map?

_____

22. What non-Indo-European language is spoken in southern Europe?

_____

23. To what language family do most of the languages spoken in northern Europe belong?

_____

24. What does this map show?

_____

25. To what family of languages does Greek belong?

_____

26. Besides Portuguese, what other two Romance languages are spoken on the Iberian Peninsula?

SHORT ANSWER

C. Critical Thinking
Directions: Answer the following questions on the back of this paper or on a separate sheet of paper.

27. Formulating Questions Read the following selection. Then, write three questions about the selection, the answers to which would give you a greater understanding of the topic.
In the tenth century a.d., long wooden ships began edging westward into the Atlantic. The heads of fearsome monsters decorated the prows; brightly colored shields hung off the sides. "The ships alone," wrote one observer, "would have terrified any enemy."
These were the Viking "dragonships." Viking warriors used them to conquer large parts of Western Europe and to sail into uncharted waters. They built colonies in Iceland and Greenland. Then, in the year 1000, the Vikings set up a short-lived colony in North America.

28. Perceiving Cause-and-Effect Relationships Why did industrial development take place in such areas as the Rhine River region, Belgium, and central England?

29. Drawing Conclusions How might the European Union help the countries of Western Europe?

30. Formulating Questions Read the following selection. Then, write three questions about the selection, the answers to which would give you a greater understanding of the topic.
On October 12, 1492, a sailor aboard a ship commanded by Christopher Columbus shouted out "Tierra! Tierra!" ("Land! Land!") Columbus did not know it, but these words foreshadowed the European discovery of two continents—North and South America. As Columbus landed on islands in the Caribbean, he claimed them for the king and queen of Spain without regard to native people living there.

31. Making Inferences What might you infer about the factors that led to repeated conflict in Europe over the centuries?

32. Drawing Conclusions Why did the people of England, Norway, Italy, and Greece become involved in trade by sea?

Answer Key   Chapter 14

SHORT ANSWER

1. The summits, or highest points, of the mountains in southern Europe ar
than those in northern Europe.

2. The prevailing westerlies are the winds
that blow constantly from west to east in
the earth's temperate zones.

3. Because of the many different languages
spoken in Western Europe, the region is
said to be multilingual.

4. Many Western European nations have joined
together economically in the European
Union.

MULTIPLE CHOICE

5. b	6. a
7. a	8. d
9. b	10. b
11. c	12. a
13. c	14. a
15. b	16. c
17. c	18. c
19. a	20. b

GRAPHIC STUDY

21. to show the major languages spoken in Western Europe

22. Basque   23. Germanic

24. the major languages spoken in Western Europe

25. Hellenic   26. Spanish and Catalan

SHORT ANSWER

27. What were the Viking sailors like? How
    much of Western Europe did the Vikings
    rule at the peak of their conquest? Why
    was the Viking colony in North America
    short-lived?

28. Industrialization took place in the Rhine
    Valley, Belgium, and central England because
    these areas were close to coal deposits and
    had access to transportation of goods.

29. By allowing people, goods, services, and
    capital to move freely within the region, the
    European Union will give Western Europe the
    opportunity to become a world economic power
    in the twenty-first century.

30. When did the Europeans actually land on the
    continents of the Americas? How did the
    native Caribbean people arrive on the
    islands? Why did Columbus disregard the
    feelings of the islanders when he claimed
    their lands for Spain?

31. Division into many languages suggests the
    presence of many different ethnic groups.
    They may have come into conflict because of
    cultural differences or in competition for
    scarce resources, since Europe is not a large
    region.

32. England, Norway, Italy, and Greece are all
    coastal countries, with easy access to the sea.
    Norway and Greece have mountains and poor soils;
    England and Italy are small in size. Developing
    a strong trading capacity helped these countries
    obtain needed resources.

Chapter 15   The British Isles and Nordic Nations

MATCHING

A. Vocabulary
Directions: Match the definitions with the terms. Write the correct letter in each blank. You will not use all the terms.

a. estuary
b. glen
c. bog
d. annex
e. firth
f. cay
g. fjord
h. peat
i. escarpment
j. ore
k. moor

1. _____ formally add land to a country's territory

2. _____ narrow valley

3. _____ flooded glacial valley

4. _____ broad, treeless plain in Scotland

5. _____ spongy material that can be used as fuel

6. _____ flooded river valley at the wide mouth of a river

7. _____ wet, spongy ground found on the Scottish moors

8. _____ rocky material containing a valuable mineral used in the production of steel

FILL-IN-THE-BLANK

Directions: Complete each sentence by writing the correct term in the blank. You will not use all the terms.

annex
glen
cay
fjords
escarpments
firth
ore
moors
peat
estuary
bogs

9. The _____ on the Thames is a flooded valley at the mouth of the river.

10. England possesses large reserves of iron _____, a rocky material containing a valuable mineral used in the production of steel.

11. Large areas of the Scottish Highlands contain broad, treeless plains called _____.

12. These plains are covered with _____, areas of wet, spongy ground.

13. A(n) _____ is a narrow valley.

14. One sixth of Ireland is covered with _____, a spongy, brownish material containing waterlogged mosses and plants.

15. The plan of the United Kingdom to _____ Ireland was carried out i 1801 when Ireland was formally added to the country's territory.

16. Melted glaciers in Scandinavia created flooded glacial valleys, called _____.

MULTIPLE CHOICE

B. Key Geographic Concepts and Skills
Directions: Write the letter of the correct ending in the blank.

17. _____ Along with England, all of the following regions constitute the United Kingdom except
    a. Wales.
    b. the Republic of Ireland.
    c. Scotland.
    d. Northern Ireland.

18. _____ Britain was known as the "workshop of the world" during the Industrial Revolution because the nation
a. made many products abroad.
b. used water power to run spinning machines.
c. had an abundant supply of raw materials.
d. produced and traded many manufactured goods.

19. _____ The major economic activities in the Scottish Highlands are
a. fishing and sheep herding.
b. shipbuilding and heavy industry.
c. farming and livestock raising.
d. tourism and textile production.

20. _____ Although politically united with England since 1707, Scotland has retained all of the following except its own
a. system of laws.
b. religion.
c. parliamentary system.
d. system of education.

21. _____ Heavy industries in Wales have declined since the mid-1900s because of the
a. use of more land for farming.
b. lack of modern technology.
c. emphasis on service industries such as tourism.
d. migration of many people to rural areas.

22. _____ Most of the Nordic region has a mild marine west coast climate because
a. winds blowing over the North Sea bring abundant rain to the region.
b. the warm currents of the North Atlantic Drift moderate the weather and keep the coast free of ice.
c. the region lies in the northern latitudes and reaches into the Arctic Circle and the polar zones.
d. mountains running through Norway prevent the warm, moist ocean winds from reaching the area.

23. _____ Icelanders call their island "a land of fire and ice" because
a. the island experiences temperature extremes.
b. volcanoes and glaciers exist side by side on the island.
c. many lochs carved out by retreating glaciers line its coasts.
d. thousands of lakes and high rugged mountains cover much of the island.

24. _____ The Nordic nations share all of the following except
a. a common landform pattern.
b. related languages.
c. a northern location.
d. a common religion.

© Prentice-Hall, Inc.

25. _____ The political divisions of Ireland are
    a. North Ireland and South Ireland.
    b. Great Britain and the Republic of Ireland.
    c. Northern Ireland and the Republic of Ireland.
    d. Great Britain and the United Kingdom.

26. _____ Great Britain consists of all of the following regions except
    a. England.
    b. Wales.
    c. Northern Ireland.
    d. Scotland.

27. _____ The most densely populated region in the United Kingdom is
    a. Wales.
    b. Scotland.
    c. Northern Ireland.
    d. England.

28. _____ Britain's relative location improved in the 1500s when
    a. the Industrial Revolution arrived on the island.
    b. trade across the Atlantic decreased.
    c. improvements in ships and navigation devices increased trade in the
       Atlantic.
    d. the center of trade shifted from the Atlantic Ocean to the
       Mediterranean Sea.

29. _____ Which of the following statements is not true?
    a. Scotland and England have been bound politically for almost 300
       years.
    b. Wales has been united with England since the late 1200s.
    c. The people in Scotland and Wales have not maintained cultural
       identities apart from England.
    d. Together with England, Scotland and Wales constitute the island know
       as Great Britain.

30. _____ Scotland's lakes and rugged highlands were created by
    a. the movement of glaciers.
    b. tectonic shifts.
    c. volcanic activity.
    d. weather and erosion.

31. _____ Ireland's basic landscape pattern consists of
    a. hills ringing most of the coastline with a plain in the middle.
    b. highlands to the north and lowlands along the southern coast.
    c. elevated plains spreading across the entire region.
    d. low hills in the east with a large, high plateau in the west.

32. _____ All of the following are products of glacial movements during the
    last ice age except
    a. Denmark's fertile topsoil.
    b. Scandinavia's thousands of lakes.
    c. Iceland's volcanoes.
    d. Scandinavia's coastal fjords.

33. _____ Because of the moderating effects of the warm currents of the North Atlantic Drift, most of the Nordic region has a
    a. marine west coast climate.
    b. cold, dry climate.
    c. polar climate.
    d. continental climate.

34. _____ Differences in the landscapes and resources of the Nordic nations have produced different
    a. political systems.
    b. languages and religions.
    c. economic activities.
    d. relative locations.

GRAPHIC STUDY

Directions: Use the time line below to answer the following questions. Write your answers on the lines provided.

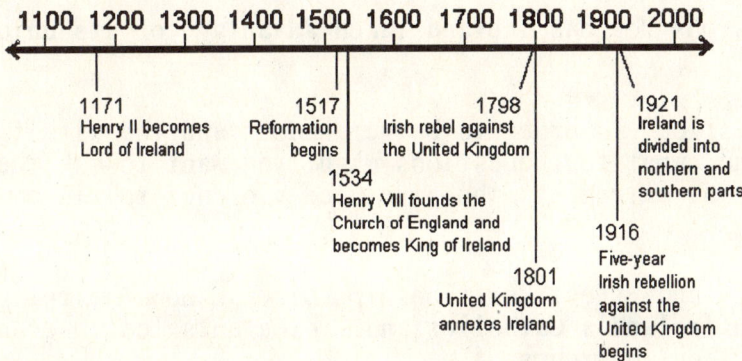

1100 1200 1300 1400 1500 1600 1700 1800 1900 2000

1171 Henry II becomes Lord of Ireland

1517 Reformation begins

1798 Irish rebel against the United Kingdom

1921 Ireland is divided into northern and southern parts

1534 Henry VIII founds the Church of England and becomes King of Ireland

1801 United Kingdom annexes Ireland

1916 Five-year Irish rebellion against the United Kingdom begins

35. How many years does the time line cover?

   _____

36. How many years passed between the beginning of the Reformation and the founding of the Church of England by Henry VIII?

   _____

37. What event on the time line led to the political division of Ireland into two parts?

   _____

38. Into what intervals of time is this time line divided?

   _____

39. How many years after the first Irish rebellion began did the United Kingdom annex Ireland?

_____

40. What events on the time line help show Britain's increasing control over Ireland?

_____

SHORT ANSWER

C. Critical Thinking
Directions: Answer the following questions on the back of this paper or on a separate sheet of paper.

41. Synthesizing Information How has Britain's relative location benefited the country since the 1500s?

42. Drawing Conclusions How has Iceland taken advantage of its unique geology?

43. Formulating Questions In order to better understand the situation in Northern Ireland, what four questions might you want to ask the Catholic and the Protestant extremists who have used violence to win control of the region?

44. Perceiving Cause-and-Effect Relationships Discuss how the religious battles between Ireland's Catholics and Protestants led to economic differences in the two groups of people.

45. Demonstrating Reasoned Judgment Name two possible economic advantages that neutrality gives the Nordic nations.

46. Perceiving Cause-and-Effect Relationships Name at least two changes brought about in the United Kingdom as a direct result of the Industrial Revolution.

Answer Key   Chapter 15

MATCHING

1. d	2. b
3. g	4. k
5. h	6. a
7. c	8. j

FILL-IN-THE-BLANK

9. estuary	10. ore
11. moors	12. bogs
13. glen	14. peat
15. annex	16. fjords

MULTIPLE CHOICE

17. b	18. d
19. a	20. c
21. b	22. b
23. b	24. a
25. c	26. c
27. d	28. c
29. c	30. a
31. a	32. c
33. a	34. c

GRAPHIC STUDY

35. 900 years   36. 17 years

37. Five-year Irish rebellion that began in 1916

38. 100-year periods

39. three years

40. 1171—Henry II becomes Lord of Ireland;
    1534—Henry VIII becomes King of Ireland;
    1801—United Kingdom annexes Ireland

SHORT ANSWER

41. Britain's location in the Atlantic Ocean
    made it ideal for trade. Since the 1500s,
    the country has made use of improvements
    in ships and navigation devices to develop
    a strong shipping industry. During the
    Industrial Revolution, British goods were
    shipped all over the world.

42. Iceland uses the volcanic activity of the
    island to produce geothermal energy. This
    form of energy accounts for a large part
    of the power used for heat and electricity
    in the country.

43. Questions to the Catholics: In what ways
    would your life be different if your country
    were reunited with the rest of Ireland? Do
    you think violence can help achieve political
    goals? To the Protestants: Why do you think
    that Northern Ireland should continue under
    English rule? Do you think violence can help
    control a region?

44. Descendants of Henry VIII fought many battles
    with the Irish Catholics who refused to
    convert to Protestantism. The victorious
    English imposed harsh laws on the Irish and
    gave away large parcels of Irish land to
    Protestant settlers. The Protestant minority
    came to control much of the wealth, while the
    defeated Irish Catholics fell into poverty.

45. Neutrality allows the Nordic nations to
    channel money that might otherwise be used
    for defense into other areas of economic
    growth. Neutral countries also have the
    advantage of being able to trade freely with
    any nation regardless of its political
    affiliation.

46. New manufacturing centers emerged near the sites of coal and iron mines; factories and mines damaged parts of the English landscape; the Industrial Revolution stimulated trade and generated wealth.

Name _____ Class _____ Date _____

Chapter 16   Central Western Europe

MATCHING

A. Vocabulary
Directions: Match the definitions with the terms. Write the correct
letter in each blank. You will not use all the terms.

a. recession
b. canton
c. polder
d. inflation
e. dike
f. nationalize
g. confederation
h. reparations

1. _____ land reclaimed from the sea

2. _____ loose organization of independent states

3. _____ extended decline in general business activity

4. _____ money for war damages

5. _____ to bring industries under state control

Directions: Match the definitions with the terms. Write the correct
letter in each blank. You will not use all the terms.

a. recession
b. canton
c. polder
d. inflation
e. dike
f. nationalize
g. confederation
h. reparations

6. _____ embankment of earth and rock built to hold back water

7. _____ loose organization of independent states

8. _____ to establish government control over an industry

9. _____ extended decline in general business activity

10. _____ general increase in prices

MULTIPLE CHOICE

B. Key Geographic Concepts and Skills

Directions: Write the letter of the correct answer in the blank.

11. _____ Which two French regions lie in south central and southeastern France?
    a. Alsace and Lorraine
    b. the Massif Central and the Alps
    c. the Paris Basin and the Côte D'Azur
    d. Normandy and Provence

12. _____ Which of the following statements is not true?
    a. Paris is a major manufacturing center.
    b. Farming is the major activity in the Alps.
    c. World-famous wines are produced in the Bordeaux region.
    d. Marseille is a busy seaport on the Mediterranean coast.

13. _____ What factor has helped the French maintain a strong sense of national identity despite a troubled political history?
    a. a belief in the historical unity of France
    b. stable governments since the French Revolution
    c. a lack of foreign invasion
    d. Charlemagne's death in 814

14. _____ Which of the following describes Germany's basic landscape pattern?
    a. gentle hills and mountains in the north; high, rugged land in the south; flat lands in the center of the country
    b. rugged mountains stretching east and west in the northern and southern sections; elevated plateaus in the center of the country
    c. rugged mountains in the south; hills, low mountains, and tall plateaus in the center; flat plains in the north
    d. elevated plains spreading across the entire region

15. _____ Where are Germany's most important industrial centers located?
    a. near the Bavarian Alps
    b. along the country's southern border
    c. in the northern plains region
    d. in the central part of the country

16. _____ How have the people in the Netherlands interacted with their environment?
    a. by polluting the coastline
    b. by damaging the land through heavy mining
    c. by diking land once covered by the sea
    d. by cultivating forests

17. _____ Which of the following statements is not true?
   a. About 30 percent of all Belgians speak French, while 55 percent speak Flemish.
   b. The Belgian government has passed laws to decentralize its government.
   c. Relations between Belgium's two ethnic groups improved after the country gained its independence from the Netherlands in 1830.
   d. Both French and Flemish are official languages of Belgium.

18. _____ What is an important economic activity in Luxembourg?
   a. manufacturing steel
   b. raising livestock
   c. making watches
   d. exporting lumber

19. _____ Which of the following is not an official language of Switzerland?
   a. French
   b. Italian
   c. Swiss
   d. German

20. _____ How do Switzerland's 26 cantons differ?
   a. in language
   b. in religious practices
   c. in economic activities
   d. all of the above

21. _____ Which statement about Austria and Switzerland is not true?
   a. The Alps cover more than half of the land area in both countries.
   b. Unlike Switzerland, Austria has mineral resources such as iron ore.
   c. Switzerland has used Austria as a model for economic renewal.
   d. Dairy farming and specialized industries are important in both countries.

22. _____ Which resource-rich regions along the Rhine River lie in eastern France?
   a. the Ruhr Valley and Alsace
   b. Bordeaux and Normandy
   c. the Riviera and the Massif Central
   d. Alsace and Lorraine

23. _____ Where is France's chief manufacturing center located?
   a. around the Massif Central
   b. in Paris and its suburbs
   c. in Bordeaux and its surrounding area
   d. along the Riviera

24. _____ The French have a strong national identity because
   a. they believe in their historical unity and take pride in their language and culture.
   b. the nation consists of only one ethnic group.
   c. they fought a bloody revolution to end the monarchy.
   d. their culture emphasizes cooperation and respect for authority.

25. _____ Why is the Ruhr Valley important to Germany's economy?
   a. It produces most of Germany's iron and steel.
   b. It is the cultural center of Germany.
   c. It is popular with tourists.
   d. It is a leading center of trade and finance.

26. _____ Which of the following is true of Germany?
   a. Its borders have remained the same for hundreds of years.
   b. The country was divided after World War I and awaits reunification.
   c. Its history has been one of long periods of peace.
   d. It ranks as a major world economic power.

27. _____ Which of the following statements is not true?
   a. The Dutch have taken one fifth of their land from the sea, lakes, and swamps.
   b. Despite its location on the North Sea, the Netherlands has no important foreign trade ports.
   c. The Netherlands has an extremely high population density.
   d. Dutch farmers fertilize heavily and use modern agricultural methods in order to make the best possible use of their land.

28. _____ What European region is the most densely populated?
   a. Switzerland and Austria
   b. France
   c. the Benelux countries
   d. Germany

29. _____ Which of the following statements is not true?
   a. Luxembourg has one of the lowest standards of living in Europe.
   b. Important economic activities in Luxembourg include steel manufacturing and service industries.
   c. Luxembourg has close cultural ties to Germany, France, and Belgium.
   d. Luxembourg is smaller than the state of Rhode Island.

30. _____ Which statement best characterizes Switzerland's 26 cantons?
   a. They are unified because they share the same language.
   b. They have a great deal of control over their own affairs.
   c. They have a similar history to the states in the United States.
   d. They are working to standardize their customs.

31. _____ Which of the following statements is not true?
   a. Switzerland has one of the highest standards of living in the world.
   b. Dairy farming is the most important agricultural activity in Switzerland.
   c. An abundance of mineral resources has enabled the Swiss to develop a strong economy based on heavy industry.
   d. The banking and tourism industries are important to Switzerland's economy.

32. _____ When did Austria become an independent nation?
a. in the early 1600s
b. in the late 1800s
c. in 1910
d. at the end of World War I

GRAPHIC STUDY

Directions: Use the map below to answer the following questions. Write
your answers on the lines provided.

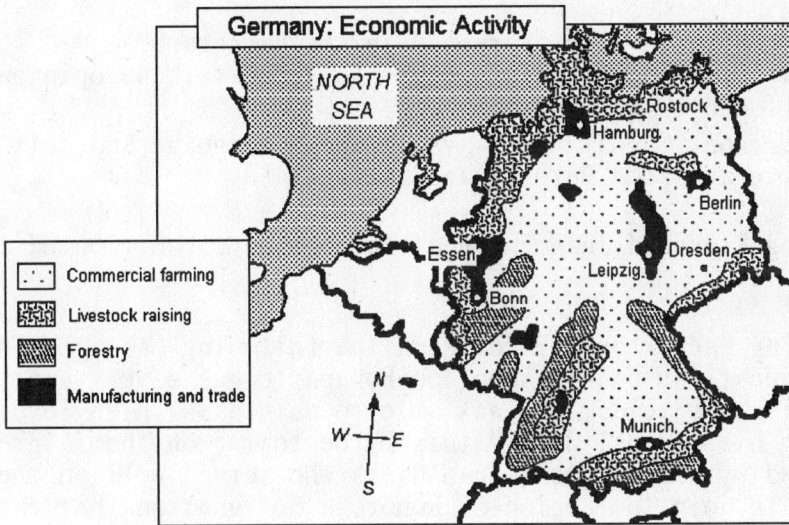

Germany: Economic Activity

33. What is Germany's greatest land use?

_____

34. How is most of the land between Essen and Bonn used?

_____

35. What is the greatest land use around the city of Rostock?

_____

36. What is the greatest land use in the southwestern part of the country?

_____

SHORT ANSWER

C. Critical Thinking
Directions: Answer the following questions on the back of this paper or
on a separate sheet of paper.

37. Distinguishing Fact from Opinion Read the following passage. Then,
answer the following questions. The years immediately after World War I
were the worst in Germany's long history. Inflation was uncontrollable
and paper money became as worthless as paper towels. Between 1914 and
1923, the value of the German mark fell from 4.2 marks for 1 dollar to
4.2 trillion.
   (a) What opinions are expressed in the paragraph?
   (b) What fact does the author use to support these opinions?

38. Making Comparisons Compare the ways in which language and cultural
diversity have affected Belgium and Switzerland.

39. Demonstrating Reasoned Judgment What factors have contributed to a sense
of French unity?

40. Distinguishing Fact from Opinion Read the following passage. Then,
answer the questions below. Napoleon Bonaparte was a very smart and
effective military leader who was able to maintain a high level of
morale among his troops. He did this by bestowing on them a great deal
of praise and by allowing those soldiers who served well on the
battlefield to join the Legion of Honor, a designation that entitled
them to both a special star-shaped medal and extra pay.
   (a) What opinion is expressed in the paragraph?
   (b) What facts does the author use to support this opinion?

41. Perceiving Cause-and-Effect Relationships How did economic factors at
the end of World War I help the Nazis rise to power in Germany?

42. Making Comparisons How are the physical landscapes and uses of land
similar in both Switzerland and Austria?

Answer Key   Chapter 16

MATCHING

1. c	2. g
3. a	4. h
5. f	6. e
7. g	8. f
9. a	10. d

MULTIPLE CHOICE

11. b	12. b
13. a	14. c
15. d	16. c
17. c	18. a
19. c	20. d
21. c	22. d
23. b	24. a
25. a	26. d
27. b	28. c
29. a	30. b
31. c	32. d

GRAPHIC STUDY

33. commercial farming

34. for manufacturing and trade

35. livestock raising

36. forestry

SHORT ANSWER

37. (a) The years immediately after World
    War I were the worst period in German
    history; inflation was uncontrollable
    and paper money was worthless.
    (b) Between 1914 and 1923, the value of
    the German mark fell from 4.2 marks for
    1 dollar to 4.2 trillion.

38. Relations between French-speaking Walloons
    and the Dutch-speaking Flemings have
    divided Belgium. Both groups struggle for
    power in the nation. On the other hand,
    the Swiss Italians, Germans, and French
    have maintained a balance between strong
    cultural identities and a strong national
    identity, thus keeping Switzerland united.

39. Political unity under Roman control and
    Charlemagne's empire gave France a sense of
    identity that was added to by a long sequence
    of monarchs. Supporting that identity was the
    common heritage of the French language and
    culture.

40. (a) Napoleon was a very smart and effective
    military leader.
    (b) Napoleon kept the morale of his troops
    high through praise and monetary rewards.

41. Germany's obligation to pay large sums of
    money in war damages to the Allies greatly
    strained its economy. Also, inflation made
    Germany's money worthless in the 1920s and
    the early 1930s. These difficult times made
    the Nazi promises of past glory and an
    improved economy very appealing to the German
    people.

42. The Alps cover more than half of the land
    areas in Switzerland and Austria and have
    become valuable assets to both countries
    as a result of tourism. Dairy farming and
    specialized industries are important in
    both countries.

Chapter 17   Mediterranean Europe

SHORT ANSWER

Directions: Use each term below in a sentence that shows the meaning of the term. Write your sentences on the lines provided.

1. navigable

   _____

   _____

2. Renaissance

   _____

   _____

3. graben

   _____

   _____

4. tsunami

   _____

   _____

MULTIPLE CHOICE

B. Key Geographic Concepts and Skills
Directions: Write the letter of the correct answer in the blank.

5. _____ What landform separates the Iberian Peninsula from the rest of Europe?
   a. the Dinaric Alps   b. the Meseta
   c. the Pyrenees   d. the Cantabrian Mountains

6. _____ Which of the following is not true of Spain's climate?
   a. Due to its high elevation, the Meseta in central Spain has an extremely wet climate.
   b. Moist Atlantic winds rising over the Cantabrian Mountains in the northeastern section of the country bring ample rain to this region.
   c. Dry African winds blowing over the land make southeastern Spain the driest region in the country.
   d. Most of Spain has a Mediterranean climate of mild, rainy winters and hot, dry summers.

7. _____ What is the goal of some Basques in northeastern Spain?
   a. greater use of the Basque language
   b. total independence from the rest of Spain
   c. unification with Portugal
   d. stronger ties with the central government

8. _____ How are Spain and Portugal alike?
   a. Both countries occupy their own landmass.
   b. Rainfall is abundant in all parts of the two countries.
   c. Both Spain and Portugal established colonial empires during the
      fifteenth century.
   d. Neither of the two countries is a member of the European Union.

9. _____ What mountain range separates Italy from the rest of Europe?
   a. the Alps   b. the Pyrenees
   c. the Apennines   d. the Cantabrian Mountains

10. _____ What is the significance of Vatican City?
    a. It is the site of the remains of the Colosseum and the Forum.
    b. It was once the capital of the Roman Empire.
    c. It is where the Renaissance began.
    d. It is the world headquarters of the Roman Catholic Church.

11. _____ How has Italy's economy changed since 1950?
    a. Italy has withdrawn from the European Union.
    b. Farming and tourism have become Italy's most important economic
       activities.
    c. More people are working in manufacturing and service industries.
    d. Small factories are slowly disappearing as larger ones continue to
       replace them throughout the country.

12. _____ When did the unification of Italy begin?
    a. in the early 400s   b. in the late 1700s
    c. in the early 1900s   d. in the mid-1800s

13. _____ Why is agriculture not a profitable industry in southern Italy?
    a. Modern irrigation systems are not available in the south.
    b. Many southern Italians have moved to cities in the north, leaving f
       farmers to cultivate the land.
    c. Arable land in the south is limited and farming technology is
       outdated.
    d. Poor roads in the south make it difficult to transport agricultural
       products to other parts of the country.

14. _____ Which of the following is not an important economic activity in
    Greece?
    a. manufacturing
    b. farming
    c. tourism
    d. shipbuilding

15. _____ Which of the following is not true of Greece's relationship with the sea?
a. Greece relies on both the Aegean Sea and the Mediterranean Sea for irrigation.
b. Greece has one of the world's largest commercial fleets.
c. Shipbuilding is an important industry in Greece.
d. Greece relies on the sea for trade and contact with its islands.

16. _____ Besides the Pyrenees, what other physical features isolate the Iberian Peninsula from the rest of Europe?
a. steep coastal cliffs
b. unnavigable rivers
c. desert regions
d. the French Alps

17. _____ Where are Spain's major industrial centers located?
a. in the center of the country
b. on the Meseta
c. along the southern coast
d. in the north

18. _____ Which of the following statements about Spain is true?
a. There are no cultural differences among the different regions in Spain.
b. Most of Spain's regions gained independence in the late 1940s.
c. As a result of more than 500 years of central rule, all of Spain shares a single national identity.
d. Several groups, such as the Basques and the Catalans, are fighting for greater local control of their regions.

19. _____ Which statement about Portugal is not true?
a. Only recently did the Portuguese grant independence to their largest African colonies.
b. Portugal established a huge trading empire and colonized large parts of Africa and Brazil between 1400 and 1800.
c. Portugal was the birthplace of the Renaissance.
d. Portugal's economy is heading in new directions.

20. _____ Where are Italy's flat lands located?
a. along the narrow coastal plains
b. in the center of the country
c. in Sicily
d. around Mount Etna

21. _____ Why have many Italians migrated to the north in recent years?
a. to work in northern factories
b. to be closer to the Alps
c. to escape the hot climate of the south
d. to find better farmland

22. _____ Which of the following is not true of the Po River valley?
   a. Located in northern Italy, the region is the country's most
      productive agricultural area.
   b. Hydroelectricity from the Alps powers many of the region's factorie
   c. The region is the site of Italy's major cultural center.
   d. About two thirds of Italy's factory products are made in the region

23. _____ What effect do the Alps have on Italy?
   a. The Alps isolate Italy from the rest of Europe.
   b. The Alps are the sole source of water for Italy's rivers.
   c. Because they block the moisture-laden westerlies, the Alps are
      responsible for Italy's Mediterranean climate south of the mountain
   d. The Alps are the cause of much volcanic activity in the region.

24. _____ Which of Italy's regions is known as the Mezzogiorno?
   a. the central region   b. the northern region
   c. the Po River valley   d. the southern region

25. _____ Which of the following is not the result of tectonic forces on t
   Greek landscape?
   a. Major faults sank the land area, which the Aegean Sea later flooded
   b. Older extensions of the Dinaric Alps run through northern Greece.
   c. The crush of tectonic plates thrust up mountains in the south.
   d. Rugged slopes in areas where natural forests have been destroyed
      suffer from soil erosion.

26. _____ Which factor does not help explain why Greece is considered part
   of Mediterranean Europe?
   a. membership in both the EU and NATO
   b. borders with Albania, the former Yugoslav republic of Macedonia, an
      Bulgaria
   c. geographic and historical ties to the region
   d. role as birthplace of Western culture

GRAPHIC STUDY

Directions: Use the bar graph below to answer the following questions.
Write your answers on the lines provided.

Mediterranean Trade

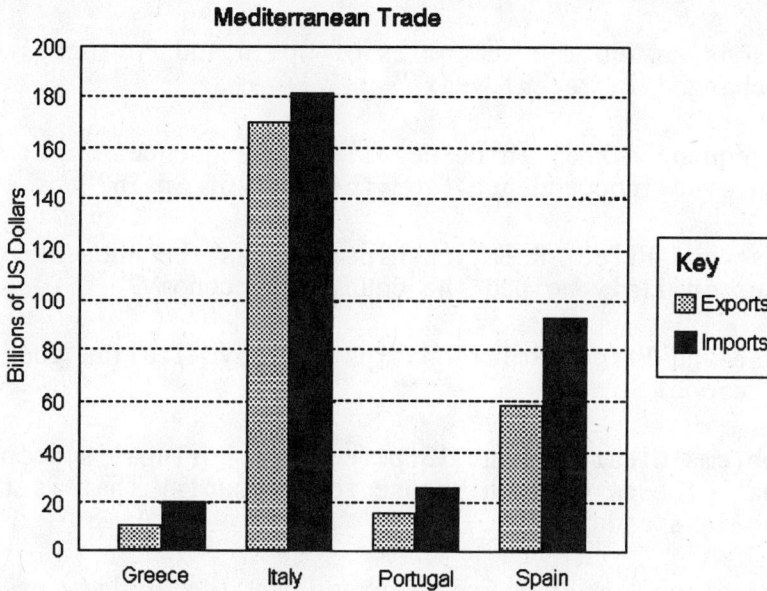

27. What does the key for the bar graph tell you?

_____

28. (a) Which country exported the most goods?
(b) Which country imported the second most goods?

_____

29. Which country had the largest trade deficit (spent more money on imports than it received for exports)?

_____

30. What does the bar graph portray?

_____

31. (a) Which country experienced the most trade activity?
(b) Which country experienced the least trade activity?

_____

32. How much more than Portugal did Spain import?

_____

SHORT ANSWER

C. Critical Thinking
Directions: Answer the following questions on the back of this paper or on a separate sheet of paper.

33. Making Comparisons How do the economies of Spain and Portugal compare? How have they changed in recent years?

34. Predicting Consequences What three negative consequences might result if the Basques achieved independence from the rest of Spain?

35. Perceiving Cause-and-Effect Relationships How has the success of metal goods industries in Italy helped the country's economy?

36. Perceiving Cause-and-Effect Relationships Why have Italian goods been successful in Europe?

37. Expressing Problems Clearly About 13 percent of Portugal's people are illiterate. What problem does this pose for a country that is trying to raise its economic standards?

38. Analyzing Information How does Greece exemplify the ability of a nation to preserve its cultural identity despite foreign invasion and occupation?

Answer Key   Chapter 17

SHORT ANSWER

1. Only one of Spain's rivers in the Meseta is navigable, or deep and wide enough to allow ships to pass.

2. The Renaissance was a great period of art, literature, and learning that began in Italy in the 1300s.

3. The Aegean Sea occupies a graben, an area of land that has dropped down between faults.

4. One Greek archaeologist theorized that tsunamis, huge ocean waves, destroyed much of the island of Crete.

MULTIPLE CHOICE

5. c	6. a
7. b	8. c
9. a	10. d
11. c	12. d
13. c	14. a
15. a	16. a
17. d	18. d
19. c	20. a
21. a	22. c
23. c	24. d
25. d	26. b

GRAPHIC STUDY

27. which bar indicates imports and which indicates exports

28. (a) Italy   29. Spain
    (b) Spain

30. imports and exports in billions of
    dollars for the Mediterranean nations

31. (a) Italy
    (b) Greece

32. more than four times as much

SHORT ANSWER

33. Traditionally, farming has been important
    to the economies of both Spain and
    Portugal. In recent years, however, both
    Spain and, to a lesser degree, Portugal
    have moved to more industrial economies.

34. Both the Basque people and the rest of
    Spain would lose natural and human resources;
    Spain would lose part of the cultural
    diversity and richness that characterize the
    nation; the non-Basques who live in Basque
    territory might lose some of their rights.

35. The boom in the metal goods industries has
    boosted Italy's steel industry and helped the
    growth of many smaller factories that supply
    parts and machinery.

36. Italy's low labor costs allowed goods to be
    exported at lower prices.

37. Illiteracy makes it difficult for workers to
    perform jobs involving reading and writing and
    to keep up on technical developments.

38. Through a history of foreign invasions and rule,
    Greece has maintained a strong national identity
    and a distinct language and culture.

Chapter 18   Regional Atlas: Eastern Europe

SHORT ANSWER

A. Vocabulary
Directions: Use each term below in a sentence that shows the meaning of the term. Write your sentences on the lines provided.

1. multiethnic

_____

_____

2. karst

_____

_____

MULTIPLE CHOICE

B. Key Geographic Concepts and Skills
Directions: Write the letter of the correct ending in the blank.

3. _____ The term Eastern Europe refers to the nations that
a. lie east of the Urals.
b. were defeated by the Soviet Union in 1917.
c. formed a buffer between the West and the Soviet Union after World War II.
d. had democratic governments after World War II.

4. _____ The inhabitants of Eastern Europe who arrived about 2,000 years ago and stayed to settle the land are
a. the Celts, who later settled Ireland.
b. the Magyars, who helped break the power of Rome.
c. the Slavs, who first settled around the Carpathian Mountains.
d. the Bulgars, who settled near the Black Sea.

5. _____ The landform region in Eastern Europe that is dominated by the Danube River is the
a. Carpathian Mountains.
b. Hungarian Basin.
c. North European Plain.
d. Balkan Peninsula.

6. _____ The Dinaric Alps lie along the coast of the
a. Mediterranean Sea.
b. Black Sea.
c. North Sea.
d. Adriatic Sea.

7. _____ The climate of Eastern Europe
   a. is the same as that of Western Europe.
   b. is hotter and rainier than the climates of Western Europe.
   c. reflects a transition between the climates of Western Europe and
      those of Northern Eurasia.
   d. is subarctic because of winds from the Baltic Sea.

8. _____ Eastern Europe's cultural diversity is best characterized by the
   many different
   a. political systems present in the region.
   b. languages spoken throughout the region.
   c. styles of clothing worn in the different countries.
   d. economic activities practiced throughout the region.

9. _____ Most Eastern Europeans are descendants of the
   a. Celts.   b. Romans.
   c. Magyars.   d. Slavs.

10. _____ The people who invaded and settled the Hungarian Basin from Asia
    centuries ago were the
    a. Croats.   b. Magyars.
    c. Russians   d. Serbs.

11. _____ Under Communist rule, Eastern Europe had a
    a. system of government that exercised complete control over people's
       lives.
    b. representative form of government that supported a market economy.
    c. decentralized political system with powerful regional governments.
    d. government that encouraged a classless society and common ownership
       of all economic resources.

12. _____ The plain that the Hungarians call the pustza
    a. is a barren, rocky expanse.
    b. used to be covered with grassland but is now farmland.
    c. has little economic value.
    d. is covered with snow for nine months of the year.

13. _____ Changes occurred in Eastern Europe in the late 1980s and the ear
    1990s when the region
    a. experienced widespread agrarian reforms.
    b. strengthened its ties with the Soviet Union.
    c. changed from an industrial to an agricultural society.
    d. moved away from communism.

14. _____ All of the following countries are located on the Balkan Peninsu
    except
    a. Poland.   b. Romania.
    c. Bulgaria.   d. Albania.

15. _____ One of Eastern Europe's most valuable natural resources, sometimes called its "lifeline," is the
a. Volga River.   b. Danube River.
c. Rhine River.   d. Oder River.

16. _____ Poland's major landform is the
a. Carpathian Mountains
b. Balkan Peninsula.
c. North European Plain.
d. Hungarian Basin.

17. _____ Almost half of the land in Eastern Europe is used for
a. farming.   b. mining.
c. forestry.   d. manufacturing.

18. _____ The major landform found in the Balkan Peninsula is
a. mountain ranges.
b. expansive plains.
c. gentle hills.
d. elevated plateaus.

19. _____ The climate in the northeastern part of Eastern Europe is generally
a. warmer than the climate of Western Europe.
b. colder than the climate of the land to the north.
c. wetter than the climate of the lands bordering the Mediterranean Sea.
d. cooler and drier than the climate of most countries on the Balkan Peninsula.

20. _____ Besides the North European Plain, all of the following landform regions appear in Eastern Europe except the
a. Carpathian Mountains.
b. Hungarian Basin.
c. mountainous Balkan Peninsula.
d. Ural Mountains.

21. _____ Most Hungarians are descended from the
a. Magyars.   b. Russians.
c. Slavs.   d. Bulgars.

22. _____ Communist governments in Eastern Europe were established by the
a. Poles during the 1800s.
b. Russians after the Russian Revolution in 1917.
c. Soviet Union at the end of World War II.
d. Soviet Union during the Cold War.

23. _____ The largest city in Eastern Europe is
a. Bucharest, Romania.
b. Belgrade, Yugoslavia.
c. Krakow, Poland.
d. Zagreb, Croatia.

24. _____ The northernmost landform region of Eastern Europe is
a. the Carpathian Mountains.
b. the Dinaric Alps.
c. the Northern European Plain.
d. the Balkan Peninsula.

25. _____ Most of the countries on the Balkan Peninsula have a
a. Mediterranean climate.
b. humid continental climate.
c. highland climate.
d. tundra climate.

26. _____ The Danube River winds its way
a. along the western slopes of the Ural Mountains.
b. along the coast of the Adriatic Sea.
c. from south to north from Albania to Poland.
d. from northwest to southwest through Eastern Europe.

GRAPHIC STUDY

Directions: Use the maps below to answer the following questions. Write your answers on the lines provided.

27. What new countries were created after World War I?

_____

28. From which countries was Poland created?

_____

29. From which countries was Yugoslavia created?

_____

30. Which Eastern European country was larger after World War I?

_____

31. What new countries were created after World War I?

_____

32. From which country was Czechoslovakia created?

_____

33. Which countries did not exist after World War I?

_____

34. Which Eastern European country was larger after World War I?

_____

SHORT ANSWER

C. Critical Thinking
Directions: Answer the following questions on the back of this paper or
on a separate sheet of paper.

35. Drawing Conclusions Why is the Danube River important to countries in
Eastern Europe?

36. Perceiving Cause-and-Effect Relationships What effect did
industrialization probably have on the population distribution of
Eastern Europe after World War II?

37. Determining Relevance How has the relative location of Eastern Europe
led to ethnic diversity in the region?

38. Drawing Conclusions What attitude have Eastern Europeans developed
toward communism in recent years? Explain.

Answer Key   Chapter 18

SHORT ANSWER

1. Eastern Europe is a multiethnic region made up of many different cultu[...]
   groups.

2. Most of the rock formations in the Dinaric
   Alps are made up of a soft limestone called
   karst.

MULTIPLE CHOICE

3. c	4. c
5. b	6. d
7. c	8. b
9. d	10. b
11. a	12. b
13. d	14. a
15. b	16. c
17. a	18. a
19. d	20. d
21. a	22. c
23. c	24. c
25. a	26. d

GRAPHIC STUDY

27. Finland, Estonia, Latvia, Lithuania,
    Poland, Czechoslovakia, and Yugoslavia

28. Germany, Russia, and Austria-Hungary

29. Montenegro, Austria-Hungary, and Serbia

30. Romania

31. Finland, Estonia, Latvia, Lithuania,
    Poland, Czechoslovakia, and Yugoslavia

32. Austria-Hungary

33. Montenegro, Serbia, and Austria-Hungary

34. Romania

SHORT ANSWER

35. The Danube River provides a major transportation route for people and goods moving in and out of the region. The river probably also provides water for crops.

36. Before World War II, most of the people in Eastern Europe lived in rural areas. After World War II, the Communist governments of the region placed a heavy emphasis on industrial development. As the region industrialized, many people probably began to move from farms to cities in search of factory jobs.

37. Eastern Europe lies between the European Peninsula and Eurasia, forming a corridor that connects the two regions. This location attracted many conquerors from the east, west, and south. Many of the people who invaded stayed and settled the land.

38. Eastern Europeans have experienced many economic shortages over the years under Communist rule. Because of this, they believe that the Communist system has failed and that it should be replaced with one that will better provide for their basic needs.

Chapter 19   The Countries of Eastern Europe

SHORT ANSWER

A. Vocabulary
Directions: Use each term below in a sentence that shows the meaning of
the term. Write your sentences on the lines provided.

1. balkanize

_____

_____

2. ghetto

_____

_____

3. collective farm

_____

_____

MULTIPLE CHOICE

B. Key Geographic Concepts and Skills
Directions: Write the letter of the correct answer in the blank.

4. _____ What factor has not contributed to the strong national identity of
the Polish people?
a. Nearly everyone living in Poland is Polish.
b. Poland has dominated its neighbors for several centuries.
c. The Poles are strongly attached to their land.
d. Almost all Poles practice the same religion.

5. _____ What institution remained strong in Poland even after the
Communist takeover of the country?
a. the Roman Catholic Church
b. Solidarity
c. the Jewish community
d. the Democratic party of Poland

6. _____ Which of the following is equally true of Czechs, Slovaks, and
Hungarians?
a. They all underwent a velvet revolution.
b. None have any mineral resources.
c. They share Western outlooks and ways.
d. Their populations are largely Turkish in origin.

7. _____ How can Bosnia-Herzegovina best be described?
   a. as a nation of conflicting ethnic groups
   b. as a unified nation
   c. as a nation struggling to rebuild Communist ties to Russia
   d. as a peaceful and prosperous nation

8. _____ Which ethnic group dominates Hungary?
   a. Magyars   b. Serbs
   c. Czechs   d. Turks

9. _____ What environmental factor was blamed for the destruction of 56 percent of Czech forests by 1993?
   a. depletion of the ozone layer
   b. cutting and exporting of lumber
   c. strip mining
   d. industrial pollution and acid rain

10. _____ What Balkan republics maintained the name Yugoslavia for their union?
    a. Croatia and Serbia
    b. Macedonia and Montenegro
    c. Slovenia and Macedonia
    d. Serbia and Montenegro

11. _____ How did Albania respond in the past to feeling threatened by its neighbor?
    a. by aligning itself with strong Islamic governments
    b. by leading the push for democracy and free enterprise
    c. by isolating itself
    d. by trying to reestablish its Roman Catholic ties to Europe

12. _____ Which of the following was a reason for Bulgaria's relative tolerance of Soviet control?
    a. Both peoples share Germanic origins.
    b. Russians, fellow Slavs, supported native Bulgarians for many years.
    c. Both peoples share a belief in Roman Catholicism.
    d. The Soviet Union made Bulgaria a leader in technology and industry.

13. _____ Why are there so few Jews in all of Poland?
    a. Poland has never had a large Jewish population.
    b. Most Jews died in religious wars with Roman Catholics.
    c. Many Jews migrated to Russia after 1917.
    d. Millions of Jews were executed by the Nazis.

14. _____ Which of the following is not a problem for the Polish economy?
    a. price increases
    b. continued Russian domination
    c. unemployment
    d. difficulty attracting foreign investors

15. _____ What landform covers most of Poland?
   a. the North European Plain
   b. the Carpathian Mountains
   c. the Hungarian Basin
   d. the Dinaric Alps

16. _____ Which of the following explains how Czechoslovakia was divided
   into the Czech Republic and Slovakia in 1993?
   a. The division resulted from a civil war.
   b. The division resulted from a peaceful separation.
   c. The division was imposed by Russia.
   d. The division was imposed by the United Nations.

17. _____ What forms the basis of the Czech economy?
   a. subsistence farming
   b. arms production
   c. tourism
   d. industry

18. _____ When did the Magyars settle in the area that is now Hungary?
   a. in 1990, when the first non-Communist government was elected
   b. when the Austro-Hungarian empire was formed in the nineteenth century
   c. in the late 800s
   d. after World War II, when the Soviet Union gained control of Eastern
   Europe

19. _____ What nation ruled over the Balkans for 500 years?
   a. Prussia
   b. Austria-Hungary
   c. Russia
   d. Turkey

20. _____ Which of the following explains why the former Yugoslavia broke up
   into a number of small countries after Communist control ended in the
   late 1980s?
   a. tensions between different ethnic groups
   b. the desire of some republics to remain Communist
   c. pressure from Western European nations
   d. the lack of a common heritage

21. _____ Which Balkan country was left in economic chaos by the communist
   leader Nicolae Ceausescu?
   a. Albania   b. Bulgaria
   c. Romania   d. Yugoslavia

SHORT ANSWER

Directions: Read the passage below. Then, define the problem presented in the passage, and make a list of alternatives for solving the problem. Use the back of this paper to continue your list of alternatives if necessary.

Akyra is concerned about a litter problem at her school. She would like to organize a campaign to clean up the school grounds and to encourage students not to litter. When she voiced this idea to her friends, however, some of them made fun of her. She does not want to lose her friends.

22. Problem:

Alternatives:

GRAPHIC STUDY

Directions: Use the map below to answer the following questions. Write your answers on the lines provided.

Eastern Europe: Economic Activity

23. What is the greatest land use in the northern part of the region?

24. What is the most common economic activity around the cities of Eastern Europe?

_____

25. How is most of the land in Eastern Europe used?

_____

26. Where does most manufacturing and trade take place in Eastern Europe?

_____

SHORT ANSWER

Directions: Describe the six steps in the decision-making process called DECIDE.

27. D
    E
    C
    I
    D
    E

Critical Thinking
Directions: Answer the following questions on the back of this paper or on a separate sheet of paper.

28. Perceiving Cause-and-Effect Relationships Why did the former Yugoslavia break up into a number of small, independent nations?

29. Formulating Questions What are three questions you might ask a Polish citizen that would help you understand life in modern Poland?

30. Recognizing Bias What extreme form of bias was demonstrated by the Nazis in Poland during World War II?

31. Drawing Conclusions Why do you think the Roman Catholic Church was able to remain strong in Poland after the Communist takeover of the country?

32. Distinguishing False from Accurate Images Why do you think Polish leader Lech Walesa was accurate when he said that "they [the Soviets] wanted us to be afraid of tanks and guns, and instead we don't fear them at all"?

33. Expressing Problems Clearly What are two problems that the Czech people must confront in the 1990s?

SHORT ANSWER

1. To balkanize means to break up into small, mutually hostile political

2. A ghetto is an area of a city where a minority is forced to live.

3. A collective farm is a government-owned farm.

MULTIPLE CHOICE

4. b		5. a	
6. c		7. a	
8. a		9. d	
10. d		11. c	
12. b		13. d	
14. b		15. a	
16. b		17. d	
18. c		19. d	
20. a		21. c	

SHORT ANSWER

22. Possible answers: Problem: Akyra wants to organize a campaign against littering at school, but she doesn't want to lose friends who laugh at the idea.
Alternatives: A: She can act on her idea and ignore her friends who laugh at the idea, though it means risking the loss of their friendship. B: She can forget about her idea and not risk alienating her friends. C: She can try to win her friends over.

GRAPHIC STUDY

23. commercial farming

24. manufacturing and trade

25. commercial farming

26. around cities

SHORT ANSWER

27. Possible answers: Define the problem:
state the problem clearly. Explore the
alternatives: make a list of
possibilities. Consider the consequences:
think through what might happen.
Identify your values: think what's most
important to you. Decide and act: use
information to compose alternatives.
Evaluate the results: review your decision.

28. The former Yugoslavia consisted of many
independent ethnic groups. Ethnic
hostilities caused the breakup of the
former Yugoslavia.

29. What are the benefits and drawbacks of
the end of communism in Poland? Why is
it difficult to convert to capitalism?
Has democracy improved your life, and
if so, how?

30. The Nazis killed six million Poles in
concentration camps, about half of them
Jews. They sealed off Jewish ghettos in
Polish cities such as Warsaw. When the
Jews in the Warsaw ghetto rebelled, the
Nazis slaughtered all the people remaining
in the ghetto. Similar actions also
occurred elsewhere in Europe. This killing
and destruction was an extreme form of bias.

31. The Roman Catholic Church remained strong
because church leaders worked out a
compromise with the Communists that allowed
Catholic churches to remain open.

32. The Poles showed that they were not afraid
of Soviet tanks and guns by supporting
Solidarity even after it was outlawed and
by continuing to press for democratic reforms
until they toppled communism.

33. The Czech people must modernize their
industries in order to compete in the world
market. They must also find ways to save their
environment, which is being destroyed by acid
rain and industrial pollution.

Chapter 20   Regional Atlas: Northern Eurasia

SHORT ANSWER

A. Vocabulary
Directions: Use each term below in a sentence that shows the meaning of the term. Write your sentences on the lines provided.

1. steppe

   _____

   _____

2. taiga

   _____

   _____

3. tundra

   _____

   _____

4. chernozem

   _____

   _____

5. taiga

   _____

   _____

6. chernozem

   _____

   _____

7. tundra

   _____

   _____

8. steppe

_____

_____

MULTIPLE CHOICE

B. Key Geographic Concepts and Skills
Directions: Write the letter of the correct ending in the blank.

9. _____ The basic landform pattern of Northern Eurasia consists of
   a. plains in the west, lakes and mountains along the southern border,
      and mountains in the east.
   b. elevated plains spreading across the entire region.
   c. rugged mountain ranges stretching north and south across the whole
      expanse of the country.
   d. lakes and mountains edging the southern border, with plains in both
      the eastern and western sections.

10. _____ West of the Ural Mountains lies the
   a. European Plain.   b. Central Siberian Plateau.
   c. Western Siberian Lowland.   d. North Siberian Lowland.

11. _____ The traditional boundary between Europe and Asia is formed by th
   a. Caucasus Mountains.   b. Volga River.
   c. Ural Mountains.   d. Yenisei River.

12. _____ The major influences on the climate of Northern Eurasia are the
   region's
   a. eastern mountain ranges and western plains areas.
   b. landforms and nearness to large bodies of water.
   c. location in the high latitudes and large size.
   d. location in the middle latitudes and nearness to cold oceans.

13. _____ Most of Siberia has a climate that is
   a. Mediterranean.   b. subarctic.
   c. humid continental.   d. semiarid.

14. _____ Moscow receives its moisture from winds blowing over the
   a. Barents Sea.   b. Mediterranean Sea.
   c. Pacific Ocean.   d. Atlantic Ocean.

15. _____ The two southernmost natural vegetation regions in Northern
   Eurasia are
   a. grassland and forest.   b. desert and forest.
   c. grassland and desert.   d. tundra and forest.

16. _____ The soil of much of the steppe region of Northern Eurasia is
a. very fertile and productive.
b. lacking in minerals and unproductive.
c. too cold to produce much food.
d. heavily fertilized with chemicals to make it marginally productive.

17. _____ All of the following are Siberian rivers that provide transportation and fish as they flow north into the Arctic Ocean except the
a. Ob.
b. Lena.
c. Dnieper.
d. Yenisei.

18. _____ The most densely populated area of Northern Eurasia lies
a. in the west, where the soil is richest.
b. along the eastern coast, where minerals are abundant.
c. in the south, where the temperatures are warmest.
d. around the diamond-mining areas of northern Siberia.

19. _____ The ethnic group that dominates the European republics is the
a. Slavs.
b. Caucasians.
c. Turkics.
d. Siberians.

20. _____ All of the following statements about climate in Northern Eurasia are true except:
a. Northwestern Russia and nearby nations and most of Siberia have a semiarid climate.
b. Away from the moderating effects of ocean water, much of Northern Eurasia's interior has a continental climate.
c. Open to the chilling winds of the Arctic Ocean, the far northern reaches of Northern Eurasia have a tundra climate.
d. A humid continental climate with warm summers covers the southern part of the European Plain.

21. _____ Northern Eurasia has four
a. basic ethnic groups.
b. regions of natural vegetation.
c. countries within the Arctic Circle.
d. coastlines that touch oceans.

22. _____ Northern Eurasia's access to the Mediterranean Sea is through the
a. Caspian Sea.
b. Aral Sea.
c. Baltic Sea.
d. Black Sea.

23. _____ The mountains lying between the Black Sea and the Caspian Sea are the
a. Pamirs.
b. Tian Shan.
c. Caucasus.
d. Urals.

24. _____ Because most of the region lies far from the moderating effects of ocean water, the interior of Northern Eurasia has
a. a climate influenced primarily by landforms.
b. a continental climate.
c. a polar climate.
d. large areas of desert vegetation.

25. _____ Much of Northern Eurasia receives little rainfall because
a. there are not enough mountains to cause the rain to fall.
b. the region has a short coastline.
c. much of the region lies in the interior of the continent.
d. the region is so far north that most precipitation falls as snow.

26. _____ The two northernmost natural vegetation regions in Northern Eurasia are
a. tundra and desert.   b. grassland and forest.
c. grassland and tundra.   d. tundra and forest.

27. _____ The historic cities of the western part of Northern Eurasia include
a. Samarkand and Tashkent.
b. Moscow and Vladivostok.
c. Omsk and Minsk.
d. St. Petersburg and Moscow.

28. _____ All of the following are major ethnic groups found in Northern Eurasia except
a. Germanic people.   b. Slavic people.
c. Turkic people.   d. Caucasian people.

29. _____ The rivers of Siberia, when not frozen, have been used for centuries to transport
a. agricultural products.
b. lumber from nearby forests.
c. people to nearby factories.
d. tourists to see the natural wonders.

30. _____ Nearly half of Northern Eurasia is covered with
a. desert.   b. forest.
c. tundra.   d. grassland.

31. _____ Most areas of dense population in Siberia are located
a. around the Aral Sea.   b. near railways and rivers.
c. along the Pacific coast.   d. in the Pamirs.

32. _____ The Communist government of the Soviet Union was established in the
a. early 1600s.   b. mid-1800s.
c. early 1900s.   d. mid-1900s.

33. _____ The largest country in Northern Eurasia is
    a. Siberia.   b. Ukraine.
    c. Georgia.   d. Russia.

34. _____ Northern Eurasian cultures and ways of life
    a. are basically the same in all of the nations.
    b. are based on European traditions in most nations.
    c. are Russian everywhere except in Siberia.
    d. vary greatly from one nation to another.

GRAPHIC STUDY

Directions: Use the map below to answer the following questions. Write
the letter of the correct place in the blank provided.

35. _____ Moscow

36. _____ Black Sea

37. _____ Volga River

38. _____ St. Petersburg

39. _____ Caucasus Mountains

40. _____ Moscow

41. _____ Caspian Sea

42. _____ Ural Mountains

43. _____ Ob River

44. _____ Vladivostok

SHORT ANSWER

C. Critical Thinking
Directions: Answer the following questions on the back of this paper or on a separate sheet of paper.

45. Perceiving Cause-and-Effect Relationships What effect has climate had on the population distribution of Northern Eurasia?

46. Making Inferences Many of the people who live in the central Asian republics are Muslims. What impact do you think their religion had on relations within the Soviet Union during the era of Communist control of these republics?

47. Making Inferences Why has the Black Sea been important as a transportation route for Northern Eurasia?

48. Perceiving Cause-and-Effect Relationships What makes the steppes of the Ukraine both desirable to other countries and vulnerable to attack?

Answer Key   Chapter 20

SHORT ANSWER

1. The Soviet steppe is a fertile, temperate grassland region.

2. The taiga is a region of thinly scattered coniferous trees.

3. Only tundra vegetation—mosses and lichens—
can grow near the Arctic Circle.

4. The black soil, or chernozem, of the
steppes makes the region good for farming.

5. The taiga is a region of thinly scattered coniferous trees.

6. The rich chernozem of the steppes is an
ideal soil for growing wheat and other
grains.

7. The tundra vegetation of the far north can
grow despite the cold climate.

8. The Russian steppe is a fertile, temperate grassland region.

MULTIPLE CHOICE

9. a

10. a

11. c

12. c

13. b

14. d

15. c

16. a

17. c

18. a

19. a

20. a

21. b

22. d

23. c

24. b

25. c

26. d

27. d

28. a

29. b

30. b

31. b

32. c

33. d   34. d

35. D   36. E

37. H   38. B

39. F   40. D

41. I   42. L

43. O   44. W

SHORT ANSWER

45. Climate has determined where many
    people in Northern Eurasia live.
    Densely settled areas include those
    in which the climate favors farming,
    such as the steppe region. On the other
    hand, areas with desert conditions, such
    as east of the Caspian Sea, or with an
    extremely cold climate, such as Siberia,
    have a low population density.

46. Because communism is a form of government
    in which the state controls all aspects of
    life and tries to suppress people's
    practice of religion, relations between
    Muslims and the Communist government of the
    Soviet Union were probably poor.

47. The Black Sea provides the western part of
    Northern Eurasia with warm-water access to
    trade. Other ports of the region, which lie
    in subarctic areas, are frozen for part of
    the year, so they can't be used for shipping.

48. The steppes of the Ukraine have rich soil
    called chernozem, which makes them very
    fertile and therefore desirable to those who
    want to control this productive agricultural
    land. Because the steppes are flat and have
    no rivers or mountains that provide natural
    defenses, they are vulnerable to attack.

Name _____ Class _____ Date _____

Chapter 21 Russia and the Independent Republics

FILL-IN-THE-BLANK

A. Vocabulary
Directions: Complete each sentence by writing the correct term in the blank. You will not use all the terms.

soviet
glasnost
genocide
collective farm
permafrost
nationalism
chernozem
taiga
command economy
perestroika
heavy industry
yurt
state farm

1. Joseph Stalin initiated government plans to develop _____, the production of goods such as steel and machines used by other industries.

2. Gorbachev's policy of economic restructuring was called _____.

3. In a(n) _____, the government makes all of the decisions about the kinds and amount of goods to be produced.

4. The huge forest of Siberia, called the _____, provides a vast supply of lumber.

5. The rich _____ of the steppes is an ideal type of soil for agriculture.

6. Transportation of resources out of Siberia is hampered by the area's _____, or permanently frozen soil.

7. Armenians suffered greatly in an act of _____ by the Turks at the beginning of World War I.

8. The strong _____ in several former Soviet republics has fueled a number of movements toward independence.

MATCHING

Directions: Match the definitions with the terms. Write the correct letter in each blank. You will not use all the terms.

a. permafrost
b. perestroika
c. soviet
d. glasnost
e. taiga
f. genocide
g. heavy industry
h. steppe
i. market economy
j. nationalism
k. command economy
l. light industry

9. _____ vast grasslands south of the forests in Northern Eurasia

10. _____ system in which the government decides the kinds and amount of goods to be manufactured

11. _____ desire of a cultural group for independence

12. _____ deliberate attempt to destroy an ethnic group

13. _____ production of goods such as steel and machines that are used for other industries

14. _____ term referring to a policy of political openness in the Soviet Union

15. _____ layer of permanently frozen soil

16. _____ term referring to a policy of restructuring of the Soviet Union

MULTIPLE CHOICE

B. Key Geographic Concepts and Skills
Directions: Write the letter of the correct ending or answer in the blank.

17. _____ Which of the following is not a challenge that Russia must overcome in developing its resources?
    a. extracting resources from remote and rugged locations
    b. preserving the fragile natural environment
    c. eliminating trade barriers between Soviet republics
    d. building means to transport resources to industrial centers

18. _____ Why was it difficult to obtain such goods as clothing and food in the Soviet Union under Stalin?
a. The state wanted to keep the standard of living low.
b. The Soviet people were more interested in developing heavy industry than in buying consumer goods.
c. Because of higher salaries, most Soviets preferred to work in industry.
d. Stalin's policies made production of consumer goods a low priority.

19. _____ Which of the following statements about the Baltic nations of Lithuania, Latvia, and Estonia is not true?
a. Because of their location, the Baltic nations have been influenced by European culture.
b. The Baltic nations have more advanced economies than other nations of Northern Eurasia.
c. Because of the benefits they receive from the former Soviet Union, these Baltic states chose not to seek independence.
d. The location of the Baltic nations astride major trade routes favored them at times.

20. _____ What is the greatest source of conflict between Armenia and Azerbaijan?
a. conflicting nationalistic feelings
b. uneven distribution of oil reserves
c. different levels of industrialization
d. offshore fishing rights

21. _____ Most people in the central Asian republics are
a. Muslims.   b. Christians.
c. Jews.   d. Buddhists.

22. _____ The Soviet program of creating cotton fields in central Asia had disastrous consequences for
a. the Caspian Sea.   b. the Aral Sea.
c. Lake Baikal   d. the Black Sea

23. _____ Which of the following statements about Russia is true?
a. Russia was forced to integrate the cultures of other republics into its own.
b. Russia is primarily a Muslim country.
c. Upon becoming an independent nation, Russia entered a period of transition to a market-driven economy.
d. Russia lies in the Caucasus to the south of Armenia and Azerbaijan.

24. _____ Which of the following would be the most important factor in evaluating the accuracy of a report on Russia's economy?
a. the nationality of the author
b. the conclusions the author reached about the economy
c. the evidence the author used to support the conclusions
d. the inclusion of historical comparisons with the economies of other countries

25. _____ What effect does climate have on the movement of resources to industrial areas in Russia?
   a. Because airplanes cannot fly in the frigid Siberian climate, there is little air transportation in Russia.
   b. Many roads, rivers, and harbors freeze over in the cold, making transportation difficult.
   c. The cold and heavy snow have prevented the construction of railroads in Siberia.
   d. The warm climate of northern Siberia makes the transport of resources relatively easy.

26. _____ Lithuania, Latvia, and Estonia are found along the coast of the
   a. Black Sea.   b. Caspian Sea.
   c. Baltic Sea.   d. Pacific Ocean.

27. _____ What mode of transportation moves the greatest amount of goods in Russia?
   a. trucks   b. pipelines
   c. railroads   d. airplanes

28. _____ When did Lithuania, Latvia, and Estonia come under Soviet control?
   a. the 1800s   b. 1917
   c. 1940   d. 1989

29. _____ What are the countries of the Caucasus?
   a. Lithuania, Latvia, and Estonia
   b. Ukraine, Belarus, and Moldova
   c. Turkmenistan and Tajikistan
   d. Georgia, Armenia, and Azerbaijan

30. _____ Which of the following statements about Azerbaijan is not true?
   a. Most of Azerbaijan's people are Christians.
   b. Azerbaijan has rich petroleum deposits.
   c. The people of Azerbaijan have had troubled relations with Armenians.
   d. Nationalism is a powerful force in Azerbaijan.

31. _____ Which two republics did the Chernobyl disaster most directly affect?
   a. Belarus and Lithuania
   b. Lithuania and Russia
   c. Ukraine and Belarus
   d. Turkmenistan and Armenia

32. _____ Which account of an Azerbaijani demonstration for independence that turned into a riot do you think would be the most reliable?
   a. the account in an Armenian newspaper
   b. the account of an Azerbaijani protester
   c. the account of a Swedish reporter
   d. the account of a Muslim leader

Name _____ Class _____ Date _____

GRAPHIC STUDY

Directions: Use the map of Northern Eurasia to answer the following
questions. Write the letter of the correct nation in the blank provided.

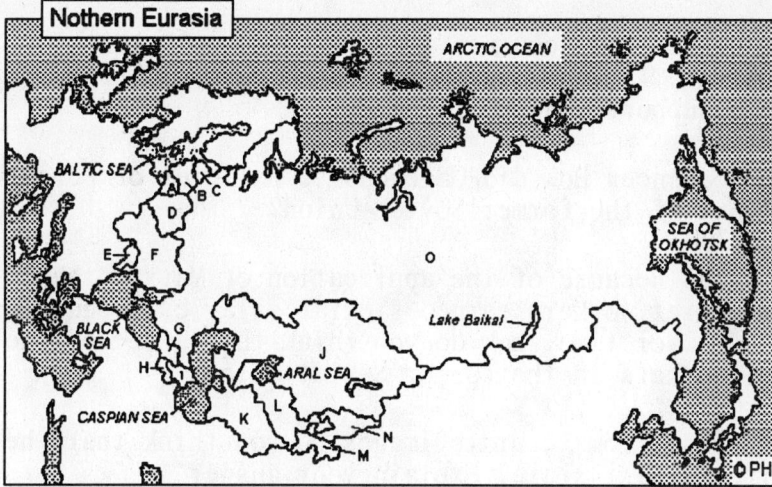

Nothern Eurasia

33. _____ Kazakstan

34. _____ Turkmenistan

35. _____ Russia

36. _____ Lithuania

37. _____ Ukraine

38. _____ Armenia

39. _____ Georgia

40. _____ Belarus

41. _____ Estonia

42. _____ Russia

SHORT ANSWER

C. Critical Thinking
Directions: Answer the following questions on the back of this paper or on a separate sheet of paper.

43. Distinguishing False from Accurate Images Many people think of Northern Eurasia as "Russia." Is this image false or accurate? Offer at least three details to support your position.

44. Recognizing Consequences How did Gorbachev's policies of perestroika affect the economy of the former Soviet Union?

45. Drawing Conclusions Because of the application of Marx's theory of equality, most Soviet workers earned similar salaries, regardless of how hard they worked. Over time, how do you think this affected the productivity of workers in the former Soviet Union?

46. Distinguishing False from Accurate Images Do you think that the Soviet Union was a true Marxist state? Explain your answer.

47. Perceiving Cause-and-Effect Relationships How did Stalin's economic plans affect the standard of living in the Soviet Union?

48. Drawing Conclusions Why might problems arise in a country whose political system consists of only one party?

Answer Key   Chapter 21

FILL-IN-THE-BLANK

1. heavy industry

2. perestroika

3. command economy

4. taiga

5. chernozem

6. permafrost

7. genocide

8. nationalism

MATCHING

9. h

10. k

11. j

12. f

13. g

14. d

15. a

16. b

MULTIPLE CHOICE

17. c

18. d

19. c

20. a

21. a

22. b

23. c

24. c

25. b

26. c

27. c

28. c

29. d

30. a

31. c

32. c

GRAPHIC STUDY

33. J

34. K

35. 0

36. A

37. F   38. H

39. G   40. D

41. C   42. 0

SHORT ANSWER

43. False—The various nations comprise people
    of different national groups who speak
    different languages and have different
    religions. The nations differ in their
    standards of living, resources, industries,
    and abilities to exist independently.

44. The new policies called for a gradual change
    from a command system. The policies offered
    the possibility of long-term growth, but
    they took away some forms of security on
    which the people depended.

45. Over time, the productivity of Soviet workers
    probably decreased because workers who could
    not directly profit from their own hard work
    had little incentive to work harder.

46. No. According to Marx, all businesses and land
    were to be owned by all people in common, with
    workers sharing equally in profits. Under the
    Soviet system, power lay in the hands of a few
    strong party leaders who made decisions on
    every aspect of Soviet life.

47. The economic plans emphasized the rapid
    development of heavy industry at the expense of
    the production of consumer goods, so the
    standard of living in the Soviet Union remained
    low.

48. Lack of competition and opposition in a one-party
    system can lead to decision-making policies that
    are rarely challenged. This, in turn, may minimize
    the pressure to change policies that have proven
    to be unsuccessful.

Chapter 22   Regional Atlas: Southwest Asia

MATCHING

A. Vocabulary
Directions: Match the definitions with the terms. Write the correct letter in each blank. You will not use all the terms.

a. muezzin
b. Hajj
c. desert
d. mosque
e. prophet
f. oasis
g. Muslim
h. arable
i. monotheism
j. minaret

1. _____ pilgrimage to Mecca

2. _____ suitable for farming

3. _____ Islamic place of worship

4. _____ person who calls Muslims to prayer

5. _____ follower of Islam

6. _____ tall, thin tower attached to Islamic house of worship

7. _____ fertile place in a dry region formed by a source of water

8. _____ person whose teachings are believed to be inspired by God

FILL-IN-THE-BLANK

Directions: Complete each sentence by writing the correct term in the blank. You will not use all the terms.

muezzin
deserts
monotheism
oases
prophet
mosque
Muslims
arable
minaret
Hajj

9. The religious journey to Mecca is known as the _____.

10. A person whose teachings are believed to be inspired by God is a _____.

11. A belief in one God is _____.

12. Underground springs of fresh water that force their way to the surface form areas in the desert called _____.

13. Muslims are called to prayer five times each day by a(n) _____.

14. Land that can be farmed is _____ land.

15. The followers of Islam are _____.

16. The Islamic place of worship is a(n) _____.

MULTIPLE CHOICE

B. Key Geographic Concepts and Skills
Directions: Write the letter of the correct ending in the blank.

17. _____ Much of the land in Southwest Asia is made up of
    a. semiarid, rocky mountains.
    b. dried-up gullies and deep river valleys.
    c. dry, hot desert.
    d. fertile coastal plains.

18. _____ Because most of the inhabitants in Southwest Asia live near reliable sources of water, the population of the region is
a. unevenly distributed over the area.
b. concentrated in small desert villages.
c. greatest in highland areas.
d. more than 90 percent Muslim.

19. _____ Small rivers are important to the region because
a. there are no large rivers in the area.
b. only small rivers deposit rich soil when they flood.
c. rivers are the major source of water in the region.
d. rivers are the main means of transportation in the area.

20. _____ In the Tigris-Euphrates basin, the vegetation is
a. grassland.   b. mixed forest.
c. evergreen forest.   d. desert.

21. _____ All of the following are among the Pillars of Islam except
a. performing daily prayers.   b. memorizing the Koran.
c. giving to charity.   d. making a Hajj.

22. _____ As the rural population of the region grows, many farm families are forced to
a. become nomadic herders.
b. work to build dams and irrigation systems.
c. move to the cities to earn a living.
d. move to farming villages along the major rivers.

23. _____ A Mediterranean climate region is found
a. throughout Southwest Asia.
b. from the Mediterranean coast east to Saudi Arabia.
c. around the Persian Gulf.
d. on the west coast of the Mediterranean.

24. _____ All of the following religions began in Southwest Asia except
a. Judaism.   b. Christianity.
c. Islam.   d. Buddhism.

25. _____ All three of the major religions that developed in Southwest Asia
a. are monotheistic.
b. originated in Iran.
c. were based on the teachings of Muhammad.
d. used Arabic as the language of their holy books.

26. _____ Water is a precious resource in Southwest Asia because
a. there are few harbors in the region.
b. temperatures rise dramatically during the day.
c. there are few underground springs in the area.
d. most of the region receives less than 10 inches (25 cm) of rain a year.

27. _____ Southwest Asia can best be characterized as
a. an area with few resources.
b. a desert with an arid and semiarid climate.
c. a region of forests.
d. an area of forests and grasslands.

28. _____ The most important source of water for the region is
a. rainfall.   b. underground springs.
c. rivers.   d. the Mediterranean Sea.

29. _____ Life in the desert is spread out over great distances primarily because
a. water is scarce.
b. people prefer to live apart from each other.
c. the desert is too hot in some areas.
d. the soil is richer in areas of high elevation.

30. _____ The predominant religion in Southwest Area is
a. Christianity.   b. Islam.
c. Judaism.   d. Hinduism.

31. _____ The teachings of Muhammad have been recorded in the
a. Torah.   b. Koran.
c. Five Pillars of Islam.   d. New Testament.

32. _____ The most important factor determining population distribution in Southwest Asia is the location of
a. oil reserves.   b. reliable sources of water.
c. Islamic houses of worship.   d. centers of trade.

33. _____ Farmers in Southwest Asia have adapted to the dry climate of the region by
a. building dams and irrigation systems.
b. covering large areas with forests.
c. becoming nomads who search for fertile soil.
d. settling in small villages and towns near markets.

34. _____ Each of the following is one of the Five Pillars of Islam except
a. performing daily prayers.
b. fasting during the holy month of Ramadan.
c. adopting the Arabic language.
d. traveling to Mecca once in a lifetime to pray.

Directions: Use the climate graph below to answer the following
questions. Write the letter of the correct ending in the blank.

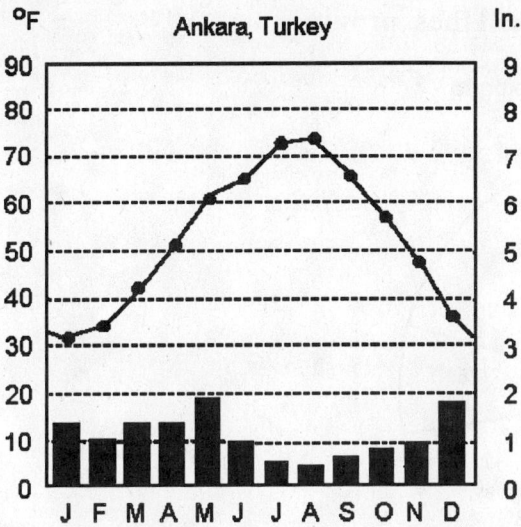

Ankara, Turkey

Line graphs show temperature. Bar graphs show precipitation.

35. _____ In Ankara, Turkey, the hottest month is
a. June.   b. July.
c. August.   d. September.

36. _____ The average December temperature in Ankara is about
a. 10°F.   b. 30°F.
c. 35°F.   d. 60°F.

37. _____ Precipitation in January and February averages
a. less than one-half inch.
b. just over an inch.
c. about 2 inches.
d. more than 3 inches.

38. _____ Ankara receives the most rainfall in
a. August.   b. March.
c. May.   d. June.

39. _____ Ankara's temperature is lowest in January and
a. February.   b. March.
c. August.   d. December.

40. _____ The highest average temperature in Ankara is approximately
a. 53°F.   b. 63°F.
c. 74°F.   d. 83°F.

GRAPHIC STUDY

Directions: Use the circle graph below to answer the following questions. Write your answers on the lines provided.

Southwest Asia: Value of Exports
$149.5 billion*

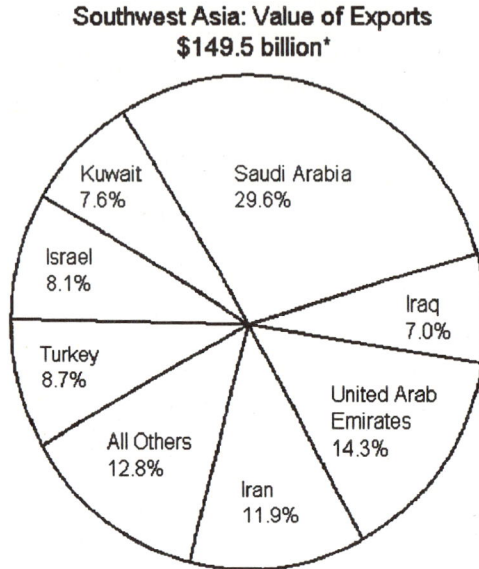

Kuwait 7.6%
Saudi Arabia 29.6%
Israel 8.1%
Iraq 7.0%
Turkey 8.7%
United Arab Emirates 14.3%
All Others 12.8%
Iran 11.9%

Source: CIA, *The World Factbook 1992.*   *Total value of Southwest Asian exports for 1990

41. What is the subject of the circle graph?

_____

42. What percentage of the total dollar value of Southwest Asian exports comes from Iraq?

_____

43. What percentage of the total dollar value of Southwest Asian exports comes from Turkey and Israel combined?

_____

44. The exports of which Southwest Asian country have the highest dollar value?

_____

45. What is the total dollar value of Southwest Asian exports?

_____

46. What percentage of the total dollar value of Southwest Asian exports comes from Iran?

_____

47. What percentage of the total dollar value of Southwest Asian exports comes from Iraq and the United Arab Emirates combined?

_____

48. The exports of which Southwest Asian country have the lowest dollar value?

_____

SHORT ANSWER

C. Critical Thinking
Directions: Answer the following questions on the back of this paper or on a separate sheet of paper.

49. Perceiving Cause-and-Effect Relationships Discuss two ways that explain how the physical geography of Southwest Asia has affected the way of life in this region.

50. Making Comparisons How are the religions of Judaism, Christianity, and Islam alike? Identify at least four features the three religions have in common.

51. Perceiving Cause-and-Effect Relationships Why are the populations of Southwest Asian cities increasing at such a rapid rate?

52. Identifying Central Issues The countries of Southwest Asia are united by several characteristics and divided by others. Name three characteristics that unite the countries and two that cause conflict or tension.

Answer Key   Chapter 22

MATCHING

1. b	2. h
3. d	4. a
5. g	6. j
7. f	8. e

FILL-IN-THE-BLANK

9. Hajj	10. prophet
11. monotheism	
12. oases	13. muezzin
14. arable	15. Muslims
16. mosque	

MULTIPLE CHOICE

17. c	18. a
19. c	20. a
21. b	22. c
23. d	24. d
25. a	26. d
27. b	28. c
29. a	30. b
31. b	32. b
33. a	34. c
35. c	36. c
37. b	38. c
39. a	40. c

GRAPHIC STUDY

41. dollar value of Southwest Asian exports for 1990

42. 7.0%   43. 16.8%

44. Saudi Arabia

45. $149.5 billion

46. 11.9%   47. 21.3%

48. Iraq

SHORT ANSWER

49. Southwest Asia is a desert region with a dry climate and unpredictable rainfall. As a result, people live and work in areas with reliable sources of water. Agriculture is concentrated along rivers and in coastal, mountain, and plateau areas that receive rainfall. Where there is little water, the people live as nomadic herders and sell the products of their livestock in nearby towns and cities.

50. All three are monotheistic, have origins in Southwest Asia, consider Jerusalem a holy city, and have holy books in which the history and teachings of the religion have been recorded.

51. With economic opportunities limited in rural areas, many farmers seek work in cities.

52. Characteristics that unite the countries: the harsh climate, the lack of water and arable land, and the Islamic culture. Characteristics that divide the countries: uneven distribution of oil reserves, uneven distribution of water.

Chapter 23   The Countries of Southwest Asia

MATCHING

A. Vocabulary
Directions: Match the definitions with the terms. Write the correct letter in each blank. You will not use all the terms.

a. falaj system
b. anarchy
c. shah
d. infrastructure
e. secular
f. ayatollahs
g. mandate
h. embargo
i. desalination
j. drip irrigation
k. militia
l. Zionists
m. Knesset
n. self-determination

1. _____ agreement under which a foreign power governs a country until it is ready for independence

2. _____ Jews who believe that the return of Palestine to the Jewish people is their historic right

3. _____ method of allowing precise amounts of water to drip from pipes onto plants

4. _____ Israel's parliament

5. _____ army

6. _____ state of lawlessness or political disorder

7. _____ process of purifying seawater of salt

8. _____ country's basic support facilities

9. _____ ancient network of underground and surface canals in Oman

10. _____ conservative Islamic religious leaders

FILL-IN-THE-BLANK

B. Key Geographic Concepts and Skills

Directions: Complete each sentence by writing the correct term in the blank. You will not use all the terms.

falaj system
anarchy
shah
infrastructure
ayatollah
mandate
self-determination
desalination
militia
Zionist
Knesset
secular
drip irrigation

11. France governed Syria and Lebanon under a(n) _____ issued by the League of Nations.

12. A Jew who believes that the return of Palestine to the Jewish people is their historic right is called a(n) _____

13. Farmers use _____ to preserve water.

14. Israel's parliament is called the _____.

15. Each religious faction in Lebanon has its own _____, or army.

16. The process of removing the salt from seawater so that it can be used for drinking and irrigation is called _____.

17. A country's _____ is its basic support facilities, including its roads, schools, and communication systems.

18. A complete state of lawlessness is called _____.

19. Farmers in Oman depend on an ancient network of underground and surface canals called the _____ for water.

20. An Islamic religious leader is a(n) _____.

MULTIPLE CHOICE

B. Key Geographic Concepts and Skills
Directions: Write the letter of the correct answer in the blank.

21. _____ What occurred after the fall of the Ottoman Empire?
    a. The Seljuk Turks conquered almost all of Southwest Asia.
    b. The followers of Muhammad invaded Mesopotamia, Palestine, and Persia.
    c. Islam successfully governed the people in Southwest Asia as one political region for 150 years.
    d. Southwest Asia was divided into several countries and political entities.

22. _____ Which of the following was not part of the United Nations' solution to the problem of Palestine in 1947?
    a. Palestine was divided into an Arab state and a Jewish state.
    b. The city of Jerusalem was designated as an international city.
    c. Palestine was divided among Jews, Palestinians, Egyptians, and Jordanians.
    d. Palestine's Jewish minority gained control of more than half of the country's lands.

23. _____ What event left the Palestinians without a homeland?
    a. the Arab-Israeli war of 1948   b. World War I
    c. the Arab-Israeli war of 1967   d. World War II

24. What is Israel's greatest resource?
    a. fertile land   b. a skilled work force
    c. oil   d. water

25. _____ Which of the following statements is true?
    a. Arabs living in Israel are Israeli citizens who have full political rights.
    b. Israeli Arabs and Jews live in the same communities and attend the same schools.
    c. Arabs are allowed to serve in Israel's army.
    d. Arabs make up more than 80 percent of Israel's population.

26. _____ Which statement about Iraq is not true?
    a. Outdated farming methods have affected Iraq's agricultural output.
    b. Profits from Iraq's oil industry have been used to develop the country.
    c. A war with Iran severely strained Iraq's financial resources.
    d. Farming is Iraq's most important economic activity.

27. _____ Why have countries on the Arabian Peninsula invested large sums of money to develop industries other than the oil industry?
a. Oil revenues are too low to support their economies.
b. The countries need to provide jobs for their large populations.
c. The countries realize that one day they will run out of oil.
d. Most countries on the Arabian Peninsula have large amounts of other resources.

28. _____ In what two countries has life changed very little over the centuries?
a. Bahrain and Qatar
b. Kuwait and the United Arab Emirates
c. Oman and Yemen
d. Saudi Arabia and Jordan

29. _____ What is one of the changes that Turkey's president Mustafa Kemal or Atatürk, brought to the country?
a. He created a bond between Islam and the Turkish government.
b. He replaced public secular schools with traditional Islamic schools
c. He gave women many political and legal rights.
d. He replaced European law with Islamic law.

30. _____ How are Turkey, Iran, and Israel different from other countries Southwest Asia?
a. Most of the people in Turkey, Iran, and Israel are Christians.
b. Arabic is not the major language of the three countries.
c. There has been very little conflict in these countries over the years.
d. They have no oil reserves.

31. _____ What was the result of Iran's 1979 revolution?
a. The Sunnis defeated the Shiites in their struggle for control of Iran.
b. Iran cut off Western influence and became an Islamic republic.
c. The Iranian Persians defeated the Iraqi Arab rule.
d. Iran became a modern, Western nation.

32. _____ Which group of people established the last great empire of Southwest Asia?
a. the Persians   b. the Ottoman Turks
c. the Arabs   d. the Seljuks

33. _____ What was not a result of the Sykes-Picot Agreement?
a. Saudi Arabia and Yemen made up an independent Arab state.
b. France ruled Syria under mandate.
c. The area from southern Turkey to southern Arabia, and from the Mediterranean Sea to the borders of Iran, formed an independent Arab state.
d. Great Britain ruled Palestine and Iraq under mandates.

34. _____ What effect did the Arab-Israeli War of 1948 have on the Palestinians?
    a. The Palestinians gained control of almost three fourths of Palestine.
    b. The Palestinians lost one half of the country to the Israelis.
    c. The Palestinians were left without a homeland.
    d. The Palestinians established an independent homeland with territories given to them by Egypt and Jordan.

35. _____ How did the Israelis overcome the challenge of limited farmland?
    a. by using traditional irrigation methods
    b. by growing fewer crops
    c. by developing oil resources
    d. by draining swamps and building irrigation systems

36. _____ What group of people makes up 17 percent of Israel's population?
    a. Sephardic Jews   b. Arabs
    c. European Jews   d. Oriental Jews

37. _____ Which of the following led to Lebanon's civil war?
    a. disagreements among Lebanon's religious groups
    b. PLO attacks on Israelis based in Lebanon
    c. anger over an Arab-Israeli peace agreement
    d. conflicts between the military and the government

38. _____ Which of the following statements about Syria is not true?
    a. Many Syrians have left their farms in recent decades to work in cities.
    b. Syria has very little fertile farmland.
    c. Damascus and Aleppo have long been centers of trade.
    d. Dams built by Turkey may affect Syria's future.

39. _____ How have countries on the Arabian Peninsula prepared for the eventual depletion of their oil supplies?
    a. by developing other industries
    b. by searching for new sources of energy
    c. by allowing only nationals to work in their countries
    d. by preserving traditional lifestyles

40. _____ How do most people in Yemen and Oman make their living?
    a. from oil   b. from mining
    c. from fishing   d. from farming and herding

41. _____ Which of the following statements about Turkey is true?
    a. Turkey is one of the most industrialized countries in the Middle East.
    b. Turkey is an almost entirely agricultural nation.
    c. Women in Turkey have very few political or legal rights.
    d. Agriculture is no longer important to Turkey's economy.

42. _____ The civil war in Cyprus during the 1970s stemmed from conflicts between what two groups of people?
   a. Greek Orthodox Christians and Turkish Muslims
   b. Sunni Muslims and Shiite Muslims
   c. Greek Muslims and Arab Muslims
   d. ultra-orthodox Greeks and non-religious Greeks

TRUE/FALSE

Directions: Read the following information about remote sensing. For each statement that follows, write T in the blank if the statement is true and F if it is false.

Remote sensing began in the 1930s with aerial photography employing techniques developed during World War I. From that point on, it became far less necessary to determine the true nature of the earth's surface through on-site ground surveys.
Then, in the 1970s, remote sensing satellites orbiting far above the earth gathered information by measuring the electromagnetic radiation emitted from points on the earth. At approximately 560 miles (900 km) above the earth, Landsat satellites have, since the first was launched in 1972, circled the earth sending back detailed information regarding land features and vegetation patterns and detecting even such small items as city blocks and parking lots. Scientists, geographers, cartographers, city planners, and many others have benefited from the increasingly valuable information about the earth.

43. _____ Remote sensing began with aerial photography.

44. _____ The use of remote sensing increased the need for on-site ground surveys of the earth's surface.

45. _____ Satellites can image only a portion of the earth's surface.

46. _____ At a height of 560 miles (901 km), Landsat satellites can image only large items on the earth's surface.

SHORT ANSWER

Directions: Read the following paragraphs. For each of the groups named in the following questions, describe a possible benefit from the remote sensing program planned for the end of this century.

By the end of the twentieth century, an ambitious space program is planned to be in effect that will use sophisticated remote sensing devices to monitor conditions on earth. Current Landsat satellites will be aided by other satellites and spacecraft to gather information vital to all people.

The major areas of information gathered will include (1) weather and crop information; (2) the study of the locations of underground natural resources such as water, oil, and natural gas; (3) pollution and its spread across regions; and (4) changes in the earth's vegetation, sometimes affected by droughts, fires, and human actions. The study of these areas will involve scientists from around the world, working together to learn more about our planet through the use of remote sensing devices and aerial photography.

47. forest rangers

_____

_____

48. farmers

_____

_____

49. environmentalists

_____

_____

50. government officials

_____

_____

C. Critical Thinking
Directions: Answer the following questions on the back of this paper or on a separate sheet of paper.

51. Analyzing Information Explain what Israel's first prime minister, David Ben-Gurion, meant when he said: "If the state does not put an end to the desert, the desert is likely to put an end to the state."

52. Expressing Problems Clearly Name one or two sources of conflict that have led to instability in Southwest Asia since the end of World War I Give examples to support your answer.

53. Determining Relevance Explain the role that oil has played in the development of several countries in Southwest Asia. Give examples to support your answer.

54. Demonstrating Reasoned Judgment Do you think oil-rich countries in the region are preparing well enough for the eventual depletion of their o resources?

55. Recognizing Bias How did the actions of the Arabs reflect their attitu toward the establishment of Israel in 1948?

56. Perceiving Cause-and-Effect Relationships What were the causes of Iran revolution and of its eight-year war with Iraq? How did these conflict affect the country's economy?

Answer Key   Chapter 23

MATCHING

1. g
2. l
3. j
4. m
5. k
6. b
7. i
8. d
9. a
10. f

FILL-IN-THE-BLANK

11. mandate
12. Zionist
13. drip irrigation
14. Knesset
15. militia
16. desalination
17. infrastructure
18. anarchy
19. falaj system
20. ayatollah

MULTIPLE CHOICE

21. d
22. c
23. a
24. b
25. a
26. d
27. c
28. c
29. c
30. b
31. b
32. b
33. c
34. c
35. d
36. b
37. a
38. b

39. a   40. d

41. a   42. a

TRUE/FALSE

43. T   44. F

45. F   46. F

SHORT ANSWER

47. provide information about forest fires and condition of forests

48. provide weather and crop information

49. detect pollution and its spread across regions

50. locate needed underground natural resources

51. Israel's prime minister was referring to the Negev Desert, which covers more than half of Israel's land, and to the challenge that it posed to the country. Israel's survival depended on whether the country could overcome the problem of its limited farmland.

52. Disagreements stemming from nationalism and religion have led to much instability in Southwest Asia. For example, Israel and neighboring Arab countries have been in conflict and have fought several wars since the establishment of Israel in 1948. In Iran, Shiite Muslim leaders overthrew the shah and set up a strict Islamic state in 1979. Shortly thereafter, Iran's Shiite Muslims engaged in an eight-year war with the Sunni Muslims in Iraq. In Lebanon, political and economic conflicts between the Maronite Christians and Muslim groups have led to two civil wars in that country since 1958.

53. The discovery of oil has brought great wealth to many of the countries in Southwest Asia and has enabled them to modernize and raise their standards of living. Iraq and Saudi Arabia, for example, have opened new schools and universities; built roads, airports, and hospitals; and improved communication systems. Also, knowing that they will one day run out of oil, several countries have developed petrochemical and other related industries.

54. Recognizing that they will not always be able to depend on oil, the countries of the Arabian Peninsula have invested large sums of money to develop other industries. Bahrain has become an international banking center. Saudi Arabia, Qatar, and the United Arab Emirates have built steel and petrochemical industries. If these countries invest the large amounts of money they now have in industries that will endure, their countries will probably prosper.

55. Just hours after the announcement of the independent state of Israel in 1948, neighboring Arab countries attacked Israel, demonstrating the strong opposition that Arabs felt toward the new state. The Arabs believed that their land was unfairly taken from them and used to pay the Jews for injustices suffered at the hands of the Nazis during World War II.

56. Resentment against the rule of the pro-Western dictatorship of the shah led to Iran's revolution and to the Islamic overthrow of the government. Iran's eight-year war with Iraq was the result of religious rivalry between Iran's Shiite Muslims and Iraq's Sunni Muslims. Both conflicts severely affected Iran's economy. Thousands of technicians and managers fled Iran along with the shah. As a result, industries that depended on highly skilled workers were forced to close. Also, oil exports dropped sharply because of damage to storage terminals and refineries during the war. Without money to pay for basic necessities, Iran's rapidly growing population of almost 54 million people faced serious shortages.

Chapter 24   Regional Atlas: Africa

SHORT ANSWER

A. Vocabulary
Directions: Use each term below in a sentence that shows the meaning of
the term. Write your sentences on the lines provided.

1. cataract

_____

_____

2. leaching

_____

_____

3. escarpment

_____

_____

4. cataract

_____

_____

5. erg

_____

_____

6. diversify

_____

_____

MULTIPLE CHOICE

B. Key Geographic Concepts and Skills
Directions: Write the letter of the correct ending or answer in the blank.

7. _____ The climate bands that cover Africa run
   a. east to west and include tropical, moderate, and polar regions.
   b. from low coastal elevations to inland areas and include arid and tropical regions.
   c. west to east and include highland, tropical, and moderate regions.
   d. north to south and include semiarid, tropical, and moderate regions

8. _____ The major landform in Africa south of the Sahara is
   a. low plain rising to towering mountains.
   b. vast plateau surrounded by a narrow coastal plain.
   c. low plain rising to a high plateau in the south.
   d. series of parallel high mountains.

9. _____ The African landform that was probably formed when two tectonic plates moved apart is the
   a. Western Coastal Plain.
   b. Sahara.
   c. Great Rift Valley.
   d. Congo River Basin.

10. _____ South Africa, Swaziland, and the southern tip of Mozambique are the most heavily populated areas in Africa because they have
    a. mild climates and good farmland.
    b. a large number of factory jobs.
    c. a large number of navigable rivers.
    d. fishing resources.

11. _____ The Namib and the Kalahari are
    a. desert regions in North Africa.
    b. tropical rain forests at the Equator.
    c. dry regions in Southern Africa.
    d. savanna regions near the Equator.

12. _____ Nearly three quarters of the people in Africa south of the Sahar live
    a. in growing urban areas.
    b. in rural, agricultural villages.
    c. north of the Equator.
    d. in the rain forest.

13. _____ Farming in Africa
    a. takes place only in Nigeria.
    b. offers its inhabitants a high living standard.
    c. has dramatically improved Africa's economy.
    d. is risky because of droughts.

14. _____ One of the main problems challenging the economies of many African nations today is
a. a lack of diverse exports.
b. increasing their export of raw materials.
c. competing with the industrial output of other African nations.
d. making fishing more productive.

15. _____ Which of the following statements is not true?
a. Women play a vital role in many African economies.
b. Many African governments have borrowed huge sums of money to modernize their countries.
c. Leaching of nutrients from the soil is more of a problem in deserts than in the rain forest.
d. Loan payments are a major part of the budgets in modernizing countries.

16. _____ The large area of land that the tropical rain forest covers in Africa
a. contains very fertile soil, but environmentalists will not allow people to cut down the trees to plant crops.
b. is shrinking as the savanna expands to take land away from the rain forest.
c. has poor soil because of leaching, which takes away nutrients.
d. is located along the eastern coast of the continent.

17. _____ Great cultural diversity exists in African countries, especially those
a. with small populations.
b. located along the northern coast.
c. located south of the Sahara.
d. that were independent in 1914.

18. _____ Scientists believe that the Great Rift Valley was created by
a. volcanic eruptions.
b. tectonic forces.
c. ocean flooding.
d. receding glaciers.

19. _____ Africa's tropical rain forests are located
a. in the equatorial region from Guinea to the Great Rift Valley.
b. along most of the western coast south of the Equator.
c. along the southern tip of Africa.
d. along the eastern coast on the windward side of the mountains.

20. _____ Generally, the farther away from the Equator one travels in Africa, the
a. hotter the temperatures become.
b. drier the climate becomes.
c. higher the landforms become.
d. denser the rain forest becomes.

21. _____ Which of the following statements is not true?
   a. The Nile River is a major transportation route across southern Africa.
   b. The central plateau produces many cataracts in African rivers.
   c. Africa's rivers can be used for hydroelectric power.
   d. Because of terrain, some African rivers are not navigable.

22. _____ Many African economies depend on the export of
   a. one or two products.
   b. rain forest products.
   c. African wildlife.
   d. manufactured goods.

23. _____ All of the following have contributed to slow economic growth in parts of Africa except:
   a. poor soils.
   b. large loan repayment amounts.
   c. drought.
   d. industrialization.

24. _____ Keeping people healthy is a challenge in Africa because
   a. governments are not concerned about health matters.
   b. drought and famine cause poor diets and weaken the health of many people.
   c. modern medicine has not yet reached the continent.
   d. hurricanes and earthquakes cause widespread damage.

SHORT ANSWER

Directions: Number the statements below so that they form a coherent essay.

25. _____ This land, known as the Sahel, supports vegetation that is suite only for grazing animals.
   _____ Thus, when the drought passes, the plants do not grow again, and the desert advances farther south.
   _____ Drought is a frequent problem in the broad band of the semiarid land south of the Sahara.
   _____ However, the animals, mostly goats, are usually so hungry that they eat all the plants they can find in the already sparsely vegetate zone, including their roots.

26. _____ First, many African rulers were cheated out of their riches in farmlands, minerals, and other natural resources.
   _____ Although this type of forced labor was cruel and inhumane, its practice continued in much of Africa until World War I.
   _____ The Africans were treated very harshly by Europeans during the colonial period.
   _____ Also, the African peoples were forced to work extraordinarily l[o] hours and were beaten if their work was not satisfactory to their European supervisors.

GRAPHIC STUDY

Directions: Use the map below to answer the following questions. Write your answers on the lines provided.

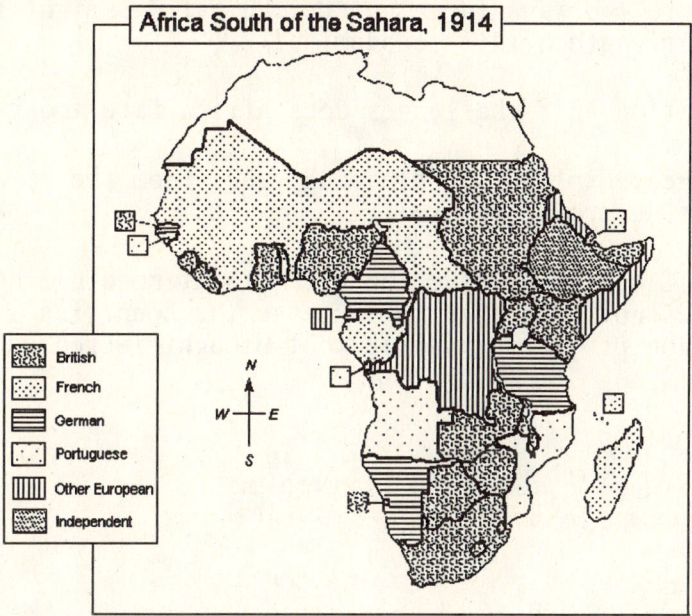

Africa South of the Sahara, 1914

British
French
German
Portuguese
Other European
Independent

27. Which two European countries controlled most of Africa south of the Sahara in 1914?

   _____

28. How many countries in the region were independent in 1914?

   _____

29. Which European country had the largest claim in West Africa in 1914?

   _____

30. Which European country had the largest claim in East Africa in 1914?

   _____

SHORT ANSWER

C. Critical Thinking
Directions: Answer the following questions on the back of this paper or on a separate sheet of paper.

31. Determining Relevance How has climate affected population patterns in Africa?

32. Perceiving Cause-and-Effect Relationships How might the existence of nearly 3,000 ethnic groups and 800 languages affect life in countries south of the Sahara?

33. Identifying Alternatives Many African nations today have weak, unstable economies as a result of their dependence on the export of just one or two products. What are two ways in which African nations might reverse this situation and strengthen their economies?

34. Synthesizing Information What challenges does Africa face today?

35. Predicting Consequences Explain why clearing trees from the rain forest would result in poor, unproductive soil.

36. Expressing Problems Clearly Why have the attempts at modernizing many of the African economies not been able to increase the countries' wealth? Why have modernization projects in Africa not brought increased wealth to the region?

Answer Key   Chapter 24

SHORT ANSWER

1. African rivers roar down enormous cataracts, or waterfalls, on their way to th
Atlantic or Indian oceans.

2. Constant heavy rains in a tropical wet
climate cause leaching of the minerals from
the soil.

3. Escarpments are steep cliffs in which the
central plateau descends to the coastal
plain.

4. African rivers roar down enormous
cataracts, or waterfalls, on their way to
the Atlantic or Indian oceans.

5. Winds in the desert move sand to create huge dunes called ergs.

6. African governments are trying to diversify
exports in order to strengthen their
economies.

MULTIPLE CHOICE

7. d	8. b
9. c	10. a
11. c	12. b
13. d	14. a
15. c	16. c
17. c	18. b
19. a	20. b
21. a	22. a
23. d	24. b

SHORT ANSWER

25. 2,4,1,3	26. 2,4,1,3

GRAPHIC STUDY

27. France and Great Britain

28. two   29. France

30. Great Britain

SHORT ANSWER

31. Extreme dry conditions in certain areas of Africa have caused droughts, desertification, and starvation. Farmers and families unable to overcome these problems have moved to the cities in search of jobs.

32. The large number of ethnic groups and languages probably makes unity within African countries very difficult. Ethnic clashes would be more likely, and everyday communication problems would exist because of the presence of so many different languages.

33. African nations can strengthen their economies by processing and manufacturing their resources, thus creating more jobs and selling highly profitable processed and finished products. African nations can also strengthen their economies by diversifying their exports, increasing their revenues by selling a variety of products, and, at the same time, protecting their economies from devastating effects if the world demand for any one particular product declines.

34. Africa faces challenges caused by natural factors such as drought and poor soils. Health problems and a low life expectancy result from famine and drought. South of the Sahara, human factors such as ethnic diversity make national unity difficult. Economic factors such as large loan repayment amounts also create challenges for African countries that are trying to modernize.

35. Clearing trees from the rain forest would deprive the soil of a constant source of fertilization—decomposing leaves—without which the soil would quickly wear out. Also, without its protective canopy, the soil would be exposed to heavy tropical rains that would leach and erode the unanchored soil.

36. Many African nations borrowed large sums of money to fund modernization projects. Loan payments have become a major part of many countries' budgets, and if governments wish to continue in their efforts to modernize, they must spend a great deal of their money paying off old loans in order to get new ones.

Name _____ Class _____ Date _____

Chapter 25   North Africa

MATCHING

A. Vocabulary
Directions: Match the definitions with the terms. Write the correct
letter in each blank. You will not use all the terms.

a. capital
b. perennial irrigation
c. caravan
d. wadi
e. pharaoh
f. reservoir
g. fellaheen
h. basin irrigation
i. bazaar
j. medina

1. _____ traditional Arab open-air market in Egypt

2. _____ practice of building walls around fields in order to trap the
water and silt overflowing from the banks of a river

3. _____ ruler of ancient Egypt who was worshipped as a god

4. _____ artificial lake created by damming a river

5. _____ older Arab section of a city in North Africa

6. _____ system that provides needed water to fields throughout the year

7. _____ large groups of merchants joined together to travel in safety

FILL-IN-THE-BLANK

Directions: Complete each sentence by writing the correct term in the blank. You will not use all the terms.

bazaar
wadi
reservoir
medina
basin irrigation
pharaoh
fellaheen
capital
perennial irrigation

8. In a(n) _____ system, farmers built walls to trap floodwaters and silt.

9. Nile floodwaters are stored in an enormous _____, called Lake Nasser.

10. An older Arab section of a North African city is a(n) _____.

11. Money used to build and support new industries is called _____.

12. A(n) _____ system provides water as needed to fields throughout the year.

13. A(n) _____ is a traditional Arab open-air market.

14. A(n) _____ was a ruler of ancient Egypt.

MULTIPLE CHOICE

B. Key Geographic Concepts and Skills
Directions: Write the letter of the correct answer in the blank.

15. _____ Water from which of the following sources keeps Egypt from becoming a desert?
    a. the Mediterranean Sea
    b. heavy rainfall
    c. the Nile River
    d. the Red Sea

16. _____ Where do the vast majority of Egypt's people live?
    a. along the Nile River and in the Nile Delta
    b. along the Mediterranean coast
    c. along the Red Sea and Lake Nasser
    d. in the Sinai Peninsula

17. _____ What event led to Great Britain's renewed interest in Egypt in the late 1800s?
   a. the opening of the Suez Canal
   b. discovery of oil in the Sinai Peninsula
   c. the building of the Aswan Dam
   d. the French invasion of Egypt

18. _____ What are Egypt's most important exports today?
   a. cotton and cotton textiles
   b. manufactured goods
   c. phosphates
   d. oil and petroleum products

19. _____ What was the major reason that Egypt tried to develop closer ties with the Arab Middle East immediately after the end of World War II?
   a. to oppose the establishment of the state of Israel
   b. to raise capital for the building of the Aswan Dam
   c. to promote trade among countries in the Middle East
   d. to protect the Suez Canal

20. _____ Which of the following problems is not a result of Egypt's growing population?
   a. overcrowded cities
   b. emigration of educated professionals to other countries
   c. a diminishing food supply
   d. widespread unemployment

21. _____ What countries make up the Maghreb nations?
   a. all Islamic nations
   b. Egypt and Libya
   c. Tunisia, Algeria, and Morocco
   d. the countries west of Egypt bordering the Mediterranean Sea

22. _____ When did North Africa enter a golden age during which the region became an important center of learning?
   a. during rule by the Carthaginians
   b. during Roman rule
   c. after the Arab conquest
   d. after European powers invaded the region

23. _____ Which of the following is true of both Libya and all the nations of the Maghreb?
   a. Most of the land area is covered by tropical rain forest.
   b. They were French colonies until the mid-1900s.
   c. The majority of their people live along the Mediterranean coast.
   d. Their economies depend on the sale of petroleum.

24. _____ Which of the following is not true of the Nile River valley?
   a. It runs the length of Egypt.
   b. It empties into the Indian Ocean.
   c. It is flanked on both sides by deserts.
   d. It is densely populated.

25. _____ What factor made ancient Egypt a tempting target for waves of invaders?
   a. arable land at the Nile Delta
   b. great treasures housed in the pharaohs' tombs
   c. its location between Asia, Africa, and Europe
   d. rich deposits of gold

26. _____ How did Great Britain gain control of the Suez Canal?
   a. by invading Egypt and seizing the Canal
   b. by disrupting Egyptian trade on the Mediterranean Sea
   c. by buying Egypt's share of ownership in the Canal
   d. by agreeing to remove British troops from Egypt in exchange for the Canal

27. _____ Which of the following was not a goal of Gamal Abdel Nasser?
   a. to end Western domination of Egypt
   b. to modernize the country
   c. to make Egypt a major influence in world politics
   d. to negotiate peace with Israel

28. _____ Why does Egypt import more than half of its food supply?
   a. to encourage cotton production on arable land
   b. to encourage rural Egyptians to give up their traditional ways of life
   c. to promote industrialization
   d. to meet the demands of a rapidly growing population

29. _____ What two major factors limit the growth of industry in Egypt?
   a. few skilled workers and lack of capital
   b. lack of foreign aid and support from other Arab nations
   c. dependence on a single export and limited oil reserves
   d. limited access to trade routes and lack of raw materials

30. _____ What is an important Arab contribution to North African culture?
   a. the Islamic religion
   b. introduction of camels from Central Asia
   c. irrigation systems
   d. organized government

31. _____ Where do most of the populations of Algeria, Libya, and Morocco live?
   a. in urban areas
   b. in rural communities
   c. in small groups throughout the Sahara
   d. in and around the oil fields

32. _____ Which of the following is a goal of Qaddafi's government?
   a. to protect the Tuareg culture
   b. to increase the revenues from foreign aid and to raise the rents on the military bases
   c. to provide Libyans with a free education from the primary grades through the universities
   d. to create a more equal distribution of wealth in Libya

GRAPHIC STUDY

Directions: Use the map of time zones in the Western Hemisphere to answer the following questions. Write your answers on the lines provided.

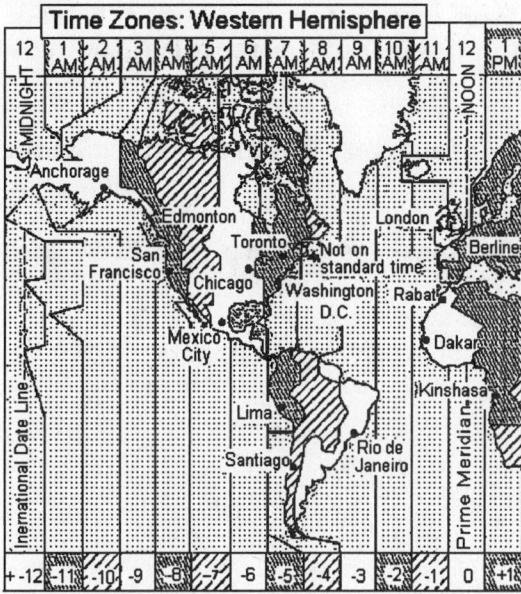

Time Zones: Western Hemisphere

33. If it is 8 p.m. in Rabat, what time will it be in a city seven time zones to the west?

_____

34. If it is 3 p.m. in Lima, what time is it in Rabat?

_____

35. When it is 6 p.m. in Rabat, what time is it in Berlin?

_____

36. If it is 3 a.m. in Rabat, what time is it in Chicago?

_____

37. If it is 12 midnight in Kinshasa, what time is it in Rabat?

_____

38. If it is 2 p.m. in Rabat, what time will it be in a city eight time zones to the west?

_____

SHORT ANSWER

C. Critical Thinking
Directions: Answer the following questions on the back of this paper or on a separate sheet of paper.

39. Identifying Alternatives What are some options government leaders in Egypt might consider to meet the demands of a rapidly growing population?

40. Making Comparisons Compare the lifestyles in North Africa's rural and urban areas.

41. Perceiving Cause-and-Effect Relationships How has the Suez Canal been a catalyst for nationalism in Egypt?

42. Making Comparisons How did the Arab conquest and rule of North Africa differ from the European conquest and rule of North Africa?

Answer Key   Chapter 25

MATCHING

1. i
2. h
3. e
4. f
5. j
6. b
7. c

FILL-IN-THE-BLANK

8. basin irrigation
9. reservoir
10. medina
11. capital
12. perennial irrigation
13. bazaar
14. pharaoh

MULTIPLE CHOICE

15. c
16. a
17. a
18. d
19. a
20. b
21. c
22. c
23. c
24. b
25. c
26. c
27. d
28. d
29. a
30. a
31. a
32. d

GRAPHIC STUDY

33. 1 p.m.
34. 8 a.m.
35. 7 p.m.
36. 9 p.m.
37. 11 p.m.
38. 6 a.m.

SHORT ANSWER

39. Options include increasing the amount of arable land through irrigation and chemical fertilization; encouraging rural Egyptians to continue farming instead of flocking to the cities; providing financial incentives for people to have smaller families; outlawing child labor and mandating public education for all children until age 16; promoting industrialization through government-sponsored training programs.

40. People in the rural areas of North Africa live and work as farmers and herders in much the same way as their ancestors. Living in one-room houses made of mud and stone, they usually have no running water and rely on wooden plows to farm. Lifestyles in the North African regions along the Mediterranean contrast sharply with village life. Modern sections of North African cities today, with their wide avenues, modern office buildings, and people dressed in Western-style clothing, look much like cities in Europe or the United States.

41. Since it opened, the Suez Canal has been the focal point of many nationalistic movements in Egypt. First, Egyptian nationalists revolted in an attempt to regain control of the Canal. British troops invaded and defeated the Egyptians and remained in Egypt for the next several decades. Later, Nasser and other nationalist army officers overthrew the Egyptian government and seized the Canal. Great Britain and France declared war on Egypt but were forced to back down because of international pressure. Nasser held the Canal, and the British troops withdrew from Egypt.

42. When the Arabs ruled North Africa, they
    assimilated the people into the Arab
    culture, giving them the Arabic language
    and the Islamic religion. The Arab rule
    marked the beginning of a long golden
    age during which North Africa became a
    center of trade and learning. On the other
    hand, North Africans gained little from
    European nations that acquired colonies
    in this region for their own benefit. In
    fact, educated professionals in Egypt
    often emigrate to Western nations.

Chapter 26   West and Central Africa

FILL-IN-THE-BLANK

A. Vocabulary
Directions: Complete each sentence by writing the correct term in the blank. You will not use all the terms.

structural adjustment program
desertification
ancestor worship
coup
inland delta
refugee
forage
mercenary
deforestation
landlocked
shifting agriculture
animism

1. When overharvested land is stripped of its trees, the process is called
   _____.

2. Food for grazing animals is called _____.

3. The loss of all vegetation in an area following a drought is called
   _____.

4. A(n) _____ flees his or her country to escape danger.

5. An area of lakes, creeks, and swamps away from the ocean is a(n)
   _____.

6. Belief in the spirits of the dead is known as _____.

7. A(n) _____ is designed to change the structure of an economy to
   make it work better.

8. A(n) _____ is a soldier who is hired to fight.

Directions: Complete each sentence by writing the correct term in the blank. You will not use all the terms.

structural adjustment program
desertification
ancestor worship
coup
inland delta
refugee
forage
mercenaries
deforestation
landlocked
shifting agriculture
animism

9. A farmer practices _____ when he prepares new farmland to replace fields in which soil has been exhausted.

10. The process of stripping the land of all its trees is called _____

11. Most of the Sahel countries are _____, or cut off from the sea.

12. A(n) _____ is a sudden, violent takeover of a government.

13. Conflict in the region has been worsened by the use of _____, or soldiers for hire.

14. The belief that ordinary things in nature contain gods or spirits is called _____.

15. A drought frequently causes _____, which is the loss of all vegetation.

16. A person who leaves his or her homeland to avoid danger or persecution is a(n) _____.

MULTIPLE CHOICE

B. Key Geographic Concepts and Skills
Directions: Write the letter of the correct answer in the blank.

17. _____ Why was the Sahel's location important to the early empire of Ghana?
    a. Its location in the Sahara made it difficult to attack.
    b. Its coastal location gave it vast fishing resources.
    c. The Sahel was the trade link between the Mediterranean coast and the rest of Africa.
    d. Its location between rain forest and desert gave it an ideal climat

18. _____ Which of the following has not contributed to the environmental destruction of the Sahel?
a. overgrazing by animals
b. damming of rivers
c. deforestation
d. desertification caused by drought

19. _____ What two rivers and their tributaries provide transportation and water for irrigation in the Sahel?
a. Congo and Zaire   b. Ubangi and Niger
c. Zaire and Benue   d. Niger and Senegal

20. _____ What two advantages do the coastal countries of West Africa have over the Sahel countries?
a. better soil and more mineral resources
b. wetter climate and access to the sea
c. cooler temperatures and flatter terrain
d. large reserves of uranium and tin

21. _____ Why have the people of West Africa started to work at the local level to help their economies?
a. They have learned that their governments alone can do little to improve economic conditions.
b. Foreign countries have stopped all economic aid to West Africa.
c. One-man rule in West Africa has been replaced by democratic governments.
d. West Africans are beginning to resist colonial rule of their countries.

22. _____ What was one result of Nigeria's dependence on its oil profits?
a. Its production of gold declined.
b. Since most nations depend on Southwest Asia for their oil supply, there was no market for Nigerian oil.
c. Enormous oil profits resulted in the corruption and destabilization of the Nigerian government.
d. Nigeria suffered serious economic problems when the price of oil fell on the world market.

23. _____ Which of the following was not part of Nigeria's structural adjustment program?
a. selling state-run businesses to private companies
b. firing some government workers
c. ceasing to sell oil on the world market
d. stabilizing wages and prices

24. _____ Which is not a result of the use of the common CFA franc in many West and Central African countries?
a. trade among the CFA countries
b. general interdependence among CFA countries
c. lack of stability in international markets for CFA countries
d. travel between the different CFA countries

25. _____ Which sentence below is a cause-effect statement?
   a. Nigerian students and workers often protested during the struc
      adjustment period.
   b. One of the surprising facts about West Africa is that the Saha
      not always a desert.
   c. Because of their location, the coastal countries of West Afric
      many advantages.
   d. The continent of Africa consists of a group of basins set in a
      plateau.

26. _____ What kind of city was Tombouctou, the capital of the Mali e
   during the reign of Mansa Musa?
   a. a major center of Islamic learning and culture
   b. a British colonial capital
   c. a major port city for the European slave trade
   d. a manufacturing center for bauxite and iron ore

27. _____ What effect has the herding of animals had on the Sahel?
   a. Grazing has removed the forage, allowing larger plants to grow
   b. Herding has helped to reverse the desertification of the Sahel
   c. Overgrazing has destroyed the plants that hold the soil in pla
   d. The Sahel has become the center of western Africa's cattle ind

28. _____ What is a major reason for the failure of West Africa's coa
   countries to create successful economies?
   a. The region has been unable to borrow money for development.
   b. The cost of the region's imports exceeds the value of its expo
   c. Most European nations avoid trading with West Africa.
   d. The region exports only manufactured goods and not raw materia

29. _____ What role do West African women play in the region's econom
   a. Tradition will not allow women to work outside the home.
   b. Women make most of the economic decisions in West Africa's
      matriarchal society.
   c. Women help grow crops and run local markets.
   d. Women own and run most of the small businesses.

30. _____ Which of the following is not a physical characteristic of
   Nigeria?
   a. rain forest   b. mountains
   c. savanna   d. swamp

31. _____ Why did the military stage a coup in Nigeria in 1983?
   a. Regional conflicts had brought the country to civil war.
   b. Foreign investors had gained control of the country's industry.
   c. The existing government was corrupt and ineffective.
   d. The economy had broken down due to the sudden fall of oil price
      the world market.

2. _____ Why is there little movement through the Congo River basin?
   a. The center of the basin is a dense rain forest.
   b. The terrain in the basin is too rugged for easy passage.
   c. Wildlife on the savanna makes it too dangerous to travel.
   d. The basin is covered by a desert.

3. _____ What factor explains why Zaire has been economically unsuccessful?
   a. corrupt national leadership and inefficient use of resources
   b. a lack of natural resources
   c. a lack of rivers that could be used for transportation
   d. poor soil and a dry climate

4. _____ What are the cause and the effect in the following statement?
   Famine relief does not reach some parts of landlocked Africa because the
   transportation system is so poor.
   a. The cause is starving people; the result is famine relief.
   b. The cause is the poor transportation system; the effect is that
      relief can't reach the people.
   c. The cause is landlocked Africa; the effect is that relief can't reach
      the people.
   d. The cause is famine relief; the result is the poor transportation
      system.

APHIC STUDY

ections: Use the map below to answer the following questions. Write
r answers on the lines provided.

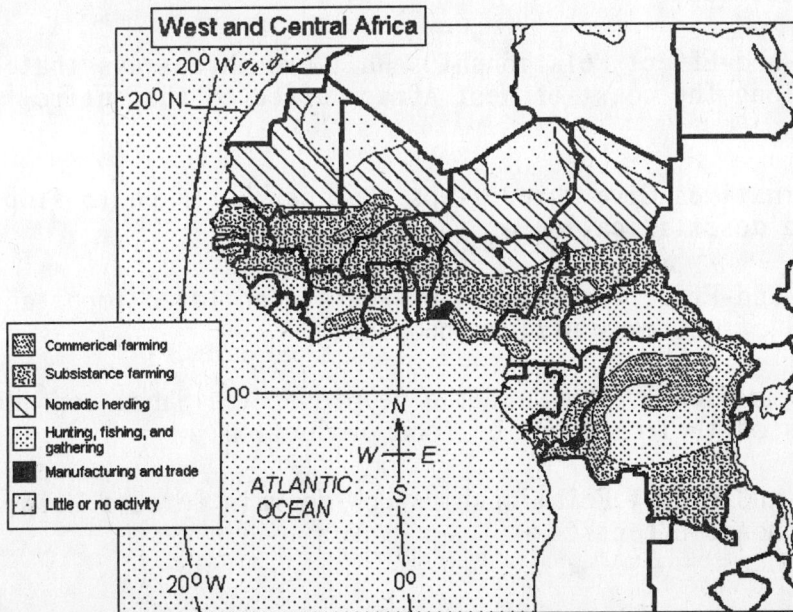

West and Central Africa

Commerical farming
Subsistance farming
Nomadic herding
Hunting, fishing, and gathering
Manufacturing and trade
Little or no activity

ATLANTIC OCEAN

35. What two economic activities occupy the least amount of land in West a Central Africa?

_____

36. What is the greatest land use in the northern part of the region?

_____

37. What three economic activities occupy most of the land in West and Central Africa?

_____

38. In what part of the region does little or no economic activity take place? Why do you think this is so?

_____

SHORT ANSWER

C. Critical Thinking
Directions: Answer the following questions on the back of this paper or on a separate sheet of paper.

39. Perceiving Cause-and-Effect Relationships Explain how drought and desertification in the Sahel have affected the inhabitants of the regi in the past two decades.

40. Perceiving Cause-and-Effect Relationships What are three ways that ear European trade along the coast of West Africa affected the entire region?

41. Identifying Alternatives Give three steps that can be taken to stop th deforestation and desertification of the Sahel.

42. Perceiving Cause-and-Effect Relationships Why are children important t the spiritual beliefs of many African peoples?

43. Expressing Problems Clearly Why must the people of the Sahel consider long-term effects of their methods of food production?

44. Perceiving Cause-and-Effect Relationships How do rain forests help to prevent the greenhouse effect?

Answer Key   Chapter 26

FILL-IN-THE-BLANK

1. deforestation

2. forage

3. desertification

4. refugee

5. inland delta

6. ancestor worship

7. structural adjustment program

8. mercenar

9. shifting agriculture

10. deforestation

11. landlocked

12. coup

13. mercenaries

14. animism

15. desertification

16. refugee

MULTIPLE CHOICE

17. c

18. b

19. d

20. b

21. a

22. d

23. c

24. c

25. c

26. a

27. c

28. b

29. c

30. b

31. d

32. a

33. a

34. b

GRAPHIC STUDY

35. commercial farming, and manufacturing and trade

36. nomadic herding

37. nomadic herding; subsistence farming; and hunting, fishing, and gathering

38. in the northern part of the region, because of arid and semiarid conditions

SHORT ANSWER

39. Drought and desertification in the Sahel wiped out farming, killed cattle, and forced people throughout the region to flee to cities. Also, many people died of starvation because of the famine caused by these conditions.

40. European trade promoted the economic growth of coastal West Africa. The new shipping routes also made trade across the Sahel and the Sahara less important, hurting that region's economies. In addition, kingdoms of the coastal area fought each other for control of trade with foreigners.

41. Trees can be planted as windbreaks to keep the topsoil from blowing away; dependence on firewood as a fuel source can be decreased; fertilizers and improved agricultural techniques can be used to produce a higher food yield from less land without exhausting the productivity of the land in the process.

42. Many Africans believe that if their children continue to honor them after death they will live on in the spirit world. Having many children ensures one's continuance as part of an extended family even after death.

43. The people of the Sahel will not be able to produce food in the future if they continue to farm land until the soil is exhausted. Nor will the land produce crops if animals are allowed to overgraze. Desertification is a serious problem in the Sahel, and it must be prevented because it cannot be remedied.

44. Rain forests absorb carbon dioxide, which, left unabsorbed in the air, would lead to a gradual rise in global temperatures.

Chapter 27　East and Southern Africa

MATCHING

A. Vocabulary
Directions: Match the definitions with the terms. Write the correct letter in each blank. You will not use all the terms.

a. animism
b. sanction
c. infrastructure
d. apartheid
e. strategic value
f. nationalism
g. land redistribution
h. diffusion
i. harambee
j. malnutrition
k. shifting agriculture
l. villagization
m. ethnocracy

1. _____ disease caused by an unhealthy diet

2. _____ value of a location for nations planning large-scale military actions

3. _____ type of government in which one ethnic group rules over other ethnic groups

4. _____ act of forcing people to move into towns and to work on collective farms

5. _____ South Africa's policy of strict racial, political, and economic discrimination against non-whites

6. _____ an economic policy of mutual cooperation, or pulling together

7. _____ economic measure taken against a country to force it to comply with international law

8. _____ act of taking land from those who have plenty and giving it to those who have little or none

FILL-IN-THE-BLANK

Directions: Complete each sentence by writing the correct term in the blank. You will not use all the terms.

animism
sanction
infrastructure
apartheid
strategic value
nationalism
land redistribution
diffusion
harambee
malnutrition
shifting agriculture
villagization
ethnocracy

9. A(n) _____ is a government in which one ethnic group rules over others.

10. Under the policy of _____, land is taken from those who have plen and is given to those who have little or none.

11. A Swahili word that means "pulling together" is _____.

12. The forcing of people to move into towns and to work on collective far is called _____.

13. Through _____, the South African government established a legal basis for the "apartness" of racial groups in South Africa.

14. Because Kenya does not grow enough food to feed its people, many of it people suffer from _____.

15. A(n) _____ is a measure that punishes a country for actions not approved of by the international community.

16. East Africa's coastal location gives some of its countries _____, the value of a location for nations planning large-scale military actions.

MULTIPLE CHOICE

B. Key Geographic Concepts and Skills
Directions: Write the letter of the correct ending in the blank.

17. _____ Under British rule in Kenya, which began in 1890,
a. Africans lost their most fertile farmland and all political power.
b. Africans continued living in their traditional homelands.
c. the Masai and the Kikuyu populations grew rapidly and became the dominant groups in the country.
d. European immigration to the country was greatly restricted.

18. _____ Kenya's social and political unrest is due largely to
a. rapid industrialization.
b. the country's move toward democracy.
c. the country's inability to supply enough food or jobs for its rapidly growing population.
d. the country's cash crop economy, which requires few farmers.

19. _____ Eritrea's long war with Ethiopia created
a. unity among its different ethnic groups.
b. sharp divisions among its different ethnic groups.
c. a postwar economic boom.
d. a thriving weapons industry.

20. _____ Sudan's many years of civil war have resulted from conflicts between
a. the northern military power and the southern economic power.
b. Muslim Arabs and Christian and animist Africans.
c. African southerners and European northerners.
d. the Hutus and the Tutsis.

21. _____ In recent years, Tanzania has
a. adopted a socialist system.
b. moved toward communism.
c. abandoned its free-enterprise system.
d. moved away from its socialist system.

22. _____ After South Africa became an independent republic in 1961,
a. many blacks moved out of the reserves into the cities.
b. the Afrikaners moved into and took control of African lands.
c. a large number of British citizens moved to South Africa to mine.
d. many Asians moved to South Africa to work in factories.

23. _____ The South African government changed its policy of apartheid in 1990 and 1991 because of
   a. the policy's failure to eliminate racial discrimination.
   b. the formation of the African National Congress (ANC) by Nelson Mandela.
   c. international sanctions and an increase in protests by black South Africans.
   d. an economically devastating civil war between black South Africans and whites.

24. _____ One problem that the countries of Rwanda and Burundi share is
   a. a lack of means for moving their goods to foreign buyers.
   b. a lack of a fresh water supply.
   c. the absence of fertile soil.
   d. very small populations.

25. _____ Zambia has become a poor country since the time the country gain independence because
   a. uncertainty about the future forced most commercial farmers to flee
   b. the economy fell when the price of copper plunged.
   c. the government failed to rebuild the country's economy after coloni rule.
   d. the economy was devastated by a civil war.

26. _____ There is enough information given in your textbook to conclude that
   a. Angola and Mozambique would have been world economic powers if they had not adopted a communist system after independence.
   b. Namibia, on the west coast of southern Africa, has proven to be the most economically independent nation of the region.
   c. Zambia and Zimbabwe would have had more economic success if they ha adopted a communist economy after independence.
   d. the countries of southern Africa are affected by the wealth and policies of the Republic of South Africa.

27. _____ The focus of movement in Kenya for centuries has been toward the
   a. coastal lowlands on the eastern shores of the country.
   b. lands around Lake Victoria in the southwest.
   c. fertile lands of the central highlands on either side of the Great Rift Valley.
   d. lands in the north and the northeast of the country.

28. _____ Kenya's government has concentrated mainly upon
   a. growing cash crops such as coffee and tea.
   b. exploiting the mineral wealth of the country.
   c. encouraging subsistence farming.
   d. developing service industries.

29. _____ Ethiopia's relative location changed because
   a. Somalia occupied its coastline.
   b. Eritrea's independence left Ethiopia landlocked.
   c. its GNP fell.
   d. its soil eroded.

30. _____ Conflicts between the Hutu and Tutsi have resulted in much violence and death in the countries of
a. Rwanda and Burundi. b. the Sudan and Uganda.
c. Djibouti and Ethiopia. d. Somalia and Tanzania.

31. _____ Tanzania's government turned around the country's failing economy by
a. forcing people to move into towns and to work on collective farms.
b. paying farmers a price for their crops that allowed them a profit.
c. creating government mining companies to mine the natural resources.
d. obtaining foreign loans that allowed the buildup of small industry.

32. _____ All of the following have contributed to South Africa's economic growth from 1950 to 1980 except
a. the country's reliance on coal as a source of energy.
b. the availability of investment capital.
c. an economic policy that rewarded its workers.
d. a vast pool of inexpensive black South African labor.

33. _____ The government of South Africa created homelands in order to
a. stop whites from taking over any more traditional black South African land.
b. control the movement of black South Africans toward the cities.
c. keep black South Africans out of the British society after the Boer War.
d. give black South Africans an amount of land proportional to their population.

34. _____ All of the following are true of Angola and Mozambique except that they
a. are coastal nations that were once Portuguese colonies.
b. have relied on South African aid to keep their economies from failing.
c. used communist economic systems to recover from colonial capitalism.
d. have rebel groups that have fought the governments in civil war.

35. _____ One major difference between the economies of Zambia and Zimbabwe is that in Zimbabwe
a. the economy was dependent on only one product, copper.
b. no infrastructure was ever developed to support the economy.
c. the president instituted a cautious policy of land redistribution.
d. the wealth of natural resources was used to develop industry.

36. _____ There is enough information given in your text to conclude that
a. Malawi and Botswana are likely to sever all economic ties with South Africa.
b. Nelson Mandela and the African National Congress (ANC) have no influence among the people of Africa.
c. pressure by Africans and international sanctions affected the South African economy and attitudes toward apartheid.
d. the Boer War was more a conflict of racial prejudice than a war to win control over the region and wealth of South Africa.

GRAPHIC STUDY

Directions: Use the map below to answer the following questions. Write
your answers on the lines provided.

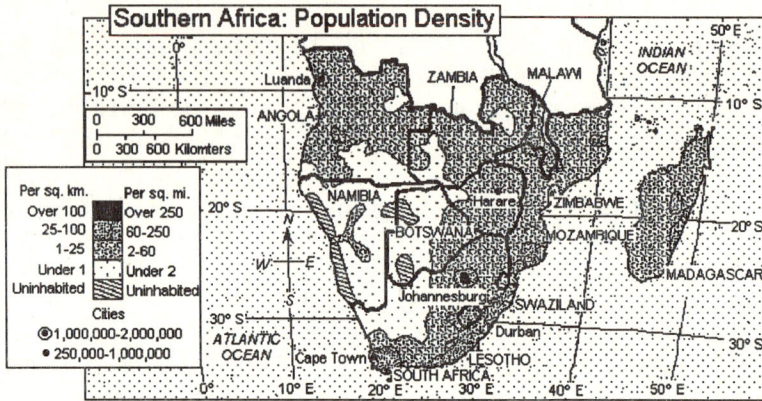

Southern Africa: Population Density

37. What is the population density in most of southern Africa?

_____

38. What large region of southern Africa has a low population?

_____

39. In what southern African city is the population density over 250 peopl
per square mile?

_____

40. What is the population density in most of Angola?

_____

SHORT ANSWER

C. Critical Thinking
Directions: Answer the following questions on the back of this paper or
on a separate sheet of paper.

41. Drawing Conclusions Read the following passage. Then, answer the
question that follows. Civil war in the Sudan has led to the destruct:
of the country's economy and to great human misery. In late 1990, the
Sudan was faced with famine on an almost unimaginable scale. Some peop
believe that one reason for the food shortage might be that the
country's president, General al-Bashir, traded 300,000 tons of food to
Libya and Iraq for weapons to use in his war against the southern
region.
What assumption can you make about the president of the Sudan?

42. Predicting Consequences What problems might arise in Kenya if the country's current economic policy is not changed?

43. Making Comparisons What is the major difference between the ethnocracies in Rwanda and Burundi? How has this difference affected the minorities?

44. Drawing Conclusions Read the following passage. Then, answer the question that follows. The South African government created arbitrary regions called homelands. Under the homelands plan, black South Africans—about 75 percent of the country's total population—were forced to live on only 13 percent of the country's land. Every black South African in the nation was assigned to a homeland and was supposed to stay in it unless a pass had been issued to him or her. What was the white government's attitude toward black South Africans in South Africa during the period of this policy?

45. Demonstrating Reasoned Judgment What three lessons might South Africa learn from the other countries of the region with regard to successfully shifting power into the hands of a democratic majority?

46. Perceiving Cause-and-Effect Relationships How did the coming of the railroad change life in Kenya?

Answer Key   Chapter 27

MATCHING

1. j   2. e

3. m   4. l

5. d   6. i

7. b   8. g

FILL-IN-THE-BLANK

9. ethnocracy

10. land redistribution

11. harambee   12. villagization

13. apartheid

14. malnutrition

15. sanction   16. strategic value

MULTIPLE CHOICE

17. a   18. c

19. a   20. b

21. d   22. a

23. c   24. a

25. b   26. d

27. c   28. a

29. b   30. a

31. b   32. c

33. b   34. b

35. c   36. c

GRAPHIC STUDY

37. 2-60 people per square mile (1-25 people per sq. km.)

38. the southwestern region including and surrounding Namibia

39. Johannesburg

40. 2-60 people per square mile (1-25 per sq. km.)

SHORT ANSWER

41. The president is a military general who is more interested in destroying his enemy than in looking after the well-being of his country's citizens.

42. Today, many Kenyans do not get enough food because the government has concentrated on growing cash crops. This situation may lead to increased social unrest in the country. Growing unrest in the country will probably increase tension between the people and the government and may lead to revolution.

43. In Rwanda, 90 percent of the population is Hutu and the rest are Tutsi. The Hutu have held power since they overthrew the Tutsi and killed 100,000 of the minority. In Burundi, only 14 percent of the population is Tutsi, but this group holds the power. The Tutsi control the army, which has been used on occasion to massacre the Hutu.

44. The white government viewed black South Africans as a threat to the white society and believed that they must be controlled and monitored. The government saw no reason to treat black South Africans equally or fairly.

45. If South Africa is to be successful in shifting the power in the country away from the minority, the new government must be certain not to cause the wealthy to flee the country. It must integrate its people to strengthen the economy by paying all people fairly for their land and labor. The country must guard against groups fighting each other in civil wars for control of the new government. It must continue to use and develop the diversified economy that has made the country strong.

46. The railroad brought English settlers to the fertile highlands of Kenya, forcing out the Masai and the Kikuyu and changing their lives.

Chapter 28   Regional Atlas: South Asia

MATCHING

A. Vocabulary
Directions: Match the definitions with the terms. Write the correct letter in each blank. You will not use all the terms.

a. rooftop of the world
b. monsoon
c. apartheid
d. Mt. Everest
e. segregation
f. subcontinent
g. precipitation
h. alluvial plain
i. Hindi

1. _____ large landmass

2. _____ broad expanse of rich, fertile land along a riverbank

3. _____ seasonal shift in the winds of Asia

4. _____ Indo-European language

5. _____ nickname for the Himalayan mountain range

FILL-IN-THE-BLANK

Directions: Complete each sentence by writing the correct term in the blank. You will not use all the terms.

precipitation
alluvial plain
segregation
apartheid
monsoon
subcontinent
tectonic plate
Hindi
rooftop of the world

6. The Himalayan range is often called the _____.

7. The _____ is the seasonal shift in the winds of South Asia.

8. About half the people in India understand the language called _____.

9. A(n) _____ is a large landmass.

10. A broad expanse of rich, fertile land along a riverbank is a(n) _____.

MULTIPLE CHOICE

B. Key Geographic Concepts and Skills
Directions: Write the letter of the correct ending in the blank.

11. _____ The Indian subcontinent includes India and all of the following countries except
a. Afghanistan and Pakistan.   b. Bangladesh and Bhutan.
c. Nepal and Sri Lanka.   d. Myanmar and Thailand.

12. _____ The Indian subcontinent is separated from the rest of Asia by th
a. Himalayas.   b. Ganges River.
c. Deccan Plateau.   d. Eastern Ghats.

13. _____ All of the following help form the large alluvial plain in the northern region of South Asia except the
a. Indus River.   b. Krishna River.
c. Ganges River.   d. Brahmaputra River.

14. _____ The heavy rains in South Asia are due to the
a. summer monsoons that pick up moisture from the warm Indian Ocean.
b. winter monsoons that bring cold air and low temperatures to the region.
c. continental air that blows from Asia's mainland over much of South Asia.
d. scorching temperatures that can reach as high as 110°F.

15. _____ Because the Western Ghats block the monsoon winds, the interior the subcontinent has a climate that is
a. hot and dry.   b. subarctic.
c. cold and wet.   d. warm and humid.

16. _____ Most areas of high population in South Asia are located along coastal regions and in northeastern India and Bangladesh where
a. the landscapes are the most attractive.
b. nomadic herding is most common.
c. there is little economic activity.
d. rainfall is abundant.

17. _____ Most of the people in South Asia make their living from
a. mining.   b. herding.
c. farming.   d. weaving.

18. _____ The landform through which the Ganges River flows is the
a. Deccan Plateau.
b. Great Indian Desert.
c. Himalaya Mountains.
d. Indo-Gangetic Plain.

19. _____ The factor that is forcing many South Asians to move to cities is
a. religious conflict in rural areas.
b. the threat of landslides in coastal areas.
c. lack of arable land due to a growing population.
d. dry conditions in the Indo-Gangetic Plain.

20. _____ The two religions with the most followers in South Asia are
a. Hinduism and Christianity.
b. Christianity and Sikhism.
c. Hinduism and Islam.
d. Sikhism and Buddhism.

21. _____ The major rivers in South Asia include all of the following except
the
a. Indus.   b. Ganges.
c. Tigris.   d. Brahmaputra.

22. _____ The landform occupying the center of the triangle that forms the
Indian subcontinent is the
a. Deccan Plateau.   b. Western Ghats.
c. Indo-Gangetic Plain.   d. Eastern Ghats.

23. _____ The climate of South Asia is mainly influenced by the region's
a. location far from large bodies of water.
b. high temperatures and monsoon winds.
c. position atop the Indo-Australian plate.
d. location in the upper latitudes.

24. _____ The monsoon rains can bring all of the following kinds of
destruction to the region except
a. floods.   b. landslides.
c. storm surges.   d. drought.

25. _____ Because the Western Ghats block winds and rain from the southwest,
the interior of the Indian subcontinent
a. is covered with mixed forest vegetation.
b. is covered with a thick tropical rain forest.
c. has a continental climate.
d. is hot and dry.

26. _____ The Indo-Gangetic Plain is one of the most densely populated areas
of the subcontinent because of its
a. lush rain forests.   b. fertile land.
c. ocean ports.   d. high mountains.

27. _____ The physical features that determine where the rain will fall in South Asia are
a. rivers.   b. coastal areas.
c. mountains.   d. plains.

28. _____ One of the greatest challenges facing South Asia today is
a. gaining independence from the British.
b. growing enough food to feed its large population.
c. increasing its population.
d. improving rail transportation throughout the region.

29. _____ Relatively little economic activity occurs
a. along the Indian coast.
b. in areas of high population density.
c. along the mountainous northern border of South Asia.
d. in the southern portion of India.

30. _____ All of the following statements are true except:
a. South Asia is one of the most densely populated regions of the worl
b. More and more South Asians are moving to cities.
c. All of the people in South Asia share a common culture and religion
d. Farming is the most important economic activity in South Asia.

GRAPHIC STUDY

Directions: Use the graph to answer the following questions. Write your answers on the lines provided.

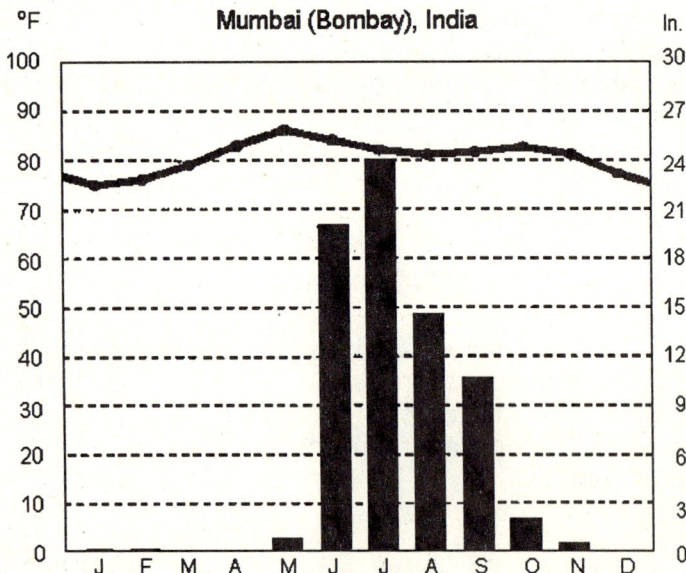

Mumbai (Bombay), India

Line graphs show average temperature.
Bar graphs show average precipitation.

© Prentice-Hall, Inc.

31. What information is presented in the graph?

_____

32. During what months of the year does Mumbai receive more than 10 inches of rain?

_____

33. During what months of the year does the average temperature remain below 80°F?

_____

34. Do you think that temperatures in Mumbai influence the amount of rain the area receives? Why or why not?

_____

35. What information is presented in the graph?

_____

36. During what months does Mumbai receive no rainfall?

_____

37. How do temperatures in Mumbai vary over the course of a year?

_____

38. When is the land in Mumbai the most productive? Why do you think so?

_____

SHORT ANSWER

C. Critical Thinking
Directions: Answer the following questions on the back of this paper or on a separate sheet of paper.

39. Demonstrating Reasoned Judgment Do you think that India's many languages have hindered or helped to create unity among its people? Explain your answer.

40. Identifying Assumptions What type of farming do you think takes place in most of South Asia? Why?

41. Perceiving Cause-and-Effect Relationships How do the monsoons and the mountains influence the climate in South Asia?

42. Making Comparisons Based on what you have learned about its physical features, culture, climate, and economy, how would you compare life in South Asia with life in the United States? List at least three points comparison or contrast.

43. Predicting Consequences What do you think would happen if most of the family-run farms in South Asia were converted to large, technologicall advanced commercial farms?

44. Checking Consistency How are monsoon rains responsible for both surviv and hardship in South Asia?

Answer Key Chapter 28

MATCHING

1. f   2. h

3. b   4. i

5. a

FILL-IN-THE-BLANK

6. rooftop of the world

7. monsoon   8. Hindi

9. subcontinent

10. alluvial plain

MULTIPLE CHOICE

11. d   12. a

13. b   14. a

15. a   16. d

17. c   18. d

19. c   20. c

21. c   22. a

23. b   24. d

25. d   26. b

27. c   28. b

29. c   30. c

GRAPHIC STUDY

31. average monthly rainfall and temperatures
    in Mumbai (Bombay)

32. June, July, August, September

33. January, February, March, December

34. Possible answer: No. Temperatures fluctuate only 10 degrees all year; rainfall ranges from 0-24 inches.

35. average rainfall and temperatures in Mumbai (Bombay)

36. March, April, December

37. Temperatures range from a high of about 86°F to a low of about 75°F.

38. Possible answer: It is probably most productive from June to September, when rainfall is the heaviest and temperatures are warm.

SHORT ANSWER

39. India's many languages have probably been an obstacle to unity. Social and commercial interactions are hindered when people find it difficult to communicate with each other.

40. Subsistence farming. The region is very densely populated, and a majority of its population works in agriculture. A large number of people farming a limited amount of land means that most people probably have small farms and grow only enough food to survive.

41. The summer monsoons pick up moisture from the seas as they blow inland. The moisture-laden winds cool as they rise to pass over the Himalayas or the Western Ghats and lose their moisture as rain on the windward slopes. Dry rain shadows form on the other side of the mountains.

42. India is strongly influenced by monsoon winds, and the United States is not; the majority of South Asia's people are farmers, while a minority of North America's people are farmers; the majority of people in South Asia practice Hinduism or Islam, while the majority of people in the United States practice Christianity.

43. Large, technologically advanced farms could produce food more efficiently and in larger quantities. However, they would displace a large portion of the labor force now working on farms. The large number of unemployed farmers migrating to cities in search of jobs would intensify existing social and health problems in South Asia's already overpopulated cities.

44. Monsoon rains bring the water that people need for drinking and growing crops. They also cause floods and landslides.

Chapter 29   The Countries of South Asia

MATCHING

A. Vocabulary
Directions: Match the definitions with the terms. Write the correct letter in each blank. You will not use all the terms.

a. caste system
b. buffer state
c. nonviolent resistance
d. joint family system
e. malnutrition
f. reincarnation
g. boycott
h. partition
i. autonomous division

1. _____ opposing an enemy by any means other than violence

2. _____ refuse to purchase or use

3. _____ divide into parts

4. _____ belief that the souls of human beings and animals go through a series of births, deaths, and rebirths

5. _____ large family made up of several related families living together

6. _____ social hierarchy in which people are born into a particular group with a distinct rank in society

7. _____ country that separates two political enemies

FILL-IN-THE-BLANK

B. Key Geographic Concepts and Skills

Directions: Complete each sentence by writing the correct term in the blank. You will not use all the terms.

caste system
buffer state
nonviolent resistance
malnutrition
purdah
boycott
partition
autonomous division
reincarnation

8. Through _____, Gandhi opposed British rule in a peaceful manner.

9. Gandhi's _____ of British cloth was one way in which he peacefull opposed British rule.

10. Conflicts between India's Hindu and Muslim groups forced British and Indian leaders to _____ India into two states.

11. The Muslim custom according to which women keep their faces covered wi a veil when outside of the home is called _____.

12. Hinduism includes the belief that the soul passes through cycles of _____.

13. According to the _____, people are born into particular groups wi distinct ranks in society.

14. Afghanistan is a(n) _____, a country that separates two political enemies.

MULTIPLE CHOICE

B. Key Geographic Concepts and Skills
Directions: Write the letter of the correct ending in the blank.

15. _____ In 1947, India and Pakistan
    a. became independent countries.
    b. came under British control.
    c. were reunited.
    d. were divided into Indian-run provinces.

16. _____ In order to avoid being ruled by a majority religion to which they did not belong, in 1947
   a. 12 million Indians migrated to other Asian nations.
   b. all of the Muslims living in Pakistan left the country.
   c. millions of Hindus moved to India and millions of Muslims moved to Pakistan.
   d. most of the Hindus living in India moved to Pakistan.

17. _____ A war between India and Pakistan in 1971 resulted in the
   a. unification of East and West Pakistan.
   b. creation of the new nation of Bangladesh.
   c. largest migration of refugees in history.
   d. establishment of East Pakistan as a colony of West Pakistan.

18. _____ All of the following statements describe rural life in India except:
   a. Most Indians follow a primarily vegetarian diet for both economic and religious reasons.
   b. Many Indian women wear saris and many cover their faces completely with a veil when outside of the home.
   c. Although all family members help in carrying out chores, life is particularly demanding for women.
   d. Radios and televisions are not part of village life.

19. _____ In recent years, many Indians have
   a. moved from rural areas to the cities in search of better educational and employment opportunities.
   b. returned to rural villages and to traditional ways of life.
   c. left India's large, overcrowded cities to live in small towns.
   d. moved from remote villages to small towns.

20. _____ Businesses such as weaving or pottery making that people set up in their own homes are called
   a. cottage industries.   b. joint family systems.
   c. buffer states.   d. partitions.

21. _____ The Indus River is important to Pakistan because the river
   a. is held sacred by the Muslims.
   b. drains the flood waters left by the monsoons.
   c. deposits rich silt behind the Tarbela Dam.
   d. provides water for irrigation.

22. _____ Because of its location and physical terrain, Afghanistan
   a. is threatened by dangerous flood waters during the summer monsoons.
   b. has been a route for merchants and soldiers crossing from China to India.
   c. is the leading agricultural and trading nation in the region.
   d. is isolated from other countries in the region.

23. _____ Most people in Afghanistan, Pakistan, and Bangladesh are
   a. Buddhists.   b. Muslims.
   c. Hindus.   d. Protestants.

24. _____ All of the following are important when predicting the consequences of events and trends except
a. having a clear and accurate understanding of the event or trend.
b. evaluating possible consequences and determining which are more likely to occur.
c. using prior knowledge and experience.
d. predicting with certainty which consequences will occur.

25. _____ Increased Indian and international pressure in 1935 resulted in the
a. destruction of the Indian cottage industry.
b. establishment of Indian-run provinces.
c. creation of a British state.
d. division of India into two states.

26. _____ After gaining independence, millions of the subcontinent's Hindu moved to India and many Muslims moved to Pakistan because
a. each group wanted to move to a country where its religion was the majority religion.
b. both groups wanted to escape British rule.
c. independence gave them the freedom to live where they wished.
d. friendly relations between the two groups allowed easy movement between the countries.

27. _____ East Pakistanis felt discriminated against by West Pakistanis fo all of the following reasons except that
a. East Pakistanis paid more taxes than West Pakistanis.
b. more than half of the country's budget was spent in West Pakistan.
c. most government and army positions were held by West Pakistanis.
d. East Pakistanis were forced to abandon their Bengali language and literary tradition.

28. _____ Most of the people in India live in
a. nomadic camps.
b. small, rural villages.
c. medium-sized towns.
d. large, overcrowded cities.

29. _____ The growth of India's middle class in recent years has resulted a(n)
a. decline in the birthrate.
b. increase in the production of consumer goods.
c. lower rate of literacy.
d. decrease in urban population.

30. _____ Built on the banks of the Ganges, the city of Varanasi is
a. India's busiest port and financial center.
b. the capital of India.
c. India's largest commercial district.
d. considered by Hindus the holiest city in the world.

31. _____ Bangladesh can be accurately described as a country that
    a. has a diversified economy.
    b. suffers from poverty, overpopulation, and natural disasters.
    c. contains rich mineral resources in the delta basin.
    d. includes large areas of light population.

32. _____ Clearing more than half of Sri Lanka's rain forest for farmland
    and other development has brought about
    a. great economic growth in the country.
    b. conflict between the Sinhalese and the Tamils.
    c. changes in the island's weather patterns and subsequent droughts.
    d. rapid urbanization of the island.

33. _____ The physical geography of Nepal and Bhutan consists of
    a. a flat, fertile river delta emptying into the Bay of Bengal.
    b. elevations ranging from 600 feet to more than 20,000 feet.
    c. the high mountain peaks of the Hindu Kush.
    d. arid lowlands that rise to barren plateaus.

34. _____ Predicting consequences of events and trends involves all of the
    following except
    a. predicting consequences for different groups involved.
    b. determining with certainty which consequences will occur.
    c. understanding the events or trends that have taken place.
    d. identifying the consequences that are more likely to occur.

GRAPHIC STUDY

Directions: Use the cartogram below to answer the following questions.
Write your answers on the lines provided.

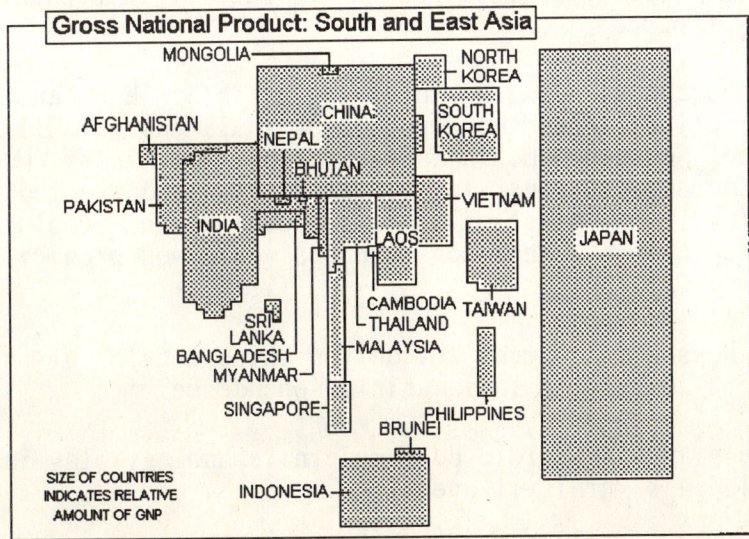

Gross National Product: South and East Asia

SIZE OF COUNTRIES INDICATES RELATIVE AMOUNT OF GNP

35. What kind of information is represented in this cartogram?

_____

36. Which South Asian country has the lowest gross national product?

_____

37. Can you tell from the cartogram exactly how much higher India's gross national product is than Pakistan's gross national product? Explain yo answer.

_____

38. Which South Asian country has the highest gross national product?

_____

39. Which region has the higher GNP, East Asia or South Asia?

_____

40. How would you explain the relatively large size of Japan in contrast t the smaller size of India?

_____

SHORT ANSWER

C. Critical Thinking
Directions: Answer the following questions on the back of this paper or on a separate sheet of paper.

41. Predicting Consequences Read the following passage. Then, answer the question that follows. When the Republic of India was established in 1947, Jawaharlal Nehru became India's first prime minister. Under his leadership, a democratic constitution was drafted and adopted under which the pariahs, the lowest of India's social castes, could no longe be discriminated against. What consequences would you predict for the pariahs?

42. Demonstrating Reasoned Judgment Why do you think nonviolent resistance was so effective in helping India gain independence?

43. Determining Relevance What role does modern technology play in the education of India's rural villagers?

44. Predicting Consequences Read the following passage. Then, answer the question that follows. In a free election held on December 2, 1988, Benazir Bhutto was elected prime minister of Pakistan. The first woman ever to be elected leader of a Muslim nation, after being sworn in, Bhutto said, "I think it's a great day for women, a great day for youth, a great day for Islam, and above all a great day for Pakistan." What consequences would you predict for Pakistani women?

45. Demonstrating Reasoned Judgment Do you think that the British influence in India was positive or negative? Explain your answer.

46. Recognizing Bias How did British actions at the time of colonization reflect bias against the Indians? What were the results of these actions?

Answer Key   Chapter 29

MATCHING

1. c   2. g

3. h   4. f

5. d   6. a

7. b

FILL-IN-THE-BLANK

8. nonviolent resistance

9. boycott   10. partition

11. purdah   12. reincarnation

13. caste system

14. buffer state

MULTIPLE CHOICE

15. a   16. c

17. b   18. d

19. a   20. a

21. d   22. b

23. b   24. d

25. b   26. a

27. d   28. b

29. b   30. d

31. b   32. c

33. b   34. b

GRAPHIC STUDY

35. the gross national products of countries in South and East Asia

36. Bhutan

37. Possible answer: No. The cartogram shows only relative sizes.

38. India   39. East Asia

40. Possible answer: Although much smaller in land area, industrialized Japan has a much higher GNP than does predominantly agricultural India.

SHORT ANSWER

41. The pariahs would probably be granted educational and employment opportunities and common privileges that traditionally had been denied to them.

42. Gandhi's philosophy of nonviolence won the support of the international community, which saw India as a nation trying to peacefully win independence from an oppressive British government. Besides having a strong military, the British occupied many of the high-level positions in India's military. Any armed rebellion against the British would certainly have resulted in more deaths and greater destruction than actually occurred under Gandhi's leadership.

43. While the government might not be able to send the villages enough people to educate the farmers personally, the government can provide the villages with public television sets. In this way, the villagers can receive televised instruction on better farming techniques, personal hygiene, and health-care management, as well as local, national, and international news.

44. Women in Pakistan have traditionally had far fewer freedoms and opportunities than men. The election of Benazir Bhutto as Pakistan's first woman prime minister might signal the beginning of greater opportunities and privileges for all of the women in Pakistan.

45. Some of the benefits of British rule
    include the abolition of slavery and the
    creation of modern transportation systems.
    However, these benefits do not make up
    for the losses that India suffered as a
    result of British rule, including
    destruction of the Indian textile industry,
    economy, and social structure.

46. The British felt superior toward the Indians
    and did not treat them as equals. For
    example, both the government and the army
    were organized with British officials in
    positions of power and Indians filling the
    lower ranks. Britain used India as a source
    of raw materials and as a market for its
    cheaper textiles. As a result, India's once
    flourishing textile industry disappeared, and
    millions of people lost their livelihoods.
    Many Indians felt great anger and resentment
    toward the British.

Chapter 30   Regional Atlas: East Asia and the Pacific World

MATCHING

A. Vocabulary
Directions: Match the definitions with the terms. Write the correct letter in each blank. You will not use all the terms.

a. volcanism
b. aquaculture
c. terrace
d. intensive farming
e. seismic
f. geysers
g. subsistence farming

1. _____ agriculture that requires great amounts of labor

2. _____ fish farming

3. _____ springs that shoot steam and heated water into the air

4. _____ level, narrow ledge built into a hillside for farming

5. _____ related to earthquakes

FILL-IN-THE-BLANK

Directions: Complete each sentence by writing the correct term in the blank. You will not use all the terms.

volcanic
terraces
aquaculture
monsoons
geysers
seismic
intensive farming

6. Activity that is caused by an earthquake is called _____ activity.

7. The use of great amounts of labor to produce food is called _____.

8. Farmers in East Asia have built _____ into hillsides in order to create more farmland.

9. Jets of steam and hot water that shoot into the air are called _____.

10. About one third of China's yearly catch is contributed by fish farming or _____.

MULTIPLE CHOICE

B. Key Geographic Concepts and Skills
Directions: Write the letter of the correct ending in the blank.

11. _____ The Himalayas, the Plateau of Tibet, and China's western mountai ranges were all created by
   a. centuries of volcanic activity in the Pacific region.
   b. the collision of the Eurasian and Indo-Australian plates.
   c. monsoon winds and ocean currents.
   d. erosion by the major rivers of China.

12. _____ The Malay and Japan archipelagoes are
   a. part of the Great Dividing Range.
   b. elevated regions of New Zealand.
   c. peaks of highlands that were covered when water levels rose.
   d. part of the Ring of Fire.

13. _____ The waters surrounding Japan and the nearby ocean currents help make Japan's climate
   a. moderate.   b. very hot.
   c. very cold and wet.   d. tropical.

14. _____ The country in this region that is formed by two main islands is
   a. New Zealand.   b. Australia.
   c. China.   d. Micronesia.

15. _____ East Asia is home to about
   a. one tenth of the world's population.
   b. one half of the world's population.
   c. one third of the world's population.
   d. two thirds of the world's population.

16. _____ People in East Asia use terrace farming to overcome the problems of farming in areas where
   a. there is not enough rain.
   b. rivers often flood the fields.
   c. slopes are too steep for planting.
   d. irrigation has not provided ample water.

17. _____ One reason why the integration of the many nations of this regio has been slow is that
   a. the area has a very low population.
   b. earthquakes have inhibited movement.
   c. natural barriers such as water and mountains have divided nations.
   d. there is no industrial development within the region.

18. _____ The industrial powerhouses of East Asia include Japan, South Korea, and
a. Laos. b. Taiwan.
c. New Zealand. d. Australia.

19. _____ The three main island groups in Oceania are
a. New Zealand, Australia, and Tasmania.
b. Antarctica, Malaysia, and Japan.
c. Tasmania, Tahiti, and Malaysia.
d. Micronesia, Melanesia, and Polynesia.

20. _____ Coral reefs are formed by
a. the skeletons of tiny sea creatures called polyps.
b. the collision of tectonic plates.
c. the Ring of Fire.
d. geysers and volcanoes.

21. _____ All of the following statements about Australia are true except:
a. Australia is the flattest continent.
b. The continent is crossed by several powerful rivers.
c. The area west of the Great Dividing Range is arid plain or dry plateau.
d. The area east of the Great Dividing Range has a moist climate.

22. _____ Many of East Asia's most important cities are located
a. near bodies of water.
b. at high elevations.
c. in Australia and New Zealand.
d. in Micronesia.

23. _____ Much of East Asia's physical landscape, including the Himalayas, was created by
a. tectonic forces. b. ocean currents.
c. monsoons. d. volcanic eruptions.

24. _____ The Ring of Fire is a line of volcanic and earthquake-related activity that
a. extends eastward from mainland China.
b. runs through the Himalayas.
c. encircles the Pacific Ocean.
d. surrounds Japan.

25. _____ Many cities in East Asia are located near
a. water. b. plains and river valleys.
c. mountain areas. d. plateau regions.

26. _____ The climate of the Southeast Asian islands on and around the Equator is
a. continental. b. cool and dry.
c. hot and dry. d. tropical wet.

27. _____ The areas of dense population in China are
a. lowland areas with mild, wet climates.
b. plateau regions with cool, dry climates.
c. coastal regions with wet, tropical climates.
d. mountain regions with semiarid climates.

28. _____ The area of Australia that receives the most rainfall over the course of a year is the
a. southern coast.   b. western coast.
c. northern coast.   d. eastern coast.

29. _____ The term Oceania refers to
a. the islands of the Pacific.
b. the islands of New Zealand.
c. the Indian and Pacific oceans.
d. the islands between Australia and China.

30. _____ Australia's landscape includes all of the following except
a. a low mountain range 20 to 200 miles inland from the eastern coast.
b. fjords that cut deep into its southern coastline.
c. vast expanses of flat land in the interior.
d. very few permanent bodies of water.

31. _____ New Zealand's North Island is narrow and hilly and includes
a. tropical grasslands.
b. desert scrub.
c. geysers and volcanoes.
d. fertile river deltas.

32. _____ The three main groups of the Pacific Islands include Polynesia, Melanesia, and
a. the Greater Antilles.
b. the Malay Archipelago.
c. Micronesia.
d. Taiwan.

33. _____ Throughout East Asia, most of the labor force works in
a. trade.   b. farming.
c. industry.   d. aquaculture.

34. _____ East Asia is home to about
a. one tenth of the world's population.
b. one quarter of the world's population.
c. one third of the world's population.
d. one half of the world's population.

GRAPHIC STUDY

Directions: Use the map on the next page to answer the following questions. Write your answers on the lines provided.

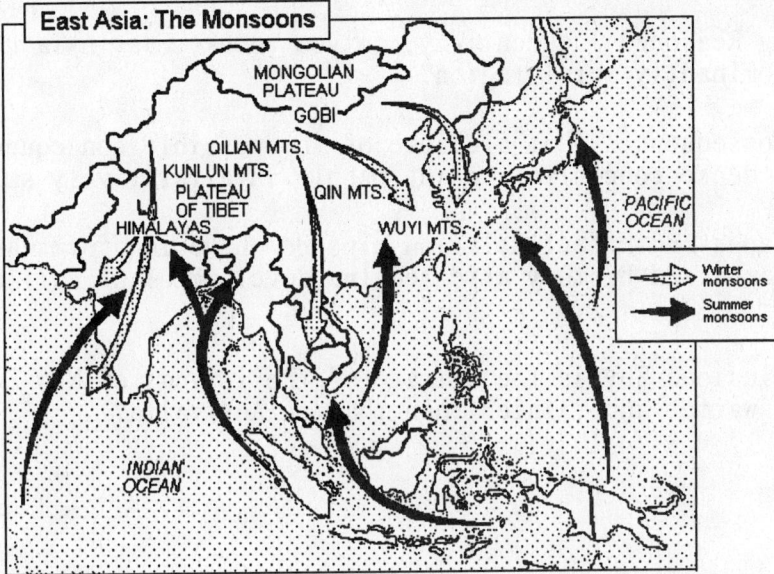

East Asia: The Monsoons

35. In which direction do the winter monsoons blow primarily?

_____

36. Over which body of water do the summer monsoons pass before they reach Indian land?

_____

37. Why does the Plateau of Tibet receive very little rainfall?

_____

38. In which direction do the summer monsoons blow primarily?

_____

39. Over which body of water do the summer monsoons pass before reaching the islands of Japan?

_____

40. The eastern plains of China receive a great deal of rainfall from the seasonal monsoons. Why?

_____

SHORT ANSWER

C. Critical Thinking
Directions: Answer the following questions on the back of this paper or on a separate sheet of paper.

41. Demonstrating Reasoned Judgment Why, do you think, East Asia continues to be a predominantly rural region?

42. Predicting Consequences What are some of the possible consequences for East Asia of dense concentrations of people in a relatively small area?

43. Perceiving Cause-and-Effect Relationships How have landforms and water bodies, climate, and history affected the development of nations in East Asia?

44. Drawing Conclusions Why is the climate of the islands of New Zealand consistently warmer and rainier than that of Australia?

Answer Key   Chapter 30

MATCHING

1. d   2. b

3. f   4. c

5. e

FILL-IN-THE-BLANK

6. seismic   7. intensive farming

8. terraces   9. geysers

10. aquaculture

MULTIPLE CHOICE

11. b   12. d

13. a   14. a

15. c   16. c

17. c   18. b

19. d   20. a

21. b   22. a

23. a   24. c

25. a   26. d

27. a   28. d

29. a   30. b

31. c   32. c

33. b   34. c

GRAPHIC STUDY

35. in a southerly direction

36. the Indian Ocean

37. The Himalayas block the summer monsoons.

38. in a northerly direction

39. the Pacific Ocean

40. Few mountains block the path of the winds over the plains.

SHORT ANSWER

41. Because the population is large and the land area is limited, an emphasis on agriculture is necessary to feed the region's people. Many areas are well-suited to growing crops. Also, although industrialization is increasing, much of the region lacks the technology to develop other economic activity.

42. Consequences might include possible food shortages, inadequate public services, and a decline in the overall quality of urban life.

43. Natural barriers of mountains and water have prevented the development of nations in some areas. Dense rain forest, caused in part by the tropical wet climate, has hindered national development in Southeast Asia. History has played a part as well, as competition among nations interested in trade and power slowed the integration of nations.

44. The climate of New Zealand is warmer and rainier than that of Australia because the islands are smaller. Although the countries have similar absolute locations, the large size of Australia causes a rain shadow in the interior of the country as the Great Dividing Range blocks moist winds off the Pacific, preventing moisture from reaching the interior. The small size of the islands of New Zealand allows the entire country to receive rainfall from the moist ocean air and allows the ocean to moderate temperatures.

Chapter 31   China

MATCHING

A. Vocabulary
Directions: Match the definitions with the terms. Write the correct
letter in each blank. You will not use all the terms.

a. ideogram
b. sphere of influence
c. provisional
d. acupuncture
e. autonomous region
f. theocrat
g. abdicate
h. double cropping
i. light industry
j. atheism
k. martial law
l. warlord

1. _____ area of a country that is controlled to some extent but not
governed by a foreign power

2. _____ regional leader with a personal army

3. _____ production of small consumer goods such as clothing, appliances,
and bicycles

4. _____ legal rule administered during periods of strict military control

5. _____ political unit with limited self-government

6. _____ picture representing a thing or an idea in written Chinese

7. _____ existing on a temporary basis

Directions: Match the definitions with the terms. Write the correct letter in each blank. You will not use all the terms.

a. ideogram
b. sphere of influence
c. provisional
d. acupuncture
e. autonomous region
f. theocrat
g. abdicate
h. double cropping
i. light industry
j. atheism
k. martial law
l. warlord

8. _____ give up the throne of a country

9. _____ regional leader who maintains a personal army

10. _____ region of a country that a foreign power controls but does not govern

11. _____ growing more than one crop a year on the same land

12. _____ someone who claims to rule by religious or divine authority

13. _____ belief that God does not exist

14. _____ practice of inserting needles at specific points on the body to cure disease or ease pain

MULTIPLE CHOICE

B. Key Geographic Concepts and Skills
Directions: Write the letter of the correct answer in the blank.

15. _____ What was the Nationalists' attitude toward reform in China?
    a. They wanted foreign powers to retain spheres of influence in China.
    b. They disliked foreign interference but were influenced by Western ideas.
    c. They advocated a working-class revolution to defeat the imperialist powers.
    d. They wanted to isolate China from foreign influence and Western thought.

16. _____ What was the purpose of the Great Cultural Revolution?
   a. to destroy the old ideology and culture and establish a socialist
      society
   b. to combine collectives into People's Communes
   c. to improve agriculture, industry, science and technology, and defense
   d. to create a cultural rebirth of the classical arts of ancient China

17. _____ How did Deng's Four Modernization's program greatly increase
China's farm production?
   a. by enabling farmers to own the land on which they farmed
   b. by establishing collective farms
   c. by giving farmers an opportunity to make more money through the
      contract responsibility system
   d. by establishing People's Communes, which contained both farms and
      industries

18. _____ What region is the center of China's government and industry?
   a. the Northeast   b. the Southeast
   c. the Northwest   d. the Southwest

19. _____ Why did the Chinese government create four Special Economic Zones
in the Southeast region of China?
   a. to encourage Chinese people to establish private industries
   b. to stimulate commercial farming through private ownership of land
   c. to attract foreign investment and technology to China
   d. to create a light industrial region and an area for tourism

20. _____ Why is the Huang He known as both the "Yellow River" and "China's
Sorrow?"
   a. The river contains large amounts of loess, a fine, yellowish soil,
      and has also created deadly floods in the Huang He Valley.
   b. Raw sewage contaminates the river and spreads yellow fever throughout
      China's most heavily populated regions.
   c. The loess in the river gives it a yellow color but makes the river
      water unsafe for human use.
   d. The Huang He is yellowish in color and deadly to humans because it
      contains large amounts of toxic waste from Beijing's factories.

21. _____ What are the most widely practiced religions in China?
   a. Buddhism and Hinduism
   b. Confucianism, Christianity, and Islam
   c. Islam and Buddhism
   d. Daoism, Buddhism, and Confucianism

22. _____ What is unusual about the written form of the Chinese language?
   a. The written characters are nonphonetic and give no clues to
      pronunciation.
   b. Few people can actually write in Chinese because the language is
      complex.
   c. Each ethnic group in China has its own version of written Chinese.
   d. There was no written form at all before the Great Cultural
      Revolution.

23. _____ Which of the following did not help spur the growth of Taiwan's economy?
   a. Foreign investments helped build new industries.
   b. The United Nations recognized Beijing as China's legal seat of government.
   c. Nationalists instituted land reform and industrial modernization.
   d. Foreign nations provided technical assistance.

24. _____ What political area will be rejoined with China in 1997?
   a. Taiwan   b. Hong Kong
   c. Mongolia   d. Tibet

25. _____ When did the Communists finally gain control of China?
   a. when Sun Yat-sen forced the emperor to give up the throne
   b. when Chiang Kai-shek defeated local warlords and took control of the country
   c. when Mao Zedong established the People's Republic of China
   d. when Deng Xiaoping defeated the Gang of Four to become China's leader

26. _____ How was the Great Leap Forward supposed to make China's production greater than that of the Western nations?
   a. by replacing private ownership of farms with common ownership
   b. by combining China's collectives into self-sufficient People's Communes
   c. by smashing the old order and establishing a new socialist society
   d. by combining elements of free-enterprise economy with socialism

27. _____ Which of the following is not a way that the Four Modernization program led to industrial development in China?
   a. It changed the focus of the economy from heavy industry to light industry.
   b. China built a transportation network connecting industry to raw materials.
   c. The program eased state control of industry.
   d. Managers and workers who improved efficiency in the factories were rewarded.

28. _____ How did the Chinese government respond to the democratic protest in Tiananmen Square?
   a. by meeting with student leaders to discuss their demands
   b. by ignoring the protests and waiting for the crowds to disband over time
   c. by barricading the square so that it was off limits to protesters
   d. by using military force to drive off the protesters from the square

29. _____ Why is the Yangzi River important to China's economy?
   a. The Yangzi supports a large fishing industry.
   b. The world's earliest industrial civilization began on the Yangzi River.
   c. The Yangzi links the port city of Shanghai to interior cities.
   d. The Yangzi provides a trade route between China and Russia.

30. _____ What landform dominates China's Southwest region?
  a. the Mongolian Plateau   b. the Plateau of Tibet
  c. the Yangzi River valley   d. an alluvial plain

31. _____ Which of the following is not a way that the Chinese government
  has attempted to control rapid population growth?
  a. The government has cut agricultural production.
  b. Special benefits, such as better housing, are offered to one-child
     couples.
  c. Penalties, such as fines and wage cuts, have been levied against
     people who have more than one child.
  d. The government has launched a publicity campaign listing the virtues
     of one-child families.

32. _____ What is significant about the Han ethnic group in China?
  a. The Han people form the cultural elite of Chinese civilization.
  b. Ninety-four percent of the entire Chinese population belongs to the
     Han ethnic group.
  c. The Han people form the distinct, Buddhist population of Tibet.
  d. The Han are the only people in China who practice Christianity.

33. _____ What is peculiar about Hong Kong's political status?
  a. It is jointly governed by both Britain and China.
  b. It is a sovereign nation that will become a Chinese colony in 2000.
  c. It is culturally a part of China but has been governed by Japan since
     1860.
  d. It is leased to the British but will become part of China in 1997.

34. _____ Which of the following describes the location and political status
  of Mongolia?
  a. Mongolia is an independent country located between Russia and China.
  b. Mongolia is a Chinese province located in the barren Northwest
     region.
  c. Although Mongolia is governed by the Chinese, it remains a Japanese
     sphere of influence in Southeast China.
  d. Mongolia is a southern province of Russia with close cultural ties to
     China.

GRAPHIC STUDY

Directions: Use the map to answer the following questions. Write your answers on the lines provided.

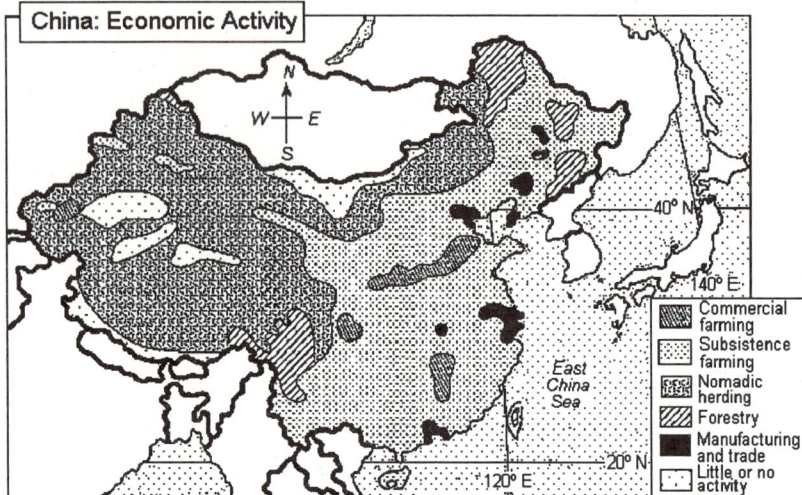

China: Economic Activity

East China Sea

40° N
140° E
20° N
120° E

Commercial farming
Subsistence farming
Nomadic herding
Forestry
Manufacturing and trade
Little or no activity

35. Where are the manufacturing regions of China located?

_____

36. What area of China do you think receives the least rainfall? Why?

_____

37. What economic activity takes up most of the land in western China?

_____

38. How do the economic activities shown on this map support what you know about the physical geography of China?

_____

Directions: Read the announcements below that were broadcast to Peking University students as they gathered to march to Tiananmen Square. Then, on the back of this paper or on a separate sheet of paper, answer the question that follows.

39. By a student leader: Citizens of the People's Republic of China enjoy freedom of speech, of the press, of assembly, of association, of procession and of demonstration! By a school official: Go back to your classes! Don't give in to the pressure from your fellow students! Beware of the consequences to yourself and your family.
Do you think either or both of the speakers were concealing or distorting the truth in their announcements? Explain your answer.

_____

Directions: Read the announcements below that were broadcast to Peking University students as they gathered to march to Tiananmen Square in protest for democracy. Then, on the back of this paper or on a separate sheet of paper, answer the question that follows.

40. By a student leader: Citizens of the People's Republic of China enjoy freedom of speech, of the press, of assembly, of association, of procession and of demonstration! By a school official: Go back to your classes! Don't give in to pressure from your fellow students! Beware of the consequences to yourself and your family. What is the point of view of the speakers of each announcement? What is the purpose of each announcement?

_____

SHORT ANSWER

C. Critical Thinking
Directions: Answer the following questions on the back of this paper or on a separate sheet of paper.

41. Perceiving Cause-and-Effect Relationships How did war and movement from 1949 to 1971 result in Taiwan's being recognized as the government of China while the large Communist state on mainland China went unrecognized?

42. Checking Consistency Give three examples of how the Chinese government has responded to political dissent within its country.

43. Determining Relevance How did the attempt to modernize Chinese technology result in the introduction of democratic ideas into China?

44. Checking Consistency When many worried that the Four Modernization's would move China towards a free-enterprise economy, Deng Xiaoping responded, "It doesn't matter if a cat is black or white as long as it catches mice." Contrast Deng's attitude with his reaction to democrati protests.

Answer Key   Chapter 31

MATCHING

1. b	2. l
3. i	4. k
5. e	6. a
7. c	8. g
9. l	10. b
11. h	12. f
13. j	14. d

MULTIPLE CHOICE

15. b	16. a
17. c	18. a
19. c	20. a
21. d	22. a
23. b	24. b
25. c	26. b
27. b	28. d
29. c	30. b
31. a	32. b
33. d	34. a

GRAPHIC STUDY

35. in the East, on or near the coast

36. Possible answer: Western China probably
    receives little rainfall, since the
    region has no economic activity except
    nomadic herding.

37. nomadic herding

38. Possible answer: In the cold, arid, and rugged Northwest there is little economic activity except nomadic herding, while in the more fertile, wetter plains of the South and the East there is farming, forestry, and industry.

39. Possible answer: Neither of the two speakers was deliberately distorting the truth. Both announcements reflect a possible outcome of the stated behavior.

40. Possible answer: The point of view for the student announcement is that of a pro-democracy protester whose purpose was to announce the democratic rights for which the people were marching. The announcement by the school official represents the state point of view. Its purpose was to discourage the protest by threatening students with negative consequences if they joined the protest.

SHORT ANSWER

41. The war between the Nationalists and the Communists caused the Nationalist government of China to flee to Taiwan, where Chiang Kai-shek set up a provisional Chinese government. The Nationalists continued to be represented in the United Nations as the official Chinese government and were supported by Western countries. Meanwhile, the newly formed Communist state of China went unrecognized until official United Nations acceptance in 1971.

42. The government has responded to dissent with violence. China put down calls for freedom in Tibet with force. Mao Zedong answered the detractors of his failed Great Leap Forward with the Cultural Revolution, which humiliated, imprisoned, and killed critics. The government silenced the protest in Tiananmen Square with military force.

43. Deng Xiaoping's Four Modernization's gave people a taste for consumer goods, an enjoyment of modernization, and a desire to have more decision-making power. These ideas led many to a desire for greater freedom and for democracy.

44. His statement about economic tolerance is inconsistent with his violent crackdown on the democratic protests and subsequent return to repressive policies.

Name _____ Class _____ Date _____

Chapter 32   Japan and the Koreas

MATCHING

A. Vocabulary
Directions: Match the definitions with the terms. Write the correct
letter in each blank. You will not use all the terms.

a. quota
b. demography
c. demilitarized zone
d. tsunami
e. tariff
f. seismograph
g. autonomous region
h. homogeneous
i. boycott
j. typhoon

1. _____ machine that registers movements of the earth's crust

2. _____ tropical storm forming over the Pacific Ocean

3. _____ sharing the same characteristics

4. _____ tax on imports

5. _____ fixed number or quantity

6. _____ strip of land free of troops and weapons

FILL-IN-THE-BLANK

Directions: Complete each sentence by writing the correct term in the
blank. You will not use all the terms.

quotas
demography
demilitarized zone
storm surges
tariffs
seismographs
autonomous regions
homogeneous
boycotts
typhoons

7. _____, machines that measure movements in the earth's crust, record
   about 7,500 earthquakes each year in Japan.

8. Tropical hurricanes that form over the Pacific Ocean are called
   _____ .

9. Japan's population is _____, meaning nearly all of the people hav
   a similar heritage.

10. The purpose of _____, taxes placed on imports, is to make foreign
    goods more expensive to buy than domestic goods.

11. The Japanese government has helped to boost the nation's economy by
    setting _____ on the number of foreign goods that can be sold in
    Japan.

12. North Korea and South Korea are separated by a _____, a strip of
    land that is free of troops and weapons.

MULTIPLE CHOICE

B. Key Geographic Concepts and Skills
Directions: Write the letter of the correct ending or answer in the
blank.

13. _____ The archipelago of Japan consists of
    a. a few small islands that were formed millions of years ago by
       volcanic activity.
    b. three large islands that lie off the coast of East Asia.
    c. thousands of small islands that are the peaks of an underwater
       mountain range.
    d. a chain of mostly large islands that lie along the rim of the Pacif
       Ocean.

14. _____ Japan experiences many earthquakes because the islands
    a. are relatively new parts of the earth's surface.
    b. have moderate climates.
    c. are part of the Ring of Fire, a region of tremendous tectonic
       activity.
    d. lie in the middle latitudes.

15. _____ Japan's climates are influenced by all of the following except
    a. latitude.
    b. its location on a large continent.
    c. monsoon winds.
    d. ocean currents.

16. _____ The high population density in Japan has
    a. affected housing and family patterns.
    b. forced many people to move to other less-populated countries.
    c. caused a huge migration of people to rural areas.
    d. been responsible for the country's lack of industrial success.

17. _____ The goal of Japan's revolutionary Meiji reforms was to
a. isolate Japan from other countries in the world.
b. modernize and industrialize the country so that Japan could deal with the West on an equal basis.
c. stop the spread of Roman Catholicism in the country.
d. restructure Japan's economy and political system according to Western models.

18. _____ The purpose of Japan's imperialist policy in the early 1900s was to
a. spread Japanese culture and religions to other parts of the world.
b. strengthen Japan's economy through obtaining additional natural resources.
c. acquire strategic defense positions in the event of a world war.
d. establish new markets for selling raw materials.

19. _____ Japan was known as the world's workshop in the years after World War II because it
a. exported more raw materials than any other nation in the world.
b. tapped and developed its abundant supply of natural resources.
c. imported raw materials and made them into finished goods for export.
d. developed a complex agricultural industry.

20. _____ The three-year Korean War, which ended in 1953, resulted in the
a. Japanese takeover of the peninsula.
b. separation of the peninsula into a communist south and a democratic north.
c. permanent division of the peninsula into North Korea and South Korea.
d. Soviet control of the entire peninsula.

21. _____ North Korea's physical landscape is dominated by
a. elevated plateaus.   b. mountains.
c. narrow plains.   d. deep valleys.

22. _____ All of the following statements about the climates on the Korean Peninsula are true except:
a. North Korea has short, cool summers and bitterly cold winters.
b. South Korea has a mostly continental climate.
c. Parts of South Korea are subtropical.
d. North Korea's climate is not greatly influenced by the moderating effects of the surrounding seas.

23. _____ Which statement best supports the conclusion that fierce competition exists in Japan for places in the best schools?
a. The school day in Japan is long, and vacations are short.
b. Japanese students are given a great deal of homework.
c. Many students take special classes after school to help them do better on examinations they must take to enter college.
d. Education has always been important in Japan.

24. _____ Japan's best farmland has been created by
a. winds blowing Mongolian loess to the western plains.
b. the alluvial deposits of its rivers.
c. volcanic ash.
d. topsoil carried by glaciers during the last ice age.

25. _____ Only 13 percent of Japan's land is arable because of
a. lack of irrigation water.
b. steep, mountainous terrain.
c. poor climate.
d. inadequate farming equipment.

26. _____ Most of the people of Japan live
a. on Shikoku, the largest of Japan's islands.
b. in mountain valleys on the island of Kyushu.
c. on Hokkaido, Japan's northernmost island.
d. along the narrow coastal plains between Tokyo and Hiroshima on the island of Honshu.

27. _____ The earliest religion of Japan was
a. Shinto.   b. Buddhism.
c. Confucianism.   d. Hinduism.

28. _____ All of the following are results of the Meiji reforms except the
a. creation of the Diet.
b. institution of a Japanese caste system.
c. establishment of a new educational system.
d. construction of the railroads.

29. _____ In an effort to help Japan recover from the devastating effects
the 1929 depression, Japanese military leaders in the 1930s
a. adopted a policy of imperialist expansion.
b. formed an alliance with Nazi Germany.
c. negotiated more trade treaties with the Soviet Union.
d. closed its doors to Western trade.

30. _____ All of the following factors contributed to Japan's rapid econom
growth after World War II except
a. a highly educated work force.
b. the dedication, cooperation, and loyalty of its workers.
c. the country's change in relative location.
d. the government's hands-off policy toward business.

31. _____ In 1950, the North Koreans launched a surprise attack on South
Korea in an effort to
a. unite the country under a single Communist government.
b. regain territory that they had lost in 1910.
c. gain control of South Korea's hydroelectric plants.
d. encourage the spread of democracy.

32. _____ Japan was occupied from 1945 until 1952 by
    a. the West German army.   b. China.
    c. the United States army.   d. South Korea.

33. _____ One result of South Korea's efforts to compete economically with Japan and other Western nations has been
    a. an absence of labor strikes in the country.
    b. major disputes between workers and business owners.
    c. a decline in the middle-class population of the country.
    d. a lower standard of living for its people.

34. _____ Which statement best supports the conclusion that Japanese employers, during the boom years, provided many benefits to their employees?
    a. Japanese workers took pride in their companies' success.
    b. Some Japanese workers are now being downsized.
    c. Many companies offered medical clinics and low-interest loans.
    d. Co-workers often vacationed together.

GRAPHIC STUDY

Directions: Use the graphs below to answer the following questions. Write your answers on the lines provided.

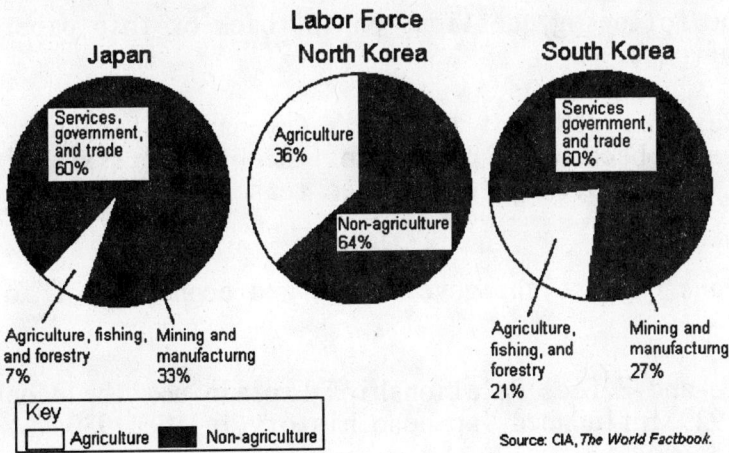

Labor Force

Japan — Services, government, and trade 60%; Agriculture, fishing, and forestry 7%; Mining and manufacturing 33%

North Korea — Agriculture 36%; Non-agriculture 64%

South Korea — Services, government, and trade 60%; Agriculture, fishing, and forestry 21%; Mining and manufacturing 27%

Key: Agriculture / Non-agriculture

Source: CIA, *The World Factbook*.

35. What percentage of the people in South Korea work in agriculture, fishing and forestry?

_____

36. What country has the highest percentage of people working in agriculture?

_____

37. Based on the information given in the graphs, what country would you expect to be the most industrialized? Explain your answer.

_____

38. What percentage of South Korea's labor force works in mining and manufacturing?

_____

39. In which country does the greatest proportion of people work in activities that are not related to agriculture?

_____

40. Based on the information presented in the graph, which of the three countries shown do you think is the least developed? Explain your answer.

_____

SHORT ANSWER

C. Critical Thinking
Directions: Answer the following questions on the back of this paper or on a separate sheet of paper.

41. Demonstrating Reasoned Judgment Japan has few natural resources, yet t country was able to become one of the most highly successful industria nations in the world. Give at least three reasons that explain how thi happened.

42. Making Comparisons Compare the governments and economies of North Kore and South Korea.

43. Perceiving Cause-and-Effect Relationships Explain how the economic depression of 1929 influenced Japanese history in the 1930s.

44. Demonstrating Reasoned Judgment How did Japan's lack of natural resources and raw materials influence the country's economy and histor during the Meiji reforms?

45. Perceiving Cause-and-Effect Relationships How does Japan's location ma it a dangerous place to live?

46. Synthesizing Information Why did the United States send Commodore Perr to Japan in 1853? What were the results of his mission?

Answer Key   Chapter 32

MATCHING

1. f
2. j
3. h
4. e
5. a
6. c

FILL-IN-THE-BLANK

7. seismographs
8. typhoons
9. homogeneous
10. tariffs
11. quotas
12. demilitarized zone

MULTIPLE CHOICE

13. c
14. c
15. b
16. a
17. b
18. b
19. c
20. c
21. b
22. b
23. c
24. b
25. b
26. d
27. a
28. b
29. a
30. d
31. a
32. c
33. b
34. c

GRAPHIC STUDY

35. 21 percent
36. North Korea

37. Japan. A relatively large percentage of
    its people work in mining and manufacturing,
    and a relatively small percentage work in
    agriculture.

38. 27 percent

39. Japan

40. North Korea, because it has the highest
    percentage of its labor force working in
    agriculture.

SHORT ANSWER

41. Japan imports raw materials and uses them to
    produce expensive, high-quality goods that
    it exports for profit; Japan's work force is
    highly educated, with Japanese employees
    being dedicated, cooperative, and loyal to
    their companies; Japan is now at the center
    of active trade networks; Japan's government
    has helped the economy by taking an active
    role in the country's business.

42. North Korea has a Communist government, and
    South Korea has a non-Communist government.
    North Korea continues to evolve from an
    agricultural to an industrial society. The
    country has rich natural resources. However,
    because the government decides what and how
    much to produce, North Korea still lags far
    behind its neighbor in its standard of
    living and gross national product. South
    Korea is one of the new industrial powers of
    the region. Over the past several decades,
    the country has experienced an impressive
    rate of economic growth, the development of
    a new middle class, and an increase in its
    role in international trade and politics.

43. The depression of 1929 took a terrible toll
    on Japanese industry. Many businesses were
    ruined, and unemployment soared. Military
    leaders argued that the way to recovery was
    through more aggressive expansion in Asia.
    An overseas empire would provide Japan with
    markets, raw materials, and new land for
    its expanding population. As conditions
    grew worse, militarists were able to gain
    control of the government. In 1931, Japan
    invaded Manchuria, and in 1937, China.

44. The lack of natural resources and raw materials was a serious obstacle to Japan's becoming an industrial power. The two major resources needed for industry, iron ore for steel and petroleum for energy, are practically nonexistent in Japan. As a result, Japan turned to imperialism in an effort to gain the resources it needed to power its developing economy. By 1910, Japan had won, through battle, territory and trading rights from China, Russia, and Korea.

45. Japan is part of the Ring of Fire, a region of great tectonic activity along the rim of the Pacific Ocean, where earthquakes and volcanoes are common. In fact, Japan experiences more earthquakes than any other country in the world. An offshore earthquake can cause a tsunami, which can devastate coastal lands. Japan's island location also places the nation at risk for damage caused by typhoons. These tropical hurricanes, which occur from late summer to early fall, often cause floods and landslides.

46. The United States sent Commodore Perry to Japan in 1853 to negotiate a trade agreement. Perry's request was backed up by a massive show of force. The Japanese knew that their weapons were no match for the warships, so they agreed to Perry's terms. During the next 15 years, Japan was forced to sign treaties with other Western nations as well. These unequal treaties gave all the economic advantages to foreigners.

Chapter 33   Southeast Asia

SHORT ANSWER

A. Vocabulary
Directions: Use each term below in a sentence that shows the meaning of
the term. Write your sentence in the space provided.

1. paddies

2. indigenous

3. insurgents

MULTIPLE CHOICE

B. Key Geographic Concepts and Skills
Directions: Write the letter of the correct answer in the blank.

4. _____ What factor made Southeast Asia one of the world's great
geographic crossroads?
a. relative location   b. natural vegetation
c. ethnic diversity   d. cultural traits

5. _____ What major activity brought the influences of Hinduism, Buddhism,
and Islam to the cultures of Southeast Asia?
a. colonization   b. trade
c. religious crusades   d. exploration

6. _____ Which statement about the European colonization of Southeast Asia
is not true?
a. Europeans planted vast areas of forest on farmland to create a lumber
industry.
b. Europeans encouraged rich local landlords to grow rice for export.
c. Europeans built roads and railroads to carry crops to ports.
d. Europeans established their own colonies, paying little attention to
existing boundaries.

7. _____ What country in Southeast Asia was influenced by Chinese culture
when China took control of the region in 100 b.c.?
a. Thailand   b. Myanmar
c. Vietnam   d. Laos

8. _____ The spread of Hinduism, Buddhism, and Islam through Southeast Asia
best exemplifies what geographic theme?
a. movement   b. location
c. place   d. human-environment interaction

9. _____ What makes Thailand unique among the countries of Southeast Asia
   a. It is the only free-market country that does not belong to ASEAN.
   b. It is the only country that was not colonized by Europeans.
   c. It is the only socialist country that has had no ties to China or t
      former Soviet Union.
   d. It is the only country that has isolated itself from the outside
      world.

10. _____ Which of the following statements about the history of Vietnam i
    not true?
    a. From about 1940 to 1945, the Japanese had control of Indochina,
       including Vietnam.
    b. In 1945, Ho Chi Minh, a Vietnamese leader, declared Vietnam's
       independence from France.
    c. In 1954, Ho Chi Minh's forces defeated the French after years of
       bitter and fierce warfare.
    d. In 1954, the Geneva peace conference established all of Vietnam as
       independent state under Ho Chi Minh.

11. _____ Which of the following did not contribute to a sense of national
    unity among the people of the Philippines?
    a. a communist ideology   b. Western cultural influences
    c. a Roman Catholic majority   d. Spanish cultural influences

12. _____ Papua New Guinea is part of what two overlapping regions?
    a. Southeast Asia and Oceania
    b. Southeast Asia and Southwest Asia
    c. Oceania and Southwest Asia
    d. South Asia and Northern Eurasia

13. _____ Which of the following statements about Malaysia and Brunei is n
    true?
    a. They reinvest their wealth in modernization.
    b. They have strong economies based on agriculture.
    c. They use oil revenues to develop industry and improve agriculture.
    d. They are two of the wealthiest countries in Southeast Asia.

14. _____ What inference can you draw from the political boundaries that
    were created by the European countries that colonized Southeast Asia?
    a. No ethnic boundaries existed when the Europeans drew their own
       boundaries.
    b. The Europeans planned to establish their colonies as independent
       countries as soon as possible.
    c. The Europeans tried to adhere closely to the existing ethnic
       boundaries.
    d. The Europeans had little regard for the existing ethnic boundaries
       and drew up boundaries for their own profit.

15. _____ Why were so many different groups of people drawn to Southeast
    Asia?
    a. It was a center of religion.   b. It was a center of education.
    c. It was a center of trade.   d. It was a center of Asian culture.

16. _____ Which of the following was not an important religion in Southeast Asia before the 1500s?
a. Hinduism
b. Islam
c. Christianity
d. Buddhism

17. _____ Why did the Chinese have little impact on the cultures of Southeast Asia?
a. Few people from China migrated to Southeast Asia.
b. Southeast Asians strongly resisted the influence of Chinese culture.
c. The Chinese did not want to spread their culture to people they considered inferior.
d. The Chinese culture was too barbaric to be of significant influence.

18. _____ How were the traditional Southeast Asian farmers affected by European colonization?
a. They became wealthy from the rising values of the cash crops they grew and exported to Europe.
b. Unable to compare with large landowners, they were forced to leave their land and work on the plantations.
c. They lost their land when European colonists converted vast tracts of farmland into forests and exported the wood to European markets.
d. They prospered when the Europeans divided large plantations into smaller parcels of land, which were distributed to small-scale farmers.

19. _____ Why has the economy of Myanmar developed much more slowly than the economies of most other Southeast Asian countries?
a. Myanmar lacks the natural resources that other countries have.
b. The government is heavily in debt.
c. Ethnic unrest and a repressive government have kept the economy from developing.
d. Myanmar tried to industrialize too quickly and now must import most of its food.

20. _____ Which of the following is not a reason that Thailand has been able to build one of the most successful economies in Southeast Asia?
a. Thailand encourages interdependence with foreign countries.
b. Thailand diversified its economy in the 1960s to promote industry.
c. Thailand encourages tourism as a major economic activity.
d. Thailand uses its oil wealth to finance modernization.

21. _____ Which of the following statements about Vietnam, Laos, and Cambodia is not true?
a. All three countries have a majority population belonging to the Khmer ethnic group.
b. All three countries were once part of French Indochina.
c. All three countries have a culture influenced by India.
d. All three countries have a mostly Buddhist population.

22. _____ From which region did the first inhabitants of Southeast Asia probably migrate?
    a. India and Australia
    b. southern China and South Asia
    c. Europe and Southwest Asia
    d. Japan and Mongolia

23. _____ What is significant about Singapore's location with regard to it economy?
    a. Singapore is located on a few islands.
    b. Singapore is located on an important trade route between Europe and East Asia.
    c. Singapore is located just north of the Equator.
    d. Singapore receives heavy rainfall year-round and has mild temperatures.

24. _____ Which of the following is not true of Papua New Guinea?
    a. The country has a sophisticated transportation system.
    b. More than 700 languages are spoken across the country.
    c. Most of Papua New Guinea's almost 4.1 million people are farmers.
    d. Gold and copper ore are mined in great quantities using modern machines.

25. _____ What information would be the most helpful in drawing inferences about why certain countries in Southeast Asia have a large number of Muslims?
    a. knowing what countries in the region were colonized by France
    b. knowing what countries were ruled by China in the past
    c. knowing the location of Southwest Asian trade routes
    d. knowing the history of the Mons, Khmers, and Thais before their migration to Southeast Asia

GRAPHIC STUDY

Directions: Use the bar graph to answer the following questions. Write your answers on the lines provided.

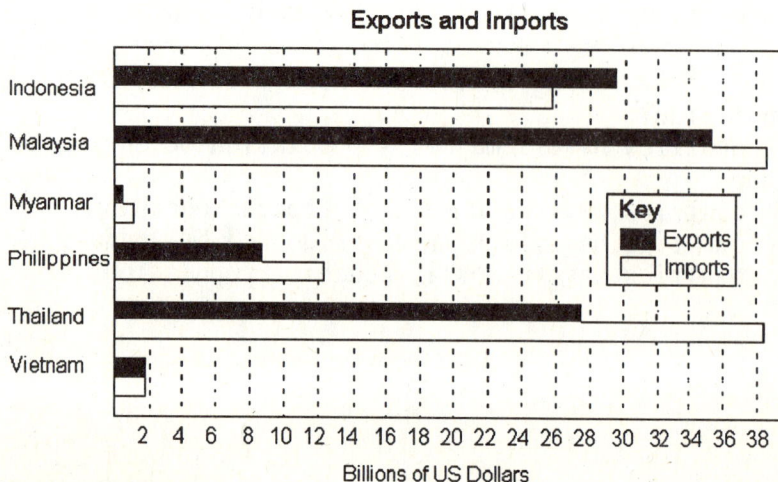

Exports and Imports

Country	Key
Indonesia	
Malaysia	
Myanmar	Exports
Philippines	Imports
Thailand	
Vietnam	

Billions of US Dollars (2, 4, 6, 8, 10, 12, 14, 16, 18, 20, 22, 24, 26, 28, 30, 32, 34, 36, 38)

Source: *World Almanac, 1993.*

26. Which country on the graph had the greatest value of exports?

_____

27. How much more was the value of Indonesia's exports than the value of its imports?

_____

28. Which two countries conducted the least amount of foreign trade?

_____

29. Which countries had a favorable balance of trade, exporting nearly as much or more than they imported?

_____

30. What was the approximate value of the Philippines' exports?

_____

31. How much more was the value of Thailand's imports than the value of its exports?

_____

SHORT ANSWER

C. Critical Thinking
Directions: Answer the following questions on the back of this paper or on a separate sheet of paper.

32. Drawing Inferences What can you infer about the effect of chronic political instability on the economic health of Myanmar, Vietnam, Laos, and Cambodia? Explain.

33. Perceiving Cause-and-Effect Relationships How did the construction of inland roads and railroads in Southeast Asia lead to the arrival of Chinese and Indian immigrants and to subsequent tensions between these groups and native Southeast Asians?

34. Determining Relevance How have the economies of many Southeast Asian countries been affected by the focus in world trade on countries bordering the Pacific Ocean?

35. Drawing Inferences Read the following passage. Then, answer the questi
below. Since World War II, Thailand has had close political ties to th
United States. Thailand felt threatened by the Communist revolution in
China in 1949. It joined with the United States to stop Communist
expansion in Southeast Asia. During the Vietnam War, Thailand allowed
the United States to use its country as a base for air attacks against
Communist forces in Vietnam, Cambodia, and Laos.
From what you know about Southeast Asia, what can you infer about the
seriousness of this historical threat of communism to Thailand? Why?

36. Perceiving Cause-and-Effect Relationships Why did many of the countrie
of Southeast Asia have deep ethnic conflicts when they became
independent?

37. Drawing Conclusions How did the peace conference in Geneva, Switzerlan
held after the French defeat in 1954, affect political tensions in
Southeast Asia?

Answer Key   Chapter 33

SHORT ANSWER

1. Rice paddies span the deltas of the Southeast Asian rivers.

2. Someone who is indigenous to Southeast Asia is native to the region.

3. Insurgents are people who rebel against their own governments.

MULTIPLE CHOICE

4. a	5. b
6. a	7. c
8. a	9. b
10. d	11. a
12. a	13. b
14. d	15. c
16. c	17. c
18. b	19. c
20. d	21. a
22. b	23. b
24. a	25. c

GRAPHIC STUDY

26. Malaysia   27. a little less than $4 billion

28. Myanmar and Vietnam

29. Indonesia and Vietnam

30. $9 billion

31. about $11.5 billion

SHORT ANSWER

32. Chronic political instability has damaged these countries' economies in three ways. First, the upheaval and destruction of internal conflict harms the productivity of economic activities by disrupting the normal flow of production. Second, political instability discourages the flow of domestic and foreign investment in these countries' economic activities. Third, political instability forces the governments of these countries to focus almost exclusively on political problems, preventing them from providing an environment that would support healthy economic productivity.

33. Inland roads and railroads, built to carry crops and other goods to the port cities for export to Europe, led to the growth of these port cities. As the port cities grew, they attracted large numbers of people from China and India. As a result, tensions sometimes developed between these new immigrants and native Southeast Asians.

34. The ASEAN countries have benefited greatly from the change in their relative location in regard to world trade.

35. The threat of communism to Thailand was very serious. Thailand's location bordering on the Indochina Peninsula put it right in the middle of the Communist revolution. The three countries on the Indochina Peninsula—Vietnam, Cambodia, and Laos—became Communist countries by the end of the Vietnam War. Myanmar, on Thailand's western border, is a country in political upheaval with a socialist economy. Thailand's agreement to provide bases for US bombing would have made the country a direct target of Communist forces. Thailand must have believed that only force could stop the threat.

36. When Europeans arrived in the region and carved out their own colonies, they paid little attention to existing ethnic boundaries. As a result, hostile groups often were united into one colony, while others that had lived together peacefully for centuries were separated. When the colonies became independent after World War II, many thus inherited deep ethnic conflicts.

37. Instead of ending the conflict, the peace conference laid the foundation for more fighting by dividing Vietnam into two parts. North Vietnam was left to the Communists under Ho Chi Minh. South Vietnam was headed by a pro-Western ruler. The Communists in North and South Vietnam wanted to reunite the two Vietnams. Another war soon began. Laos and Cambodia were also drawn into the fighting as Communists in these countries supplied the Communists in South Vietnam. By 1975, Vietnam, Cambodia, and Laos were all under Communist control.

Chapter 34   The Pacific World and Antarctica

MATCHING

A. Vocabulary
Directions: Match the definitions with the terms. Write the correct
letter in each blank. You will not use all the terms.

a. ice shelf
b. outback
c. atoll
d. geyser
e. krill
f. permafrost
g. convergence zone
h. artesian well
i. cay
j. crevasse
k. cyclone
l. subduction zone
m. pack ice
n. lagoon
o. cataract

1. _____ shallow body of water with an outlet to the ocean

2. _____ Australian name for a hurricane

3. _____ hole drilled into the earth to tap deep underground water

4. _____ flat, ring-shaped coral island surrounding a lagoon

5. _____ large crack in glacial ice

6. _____ ice that extends out over the ocean

7. _____ large, floating expanse of icebergs and ice mixed together

8. _____ point at which the frigid waters around Antarctica and the warmer
waters of the Atlantic, Pacific, and Indian oceans meet

9. _____ shrimp-like creatures that provide ample food for whales and fish

FILL-IN-THE-BLANK

Directions: Complete each sentence by writing the correct term in the blank. You will not use all the terms.

ice shelf
outback
atoll
geyser
krill
permafrost
convergence zone
artesian well
cay
crevasse
cyclone
cataract
pack ice
lagoon
subduction zone

10. The Great Barrier Reef forms a(n) _____ between itself and the mainland.

11. Darwin has twice been leveled by a(n) _____, which is what the Australians call a hurricane.

12. A(n) _____ is a hole drilled deep into the ground to tap a layer porous earth filled with ground water.

13. A volcano helps to form a(n) _____, a coral reef surrounding an inner lagoon.

14. A large crack, or _____, will often form in glacial ice.

15. Ice that extends out over the ocean forms a(n) _____.

16. Icebergs on the fringes of the Antarctic continent mix with ice in the ocean waters to form _____.

17. The _____ is the point at which the frigid waters around Antarcti and the warmer waters of the Atlantic, Pacific, and Indian oceans meet

18. Small, shrimp-like creatures called _____ are an important link i the food chain of the Antarctic waters.

Name _____ Class _____ Date _____

MULTIPLE CHOICE

B. Key Geographic Concepts and Skills
Directions: Write the letter of the correct answer in the blank.

19. _____ Where are most of Australia's eight major cities located?
   a. within the Urban Rim region
   b. in the western part of the continent
   c. in the interior of the continent
   d. along the country's coasts

20. _____ Which of the following statements about Australia's Urban Rim is not true?
   a. The Urban Rim is sparsely populated because it is one of the hottest and driest regions in the country.
   b. Three of Australia's most important cities—Sydney, Melbourne, and Canberra—lie within this region.
   c. The Urban Rim is a cup-shaped region in southeastern Australia that extends from the Great Dividing Range to the eastern coast.
   d. Moist winds from the Pacific Ocean and the Tasman Sea bring frequent rains to the Urban Rim, making it an extremely fertile area.

21. _____ Which of the following statements explains why Canberra was chosen as the capital of Australia?
   a. Canberra, the nation's largest city, has a magnificent harbor laced with small coves.
   b. Canberra has a mild climate and gentle terrain.
   c. Canberra's location was selected to balance competing political interests in several of Australia's states.
   d. Canberra is an important cultural center in Australia and home to the nation's famous Opera House.

22. _____ What is the major economic activity in the outback?
   a. dairy farming and the production of cheese
   b. mining of the many minerals found in the region
   c. ranching of sheep and cattle in the dry region
   d. forestry, for the valuable woods from Australian timber

23. _____ Which of the following statements best describes New Zealand's physical landscape?
   a. The South Island is predominantly flat, while the North Island is covered mostly with elevated plains.
   b. New Zealand's terrain is mostly mountainous, with gentle plains sloping down from the mountains on both islands.
   c. Rugged mountains form the backbone of the North Island, while the South Island is predominantly flat.
   d. The physical landscape of both islands consists mainly of coastal plains that rise to a huge interior plateau.

24. _____ Which of the following statements about New Zealand's first inhabitants is not true?
   a. The origin of the Maoris is in dispute by scholars.
   b. The Maoris lost most of their land in the 1800s to the British colonists.
   c. The Maoris are trying to reassert their claims to the land.
   d. Today, the Maoris comprise about 40 percent of New Zealand's population.

25. _____ Which of the following is an important economic activity in the Pacific Islands?
   a. manufacturing   b. ranching
   c. tourism   d. banking

26. _____ Which of the following statements does not reflect a way in which cold and ice affect the climate and weather in Antarctica?
   a. The ice reflects the sun's rays, making temperatures colder.
   b. Frigid Antarctic waters mix with warmer ocean waters and cause violent storms.
   c. The thickness of the ice distorts the earth and makes it pear-shape
   d. The coldness and elevation of the ice cause extreme dryness.

27. _____ What is the greatest Antarctic resource being utilized today?
   a. fresh water supplied by the massive icebergs
   b. oil and meat supplied by the region's whales and seals
   c. the wealth of mineral deposits beneath the ice
   d. the scientific information being shared by many nations

28. _____ Which of the following describes the lands that lie within Australia's Urban Rim
   a. well-watered and fertile
   b. mountainous and heavily forested
   c. rich in iron ore and coal deposits
   d. tropical with very little human activity

29. _____ What major city is located on the Sunshine Coast in Australia's wettest region?
   a. Perth   b. Melbourne
   c. Darwin   d. Brisbane

30. _____ Which statement explains why the Aborigines protected their environment?
   a. The Aborigines followed the example of the English settlers.
   b. The Aborigines believed that the earth was sacred.
   c. The Aborigines were concerned about global pollution.
   d. The government instituted strict conservation policies after the outback was exploited.

Name _____ Class _____ Date _____

31. ___ Which of the following is not an important economic activity in the interior of Australia?
a. raising sheep for wool
b. raising cattle for beef
c. farming fruits and sugar cane
d. mining mineral resources

32. ___ What is the primary economic activity in New Zealand?
a. mining
b. agriculture
c. manufacturing
d. service industries

33. ___ When and by whom were the islands of Melanesia first discovered and probably settled?
a. 33,000 years ago by people from Southeast Asia
b. 4,000 years ago by people from surrounding islands
c. 400 years ago by people from Australia
d. 200 years ago by people from England

34. ___ When did most islands in the South Pacific gain their independence?
a. in the 1980s and 1990s
b. in the 1960s and 1970s
c. in the 1840s and 1850s
d. in the early 1800s

35. ___ Which statement explains why Antarctica was the world's last continent to be discovered and explored?
a. Antarctica has few natural resources.
b. Summers at the South Pole are extremely hot.
c. Ships are unable to navigate around the Great Barrier Reef.
d. Antarctica is a distant continent with harsh natural conditions.

36. ___ Why have no mineral deposits in Antarctica been exploited?
a. Antarctica has no mineral deposits.
b. Antarctica's mineral deposits are very small.
c. No practical way has yet been found to mine and transport them.
d. A treaty prohibits mining of the continent's mineral deposits.

© Prentice-Hall, Inc.

Chapter 34 ■ 311

Directions: Use the map below to answer the following questions. Write your answer on the lines provided.

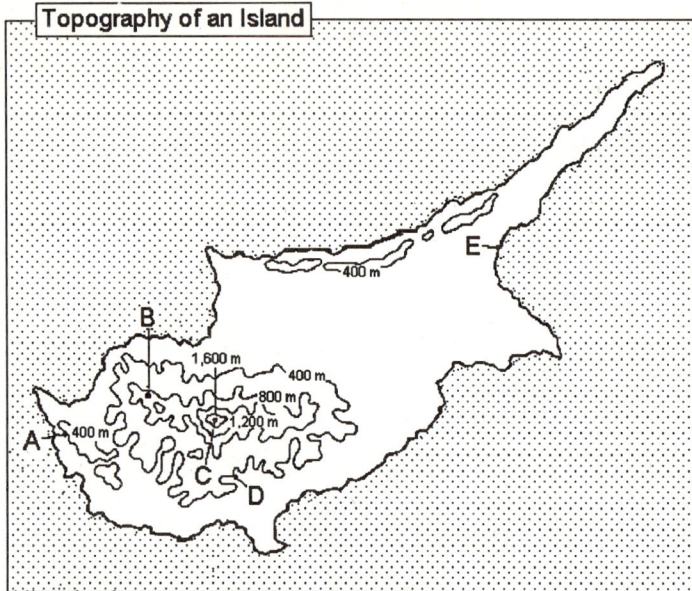

Topography of an Island

37. What is the highest elevation on the island?

_____

38. Which point is lower, point A or point B?

_____

39. Around what point is the land flattest?

_____

40. Is the land steeper between point C and point D or between point C and point E?

_____

41. What is the elevation of the island along the coastline?

_____

42. Which point is higher, point B or point C?

_____

43. Between what two points is the land the steepest?

_____

44. What is the difference in elevation between point A and point E?

_____

SHORT ANSWER

C. Critical Thinking
Directions: Answer the following questions on the back of this paper or on a separate sheet of paper.

45. Expressing Problems Clearly Australia's economy depends heavily on the export of a few mineral and agricultural products. How might this dependence cause problems for the country?

46. Distinguishing False from Accurate Images How does a south-polar projection map give an accurate depiction of Antarctica in a way that a Mercator projection does not?

47. Synthesizing Information Why has no country been able to stake a valid national claim to Antarctica?

48. Predicting Consequences In what two ways would the development of computer and telecommunication industries help Australia's economy?

49. Perceiving Cause-and-Effect Relationships How did independence in several Pacific Islands affect the native cultures there?

50. Synthesizing Information How is the convergence zone around Antarctica created? What are two important effects of the circumstances that create the zone?

Answer Key   Chapter 34

MATCHING

1. n   2. k

3. h   4. c

5. j   6. a

7. m   8. g

9. e

FILL-IN-THE-BLANK

10. lagoon   11. cyclone

12. artesian well

13. atoll   14. crevasse

15. ice shelf   16. pack ice

17. convergence zone

18. krill

MULTIPLE CHOICE

19. d   20. a

21. c   22. c

23. b   24. d

25. c   26. c

27. d   28. a

29. d   30. b

31. c   32. b

33. a   34. b

35. d   36. c

GRAPHIC STUDY

37. 1,600 meters

38. point A   39. point E

40. between point C and point D

41. sea level, or 0 meters

42. point C   43. between C and D

44. 400 meters

SHORT ANSWER

45. Australia suffers from the same problems as other countries whose economies depend on the export of a few mineral and agricultural products. When foreign demand is high, the economy booms; when foreign demand declines, the economy slumps.

46. To see Antarctica clearly, the South Pole must occupy a central position on the map. This does not happen with the Mercator map, which stretches the South Pole, distorting Antarctica into a long, slender continent. The south-polar projection places the South Pole in a central position and gives a true picture of Antarctica's shape and size.

47. In the late 1800s, the most powerful nations agreed that land had to be occupied and actively governed for a national claim to be valid. Because of the harsh climate and rugged landscape of Antarctica, no country has established a permanent settlement. Thus, no country can stake a valid national claim to the region.

48. The development of computer and telecommunication industries in Australia would help diversify the country's economy, making it less dependent on the prices of mining and agricultural products in the changeable foreign market. These industries would also help the country to reduce its remoteness and isolation.

49. Independence helped renew interest in native cultures among the people. Many of the new national governments were based on traditional forms of leadership.

50. The convergence zone is created by the frigid waters that circulate around Antarctica meeting the warmer waters of the surrounding oceans. This clash of warm and cold waters helps cause severe storms along Antarctica's coastline. The contrast in temperatures also encourages the mixing of different layers of water. Nutrient-rich, deep waters rise to the surface, feeding millions of krill, which provide food for whales and fish at the bottom of the food chain.

Unit 1   Physical and Human Geography

COMPLETION

A. Vocabulary
Directions: Complete each sentence by underlining the correct term in parentheses.

1. To say that Pittsburgh is located in the western part of Pennsylvania is to describe its (absolute, relative, census) location.

2. The imaginary line of latitude that circles the globe at its widest point is the (Equator, Tropic of Cancer, Prime Meridian).

3. (Culture, Sovereignty, Environment) includes the beliefs and actions that define a group of people's way of life.

4. The center of the earth is a (core, mantle, magma) that consists of very hot metal, mainly iron mixed with some nickel.

5. (Convection, Volcanism, Rotation) occurs when a material is heated, expands and rises, then cools and falls.

6. The movement of weathered materials—including gravel, soil, and sand— is called (erosion, equinox, frost wedging).

7. (Climate, Biome, Environment) is the term for the weather patterns that an area or region typically experiences over a long period of time.

8. The (continental drift theory, scientific method, Coriolis effect) explains why winds do not blow in a straight line.

9. Change from outside a culture comes through (convection, distortion, diffusion), the spread of cultural traits from one society to another.

10. (Sovereignty, Democracy, Acculturation) is freedom from outside control.

11. A (dictatorship, monarchy, democracy) is an authoritarian government in which the leader of the government inherits his or her position.

12. (Fossil fuels, Renewable resources, Geothermal energy) such as coal, oil, and natural gas were formed from the remains of ancient plants and animals.

13. The (manufacturing, gross national product, census) of a country is the total value of goods and services the country produces in a year.

MULTIPLE CHOICE

B. Key Geographic Concepts and Skills
Directions: Write the letter of the correct ending in the blank.

14. _____ All of the following are true of the five themes of geography except:
    a. The location of a place can be described only by its latitude and longitude.
    b. Human beings can make enormous changes in their environment.
    c. People depend on the movement of people, goods, and ideas.
    d. A place has both physical and human characteristics.

15. _____ Grouping places according to common characteristics reflects the geographic theme of
    a. location.
    b. regions.
    c. movement.
    d. human-environment interaction.

16. _____ The four general types of vegetation regions include forest and all of the following except
    a. desert.   b. tundra.
    c. grassland.   d. polar.

17. _____ The earth's landforms were first shaped by
    a. water.   b. internal forces.
    c. weathering and erosion.   d. glaciers.

18. _____ A country is defined as a political unit that must have each of the following characteristics except
    a. sovereignty.   b. a common language.
    c. a government.   d. clearly defined territory.

19. _____ Coniferous trees are well adapted to their natural environment because they
    a. shed their leaves and "hibernate" when winter approaches.
    b. have needle leaves that expose only a small surface to the cold winter.
    c. have leathery leaves that hold moisture over the dry summer.
    d. are broadleaf evergreens that absorb all available sunlight and rain.

20. _____ A country's economic system must answer all of the following basic economic questions except:
    a. What and how many goods and services will be produced?
    b. How will the products and wealth gained from their sale be distributed?
    c. How will power be divided between the regional and the national governments?
    d. How will the goods and services be produced?

21. _____ Renewable resources are
   a. continually replaced by the environment.
   b. minerals and fossil fuels formed in the earth's crust.
   c. forms of energy produced by fission.
   d. the vast coal deposits distributed throughout the world.

GRAPHIC STUDY

Directions: Use the map to answer the following questions. Write your answers on the lines provided.

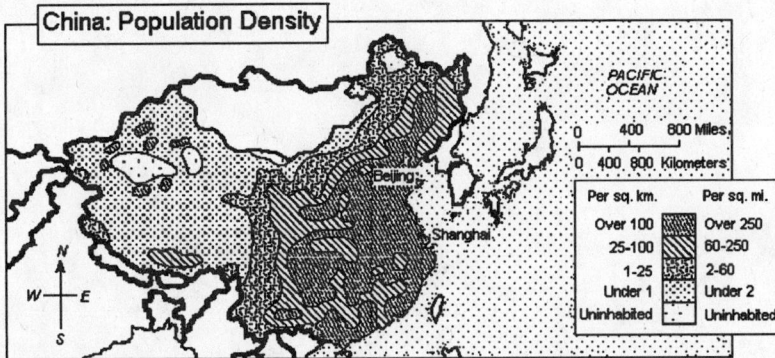

China: Population Density

22. Where are the lowest population densities located in China?

_____

23. In which part of China is the population density 2-60 people per square mile?

_____

24. Where are the highest population densities located in China?

_____

25. What physical factors do you think account for the high population densities of this area?

_____

SHORT ANSWER

C. Critical Thinking
Directions: Answer the following questions on the back of this paper or on a separate sheet of paper.

26. Distinguishing False from Accurate Images Is the image of erosion as only a destructive process a false or an accurate image? Give reasons to support your answer.

27. **Perceiving Cause-and-Effect Relationships** Explain how the process of convection distributes the sun's heat.

28. **Synthesizing Information** Explain why competition for oil is a strong force in world politics and economics.

Answer Key   Unit 1

COMPLETION

1. relative
2. Equator
3. culture
4. core
5. convection
6. erosion
7. climate
8. Coriolis effect
9. diffusion
10. sovereignty
11. monarchy
12. fossil fuels
13. gross national product

MULTIPLE CHOICE

14. a
15. b
16. d
17. b
18. b
19. b
20. c
21. a

GRAPHIC STUDY

22. in western China

23. mainly in a strip of land that runs north and south in the center

24. along the coast, sometimes reaching inland about 1,000 miles (1,600 km)

25. mild climate, fertile land, adequate water supply

SHORT ANSWER

26. A false image. Erosion is the movement of weathered materials usually by water, wind, or glaciers. Without this process, the earth's surface would be barren rock. Water deposits the sediment, and wind carries the loess that create fertile lands.

27. Convection occurs because lighter, warm gases or liquids tend to rise while cooler, heavier gases and liquids sink and displace the lighter materials. Thus, warm air and water flow from the Equator toward the poles. Cold air and water tend to move from the poles toward the tropics and the Equator. Both winds and currents help to distribute the sun's heat.

28. Most modern industrialized countries depend heavily on oil. Without enough supplies of their own, they must import much of what they use. Because oil reserves are spread unevenly throughout the world and because supplies are likely to run out in a century, political and economic competition to gain access to the limited supply of oil is high.

Name _____ Class _____ Date _____

Unit 2   The United States and Canada

MATCHING

A. Vocabulary
Directions: Match the definitions with the terms. Write the correct
letter in each blank. You will not use all the terms.

a. prairie
b. customs
c. maritime
d. hinterlands
e. tributaries
f. suburbs
g. bayous
h. standard of living
i. growing season
j. cordillera
k. aqueducts
l. free enterprise
m. rugged individualism
n. hydroelectricity
o. literacy rate
p. megalopolis

1. _____ bordering on or related to the sea

2. _____ large pipes that carry water over long distances

3. _____ rivers and streams that carry water to a river

4. _____ type of power generated by moving water

5. _____ residential areas on the outer edges of a city

6. _____ marshy inlets of lakes and rivers

7. _____ average number of days between the last spring frost and the first
fall frost

8. _____ temperate grassland

9. _____ measurement of a person's or a group's education, housing, health
care, and nutrition

10. _____ economic system allowing individuals to own, operate, and profit
from their own businesses

11. _____ areas served by larger cities

12. _____ related set of mountain ranges

MULTIPLE CHOICE

B. Key Geographic Concepts and Skill
Directions: Write the letter of the correct ending in the blank.

13. _____ The overall pattern of landforms in North America is
    a. central plains between high mountains to the west and low mountains to the east.
    b. high mountains to the west and vast rolling plains to the east.
    c. high mountains to the east, low mountains to the west, and plains in the north and south.
    d. plateaus between high eastern mountains and western coastal plains.

14. _____ The only natural vegetation that grows in the cold Arctic tundra is
    a. desert scrub.
    b. grasses and coniferous forests.
    c. deciduous forests.
    d. lichens, mosses, and a few other tiny plants.

15. _____ The populations of both the United States and Canada
    a. share similar characteristics.
    b. are approximately the same size.
    c. are descended mostly from native peoples.
    d. have strong national identities.

16. _____ The United States became a wealthy nation for all of the following reasons except
    a. abundance of natural resources.
    b. a belief in rugged individualism.
    c. advances in transportation and communication.
    d. urban hierarchies.

17. _____ The most significant factor affecting population patterns and economic activity in the West is the
    a. lack of a sound transportation system.
    b. abundance or scarcity of water.
    c. variety of rich soils.
    d. availability of natural resources such as petroleum and iron ore.

18. _____ All of the following statements about the South are correct except:
    a. The South has become a retirement and tourism center.
    b. Since the 1950s, many northern industries have relocated to the South.
    c. Almost all business activities in the South are tied to agriculture.
    d. More African Americans are currently leaving the South than are migrating in.

19. _____ The dominant factor affecting the economy of the Midwest is
    a. the auto industry.
    b. agriculture.
    c. water transportation.
    d. coal mining.

20. _____ The most valuable natural resource of the Northeast region of the
    United States and the Atlantic provinces of Canada is their
    a. waters and harbors.
    b. fertile soil.
    c. iron ore deposits.
    d. mild climate.

21. _____ Canada is well suited to working with other nations because of its
    a. high standard of living and low literacy rate.
    b. role as a superpower.
    c. location, size, and multicultural population.
    d. isolation from the United States.

GRAPHIC STUDY

Directions: Use the map to describe the weather in two regions of the
United States. Write your answers on the lines provided.

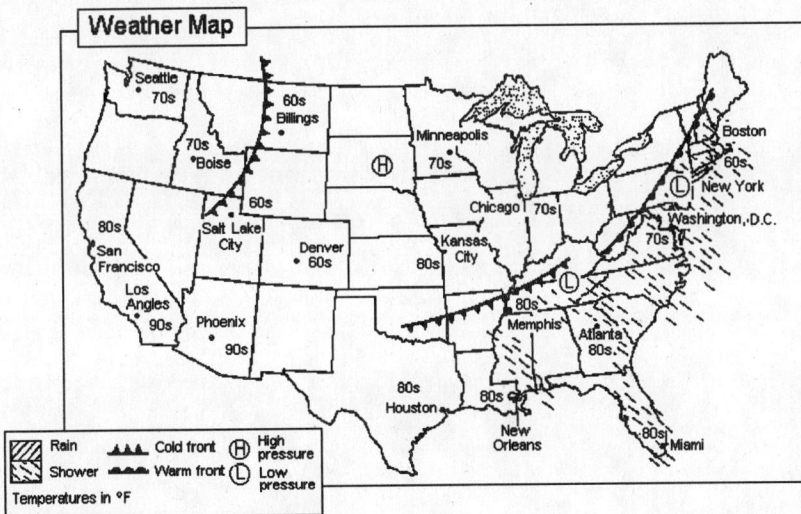

Weather Map

22. Northeast:

_____

23. West:

_____

SHORT ANSWER

C. Critical Thinking

Directions: Answer the following questions on the back of this paper or on a separate sheet of paper.

24. Identifying Central Issues Explain why the United States and Canada have been able to maintain friendly relations with each other.

25. Predicting Consequences Explain the possible economic and cultural consequences to Canada and to Quebec if Quebec secedes from Canada.

26. Testing Conclusions Support these statements with examples from your text: "Cities of similar size are not alike in all parts of the United States. They have distinct characteristics based in part on regional differences."

Answer Key   Unit 2

MATCHING

1. c	2. k
3. e	4. n
5. f	6. g
7. i	8. a
9. h	10. l
11. d	12. j

MULTIPLE CHOICE

13. a	14. d
15. a	16. d
17. b	18. c
19. b	20. a
21. c	

GRAPHIC STUDY

22. There are showers over most of the Northeast except for Maine. Temperatures are in the 60s with a warm front moving in.

23. A cold front is heading toward Billings, Denver, and Salt Lake City, where the temperatures are currently in the 60s. Farther south in Phoenix, the temperature reached the 90s. The weather in California is warm and clear.

SHORT ANSWER

24. The United States and Canada have maintained friendly relations because of strong cultural and economic ties to one another. Both countries have abundant resources and are major trading partners of each other. They share similar values as reflected in their democratic governments and free enterprise economies.

25. Secession of Quebec from Canada would result in severe economic problems for both the province and the country because Quebec, together with Ontario, is the economic heartland of Canada. Canada would lose a substantial percentage of its population, natural resources, and income. Quebec would suffer economically as English-speaking residents and businesses left the province. Also, Quebec runs the risk of losing Canada's trading partners.

26. Large cities along the Atlantic coast, such as New York and Boston, are centers of industry and international trade. The economies of large cities in the South, such as Houston and Dallas, have strong ties to regional industries such as oil, cattle, and banking. The economies or large midwestern cities, such as Kansas City and Omaha, are closely linked to economic activities related to agriculture. Denver, Seattle, and other western cities similar in size are regional metropolises.

Unit 3   Latin America

MATCHING

A. Vocabulary
Directions: Match the definitions with the terms. Write the correct letter in each blank. You will not use all the terms.

a. mestizo
b. ejido
c. altiplano
d. mulatto
e. irrigation
f. campesino
g. guerrilla
h. selva
i. hurricanes
j. isthmus
k. timber line
l. escarpment
m. tropical storms

1. _____ small farmer in South America

2. _____ name for plateau areas in Peru and Bolivia

3. _____ steep cliff that separates two level areas

4. _____ member of an armed force that is not part of the regular army

5. _____ narrow strip of land bordered on both sides by water and joining two larger bodies of land

6. _____ artificial watering of farmland, often by means of canals

7. _____ farmland owned collectively by members of a rural community

8. _____ tropical storms in the Atlantic Ocean or eastern Pacific Ocean with winds of a least 74 miles (119 km) per hour

9. _____ boundary above which continuous forest vegetation does not grow

10. _____ person of mixed European and Indian ancestry

MULTIPLE CHOICE

B. Key Geographic Concepts and Skills
Directions: Write the letter of the correct ending or answer in the blank.

11. _____ Mexico's arid and semi-arid climates in the north and wetter climates in the south are mostly influenced by
    a. latitude.   b. nearness to water.
    c. elevation.   d. the Tropic of Cancer.

12. _____ All of the following make up the landscape of Central America except
    a. wide, deep, navigable rivers.
    b. lakes and mountain streams.
    c. lowland plains and active volcanoes.
    d. mountain ranges and plateaus.

13. _____ Most of Mexico's people live and work in the central plateau region because
    a. it is the only region in Mexico that is geologically stable.
    b. temperatures are mild and there is plenty of rainfall in the southern section.
    c. the region's resort cities and beaches make tourism an important economic activity.
    d. it is rich in petroleum and natural gas.

14. _____ For most of its history, the primary cause of discontent and conflict in Central America has been
    a. a small but powerful middle class controlling the government.
    b. rivalries among Indians, African Americans, and mestizos.
    c. uneven distribution of available farmland and inequalities of income.
    d. attempts to turn the region toward communism.

15. _____ The average year-round temperature of 80°F (27°C) in the Caribbean illustrates how climate is affected by
    a. elevation and landforms.
    b. nearness to water and ocean breezes.
    c. location in the tropics where the sun's rays are most direct.
    d. rainfall and humidity.

16. _____ Brazil's leaders built the new capital city of Brasília in the Brazilian Highlands in order to
    a. promote the development of the interior of the country.
    b. draw developers away from the Amazon River basin.
    c. provide large numbers of workers for the coffee plantations.
    d. encourage Brazilians to move from rural areas to urban, industrial centers.

17. _____ Brazil has become one of the world's leading industrial nations
    because of
    a. massive government programs encouraging the growth of industry.
    b. government land redistribution programs.
    c. the elimination of poverty in the nation.
    d. the development of resources in the Brazilian Highlands.

18. _____ Venezuela is the richest country in South America primarily
    because
    a. Venezuelan farmers grow different crops due to variations in soil and
       climate.
    b. Venezuela is the world's largest exporter of bauxite.
    c. Venezuela has an oil-based economy that is rapidly diversifying.
    d. the Venezuelan government encouraged the development of heavy
       industries.

19. _____ Unlike other Andean nations, Chile has
    a. a large mestizo population.
    b. a predominantly Indian population.
    c. a population equally divided among Indians, Europeans, and mestizos.
    d. relatively few Indians.

20. _____ Which of the following statements is not true about Uruguay,
    Paraguay, and Argentina?
    a. They are bound together by the Río de la Plata.
    b. They share similar climates and terrains.
    c. They are generally wealthier than other South American countries.
    d. They have stronger ethnic ties to Europe than do other South American
       countries.

GRAPHIC STUDY

Directions: Use the population pyramid below to answer the following
questions. Write your answers on the lines provided.

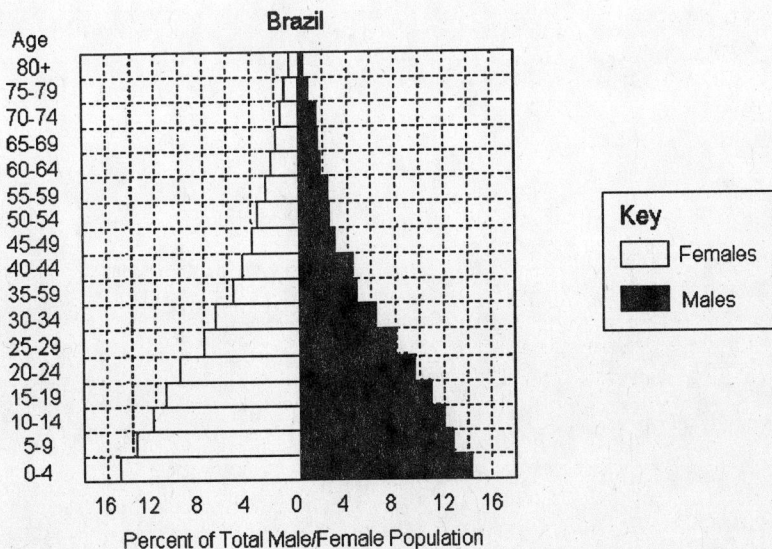

Brazil

Age

80+
75-79
70-74
65-69
60-64
55-59
50-54
45-49
40-44
35-59
30-34
25-29
20-24
15-19
10-14
5-9
0-4

16 12 8 4 0 4 8 12 16

Percent of Total Male/Female Population

Key
☐ Females
■ Males

21. What percentage of Brazil's population is between ages 20 and 24?

_____

22. What percentage is between ages 10 and 14?

_____

23. Is the population of Brazil growing or declining? How can you tell?

_____

24. How might demands for education, housing, and jobs be affected by Brazil's population?

_____

SHORT ANSWER

C. Critical Thinking
Directions: Answer the following questions on the back of this paper or on a separate sheet of paper.

25. Determining Relevance Explain the link between the European colonization of Latin America and how social structure influences the way in which many Latin Americans earn a living today.

26. Expressing Problems Clearly Describe three problems challenging the Caribbean islands today and the reasons for each problem.

27. Determining Relevance What appears to be the link between land and political conflict in Mexico and Central America? Give examples to support your answer.

Answer Key   Unit 3

MATCHING

1. f	2. c
3. l	4. g
5. j	6. e
7. b	8. i
9. k	10. a

MULTIPLE CHOICE

11. b	12. c
13. b	14. c
15. b	16. a
17. a	18. c
19. d	20. b

GRAPHIC STUDY

21. about 10 percent

22. about 12 percent

23. The population is growing, as indicated
    by the wide base of the pyramid.

24. Brazil will have to provide more housing,
    schools, and job opportunities for its
    people. Otherwise, the economy could
    weaken as poverty and unemployment rates
    increase.

SHORT ANSWER

25. European colonization of Latin America resulted in the creation of a social structure based on ethnic origin. People of European descent composed a small, elite upper class; a small number of mestizo artisans and business owners, the middle class; and large numbers of mestizos, Indians, and Africans, the lowest class. Throughout Latin America, ethnic background and social class continue to influence how people earn a living. People of European descent own the largest farms and businesses. Mestizos work as small farmers or as unskilled laborers in factories, and Indians are mostly subsistence farmers.

26. Problems Caribbean nations face today include migration of people to other countries, political instability, high unemployment rates, and poverty. Caribbean countries are poor because their economies are agricultural. Although tourism thrives, most of the revenue from this industry goes to foreign corporations that own the hotels, airlines, and cruise ships. Caribbean islanders migrate in search of jobs, especially during the plantations' eight-month dead season. Revolutions have taken place in Caribbean nations ruled by dictators who did little to raise living standards.

27. The uneven distribution of farmland in Mexico and Central America has been the primary cause of political and social conflict. Since colonization, the upper class has owned huge tracts of farmland on which peasants have worked. In Mexico before the revolution, almost all the land suitable for farming was part of haciendas. Although the government instituted a land redistribution program, three to four million Mexican rural families today are landless. In Central America, the shortage of farmland has sparked discontent and guerrilla warfare. Government leaders who favored the wealthy with their land policies have been overthrown.

Unit 4   Western Europe

FILL-IN-THE-BLANK

A. Vocabulary
Directions: Complete each sentence by writing the correct term in the
blank. You will not use all the terms.

cantons
graben
fjords
multilingual
dialect
inflation
ore
navigable
glen
moor
peat
polder
lignite

1. The people of many Western European countries are _____, speaking
   many different languages.

2. A(n) _____ is a variation of a language that is unique to a region
   or a community.

3. Iron _____, the rocky material containing iron, is melted and used
   in the production of steel.

4. A narrow valley is called a(n) _____ in Scotland.

5. Irish farmers cut and dry blocks of _____, a spongy material
   containing waterlogged mosses and plants, for fuel.

6. Many of Norway's villages are located along _____, flooded glacial
   valleys along the coasts.

7. The Dutch call the land they reclaimed from the sea a(n) _____.

8. Twenty-six _____, or states, make up Switzerland.

9. Only one river flowing across Spain's Meseta is _____, deep and
   wide enough to allow ships to pass.

10. The Aegean Sea occupies a(n) _____, a flooded area of land that
    dropped down between faults.

MULTIPLE CHOICE

B. Key Geographic Concepts and Skills
Directions: Write the letter of the correct ending in the blank.

11. _____ The physical geography of Europe can best be described in all of the following ways except
    a. a "peninsula of peninsulas."
    b. a landscape varying from soaring mountains to rolling plains.
    c. an area with few navigable rivers.
    d. a landmass half the size of the continental United States.

12. _____ The French have a strong sense of national identity because
    a. France has undergone many changes in government since the French Revolution.
    b. France has one of the strongest economies in Europe.
    c. the French take pride in their language, history, and culture.
    d. there are few regional differences within the country.

13. _____ The Ruhr Valley is important to Germany's economy because of the valley's
    a. industrial resources.
    b. fertile farmland.
    c. warm climate and resort cities.
    d. many service industries.

14. _____ Britain is no longer the world's leading industrial power primarily because
    a. most of its valuable mineral reserves have been used up.
    b. many of its industries could not compete with those of newer industrial nations.
    c. it has few service industries.
    d. it has a very small merchant marine.

15. _____ Religious and political turmoil in Ireland today can be traced back to the time when
    a. Celtic tribes first settled in Ireland.
    b. the king of England broke with the Roman Catholic Church and founded the Church of England.
    c. Ireland was divided into two parts.
    d. Great Britain sent troops to Northern Ireland to protect the Catholic majority from Protestant extremists.

16. _____ East and West Germany were reunited when
    a. Germany defeated France in the Franco-Prussian War.
    b. the Nazi party came to power in Germany.
    c. Allied forces withdrew from Berlin.
    d. East Germans overthrew their Communist government.

17. _____ The Benelux nations are called the Low Countries because
   a. much of their land is flat and low.
   b. they have such a small land area.
   c. they are located in a valley between two high mountains.
   d. they are Europe's newest independent countries.

18. _____ In foreign affairs, both Switzerland and Austria
   a. have sided with their Eastern European neighbors.
   b. are neutral.
   c. have played the role of a middle power.
   d. are members of the North Atlantic Treaty Organization (NATO).

19. _____ The Iberian Peninsula is separated from the rest of Europe by the
   a. Apennines.   b. Meseta.
   c. Pyrenees.   d. North European Plain.

20. _____ The people of both Greece and Portugal have
   a. always relied on the sea for trade.
   b. used their resources to develop heavy industries.
   c. used their land mostly for fruit and vegetable production.
   d. recently begun to enjoy a high standard of living.

GRAPHIC STUDY

Directions: Use the bar graph below to answer the following questions.
Write your answers on the lines provided.

Trade of Four Western European Countries

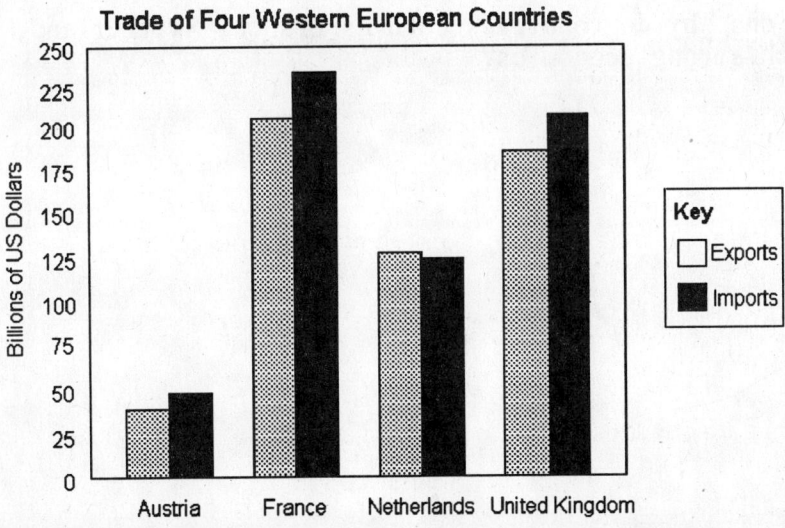

Key
☐ Exports
■ Imports

21. What information is presented in the bar graph?

_____

22. How does the dollar value of the United Kingdom's exports compare with the dollar value of its imports?

_____

23. Which country shown on the graph has a favorable balance of trade, exporting more than it imports?

_____

24. Which country exports the least amount of goods?

_____

SHORT ANSWER

C. Critical Thinking
Directions: Answer the following questions on the back of this paper or on a separate sheet of paper.

25. Identifying Central Issues How has location influenced the economic development of Western Europe? Cite at least three specific examples.

26. Making Comparisons Why are the Nordic nations unified as a region, while the United Kingdom remains a region of four countries, each with its own identity?

27. Drawing Conclusions Why do countries such as France, Switzerland, and Germany have such strong economies?

Answer Key   Unit 4

FILL-IN-THE-BLANK

1. multilingual

2. dialect   3. ore

4. glen   5. peat

6. fjords   7. polder

8. cantons   9. navigable

10. graben

MULTIPLE CHOICE

11. c   12. c

13. a   14. b

15. b   16. d

17. a   18. b

19. c   20. a

GRAPHIC STUDY

21. imports and exports of four Western European
    countries

22. The dollar value of its exports is lower
    (by about 25 billion dollars) than the dollar
    value of its imports.

23. the Netherlands

24. Austria

SHORT ANSWER

25. A favorable location has influenced the economic growth of much of Western Europe. London's relative location on the Thames River has made it one of the greatest commercial cities of the world. Rotterdam and Amsterdam on the North Sea, became important ports for foreign trade. Madrid became the capital of Spain because of its location in the center of the country.

26. The Nordic nations are unified by climate, location, and strong cultural bonds. They share a common history, religion, and political and economic philosophies. Nordic languages derive from common roots. In the British Isles, religion is one of many factors dividing the region. Ireland is divided between Protestants and Catholics. Although united politically with England for hundreds of years, Scotland and Wales have retained separate cultural identities. A sense of regional cultural pride and independence has acted as a barrier to unity in the British Isles.

27. Their economies are modern, industrialized, and diversified. France, Germany, and Switzerland have used their valuable natural and human resources to develop specialized economic activities that are highly profitable. For example, Switzerland is famous for producing chocolates, medicines, and high-quality watches.

Unit 5   Eastern Europe

MATCHING

A. Vocabulary
Directions: Match the definitions with the terms. Write the correct
letter in each blank. You will not use all the terms.

a. balkanize
b. entrepreneur
c. collective farm
d. privatization
e. multiethnic
f. karst
g. national identity
h. multilingual
i. ghetto

1. _____ section of a city where racial minorities are forced to live

2. _____ soft limestone easily eroded by wind and water

3. _____ composed of many ethnic groups

4. _____ state-owned agriculture in which workers share the profits from
their produce

5. _____ to split into many smaller states

MULTIPLE CHOICE

B. Key Geographic Concepts and Skills
Directions: Write the letter of the correct answer in the blank.

6. _____ The northernmost landform region in Eastern Europe is the
a. Carpathian Mountains.
b. Hungarian Basin.
c. North European Plain.
d. Balkan Peninsula.

7. _____ Most of the people in Eastern Europe are descended from the
a. Goths.   b. Celts.
c. Huns.   d. Slavs.

8. _____ At the end of World War II, the Soviets supported Communist governments in Eastern Europe in an effort to
   a. protect the eastern borders of these countries against invasion.
   b. encourage the growth of capitalism.
   c. establish a buffer zone of Communist states between themselves and Western Europe.
   d. stop the spread of Marxism.

9. _____ Few Jews live in Poland today because almost all of Poland's Jews
   a. were killed by the Nazis during World War II.
   b. moved to countries where Roman Catholicism was not the major religion.
   c. were forced by the Nazis to live in ghettos outside of Poland after World War II.
   d. fled from the lands overtaken by the former Soviet Union after World War II.

10. _____ Throughout their history, the Poles have maintained a strong sense of national identity as members of
    a. the Roman Catholic church.
    b. Solidarity.
    c. the Communist party.
    d. the Eastern Orthodox Church.

11. _____ Which of the following statements is not true of the Czech Republic and Slovakia?
    a. The two countries form a relatively flat area with numerous plains stretching along the Elbe and Danube rivers.
    b. Both countries share Western outlooks.
    c. The two countries were peacefully created when Czechoslovakia divided in 1993.
    d. As Czechoslovakia, the two countries were under Communist rule from 1945 until 1989.

12. _____ Which of the following statements about Romania is not true?
    a. Government policies have left Romania an impoverished country.
    b. Romania has fertile plains along the Danube River and abundant minerals in the foothills of the Carpathian Mountains.
    c. Romania is the most industrialized of the five Balkan nations.
    d. A democratic revolution in Romania in 1989 overthrew the nation's dictator.

13. _____ Which of the following statements about Bulgaria is not true?
    a. Bulgarians share Slavic origins with the Russians.
    b. Unlike other countries on the Balkan Peninsula, Bulgaria remained free of Turkish rule.
    c. Bulgaria has a very low standard of living.
    d. Bulgaria's tourist income brings in needed foreign currency.

Name _____ Class _____ Date _____

SHORT ANSWER

Directions: Read the passage below about Hungary's struggle for freedom. Then, identify Hungary's values, and evaluate the results of Hungary's action. Use the back of this paper if necessary to complete your answer.

In Hungary's struggle to break free of Soviet control in 1956, the Hungarian prime minister, Imre Nagy, pulled the nation out of the Warsaw Pact. The Soviets were alarmed by this action, and they removed Nagy from power. This Soviet action led to a widespread uprising by Hungarians, who demanded that Nagy be restored to power. The Soviets responded by sending troops into Hungary and killing thousands of people in bloody street fights.

14. Identify Hungary's values:

Evaluate the results of Hungary's action:

GRAPHIC STUDY

Directions: Use the map below to answer the following questions. Write your answers on the lines provided.

Eastern Europe: Economic Activity

15. How is most of the land in Eastern Europe used?

_____

16. Where does most trade and manufacturing take place throughout Eastern Europe?

_____

SHORT ANSWER

C. Critical Thinking
Directions: Answer the following questions on the back of this paper or on a separate sheet of paper.

17. Determining Relevance Explain how geographic location and landforms influenced the early development of Eastern Europe.

18. Recognizing Ideologies Why do you think that a movement that began with the formation of an independent workers' union (Solidarity) resulted in breaking the power of the Communist government in Poland?

Answer Key   Unit 5

MATCHING

1. i   2. f

3. e   4. c

5. a

MULTIPLE CHOICE

6. c   7. d

8. c   9. a

10. a   11. a

12. c   13. b

SHORT ANSWER

14. Hungary's most important value was to gain
    freedom from the former Soviet Union. The
    result of Hungary's action of pulling out
    of the Warsaw Pact was the removal of prime
    minister Nagy from power, which led to an
    uprising in Hungary that Soviet troops put
    down, resulting in thousands of Hungarian
    deaths.

GRAPHIC STUDY

15. for commercial farming

16. in and around major cities

SHORT ANSWER

17. Because of its strategic location connecting
    the European Peninsula with the rest of
    Eurasia, Eastern Europe has been the target
    of many foreign invasions over the years. Of
    the many groups of people who marched through
    the region, the Slavs were the ones who stayed
    and settled in the area. Arriving at the
    Carpathian Mountains, they gradually moved
    north to the Baltic, south to Greece, west to
    Germany, and east to Russia. Once settled, the
    Slavs were separated from each other by
    mountain ranges. As a result, each group
    gradually developed its own language and culture.

18. Under communism, the government controls industry and therefore is the sole employer of its citizens. Thus, when the workers struck in Poland, they were in effect protesting the policies of the Communists. The popular support Solidarity received represented a wave of popular opinion against the government, which lost control in 1990.

Unit 6   Northern Eurasia

MATCHING

A. Vocabulary
Directions: Match the definitions with the terms. Write the correct
letter in each blank. You will not use all the terms.

a. light industry
b. tundra
c. chernozem
d. taiga
e. steppe
f. command economy
g. heavy industry
h. perestroika
i. market economy
j. soviet
k. glasnost
l. nationalism
m. genocide

1. _____ temperate grassland region

2. _____ production of such goods as steel and machines that are used by
other industries

3. _____ governing council

4. _____ Russian coniferous forest region

5. _____ Russian word meaning "openness"

6. _____ the intentional destruction of an ethnic group

7. _____ vegetation such as mosses or lichens that can survive in a
subarctic climate

8. _____ Russian word used to describe an economic restructuring policy

9. _____ the desire of a cultural group to rule itself

10. _____ rich black soil suitable for growing crops

11. _____ economy in which the government makes all of the decisions about
the kinds and amount of goods to be produced

MULTIPLE CHOICE

B. Key Geographic Concepts and Skills
Directions: Write the letter of the correct ending or answer in the blank.

12. _____ Russia is
    a. the third largest country in Northern Eurasia.
    b. nearly twice the size of Canada.
    c. half the size of Europe.
    d. the largest country in the Southern Hemisphere.

13. _____ All of the following rivers flow across the Northern Eurasian plains and empty into the Arctic Ocean except the
    a. Ob.   b. Lena.
    c. Volga.   d. Yenisei.

14. _____ Because the interior of Northern Eurasia does not receive the moderating effect of the ocean, the region has a
    a. continental climate.
    b. Mediterranean climate.
    c. tropical climate.
    d. cool and humid climate.

15. _____ The main form of vegetation in the northernmost part of Northern Eurasia is
    a. forest.   b. desert.
    c. grassland.   d. tundra.

16. _____ Because of rugged land and harsh climates in much of Northern Eurasia,
    a. most people are concentrated on the eastern plains.
    b. many people have moved away from the western region.
    c. large areas of the region are sparsely populated.
    d. the population is evenly distributed along the southern border.

17. _____ Northern Eurasia faces all of the following problems except
    a. underdeveloped resources.
    b. ethnic diversity.
    c. a low standard of living.
    d. lack of mineral resources.

18. _____ The Baltic nations of Lithuania, Latvia, and Estonia are different from other Northern Eurasian nations in that the Baltic nations
    a. were never independent.
    b. have more advanced economies.
    c. have a large Muslim population.
    d. work hard to strengthen their relationship with the central government in Moscow.

© Prentice-Hall, Inc.

19. _____ Which of the following statements about Armenia is not true?
a. Most of Armenia's population is Muslim.
b. Armenia is the smallest of the nations in Northern Eurasia.
c. Armenia is landlocked.
d. Armenia has been in conflict with Azerbaijan.

20. _____ All of the following statements about the five nations of central Asia are correct except:
a. The central Asian nations are the most industrialized in Northern Eurasia.
b. All are Muslim nations.
c. Much of the land is covered by mountains or deserts.
d. All of the nations are home to a mixture of peoples.

GRAPHIC STUDY

Directions: Use the map that follows to answer the following questions. Write your answers on the lines provided.

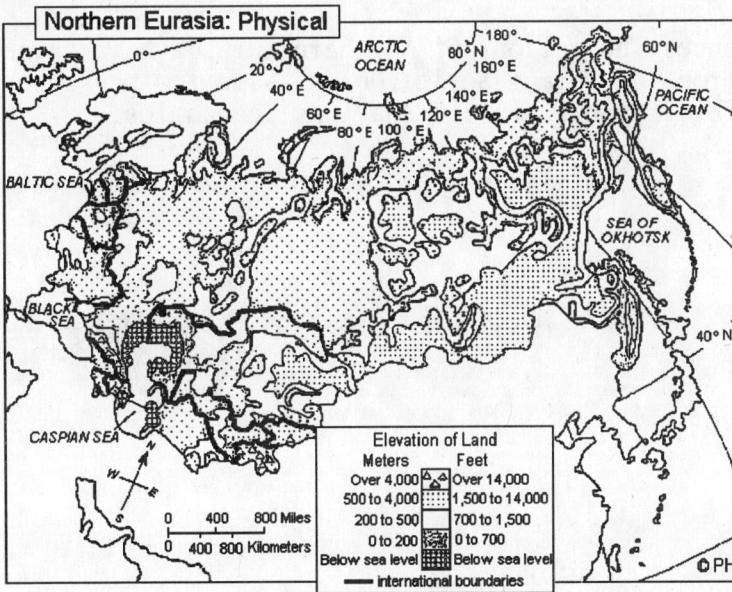

21. How might you describe changes in elevation in the land between the Caspian Sea and the Black Sea?

_____

22. What is the elevation range for the peninsula that lies between the Sea of Okhotsk and the Pacific Ocean?

_____

SHORT ANSWER

C. Critical Thinking
Directions: Answer the following questions on the back of this paper or on a separate sheet of paper.

23. Recognizing Bias Rewrite the following passage so that it is free of bias: The thousands of men, women, and children who crowded St. Petersburg should never have ventured out into the icy streets of the Russian capital on that cold Sunday in January 1905. They were foolish to believe that the crosses, religious banners, and portraits of Czar Nicholas II they carried in their peaceful march to the Winter Palace would grant them the right to see the czar and present a petition to him asking for political rights, to which they were not entitled.

24. Checking Consistency Northern Eurasia has remained relatively isolated from the rest of the world. At the same time, the influence of many foreign cultures can be seen in Northern Eurasia today. Explain why these statements are consistent.

25. Predicting Consequences The nations of Northern Eurasia have gained political freedom from the former Soviet Union. Name two possible consequences that this may have for the nations' economies.

Answer Key   Unit 6

MATCHING

1. e	2. g
3. j	4. d
5. k	6. m
7. b	8. h
9. l	10. c
11. f	

MULTIPLE CHOICE

12. b	13. c
14. a	15. d
16. c	17. d
18. b	19. a
20. a	

GRAPHIC STUDY

21. The land rises steeply and rapidly.

22. 0 to 14,000 feet (0 to 4,000 m)

SHORT ANSWER

23. Thousands of men, women, and children crowded the icy streets of St. Petersburg, the Russian capital, on a cold Sunday morning in January 1905. They carried crosses, religious banners, and portraits of Czar Nicholas II on their march to the Winter Palace to see the czar and present a petition to him asking for political rights.

24. While distance, harsh climate, and hostility have kept nations relatively isolated from the rest of the world, invasion, expansion, and trade have brought many outsiders who have left a lasting mark on the various cultures of the region.

25. A disruption in the flow of supplies to
    Northern Eurasia might lead to shortages in
    some nations and surpluses in others;
    scarcity of fuels and raw materials might lead
    to slowdowns in production, which might lead
    to high levels of unemployment.

Unit 7   Southwest Asia

FILL-IN-THE-BLANK

A. Vocabulary

Directions: Complete each sentence by writing the correct term in the blank. You will not use all the terms.

ayatollahs
drip irrigation
falaj system
Zionists
infrastructure
self-determination
monotheism
secular
mandates
mosques
anarchy
minarets
Hajj
prophet

1. _____ are conservative religious leaders in Iran.

2. Israel used _____ to bring water to the Negev Desert.

3. Farmers in Oman rely on the _____, an ancient irrigation system.

4. The _____, or pilgrimage, is one of the Pillars of Islam.

5. The belief in one God is called _____.

6. The Koran is believed to be a record of the word of Allah as it was revealed to his _____ Muhammad.

7. Islamic places of worship are called _____.

8. Jews who emigrated to Palestine to create a Jewish homeland called themselves _____.

9. A state of lawlessness is called _____.

10. The basic support facilities of a country are the country's _____.

11. After World War I, several countries that once belonged to the Ottoman Empire were ruled as _____.

MULTIPLE CHOICE

B. Key Geographic Concepts and Skills
Directions: Write the letter of the correct ending in the blank.

12. _____ Unlike other countries in Southwest Asia, Turkey has
    a. broken the bond between Islam and government.
    b. recognized Israel as an independent state.
    c. encouraged Palestinians to become part of its society.
    d. tried to increase its agricultural production.

13. _____ Saudi Arabia has changed in all of the following ways except
    a. modernization and an improved standard of living.
    b. migration from rural settlements to urban areas.
    c. dependence on other countries for food.
    d. investment in the infrastructure.

14. _____ In the 1980s, the economic development of Iran was adversely affected by
    a. the policies of the shahs.
    b. an Islamic revolution and a drop in oil exports.
    c. a civil war between Muslims and Christians.
    d. a war with Israel.

15. _____ All of the following statements about Israel are true except:
    a. Israel has a modern, industrial economy.
    b. The small Arab minority in Israel is a diverse population.
    c. European and Sephardic Jews make up about 80 percent of the population.
    d. All Israelis believe that Israel should be governed in strict adherence to Jewish law.

16. _____ As a result of the Arab-Israeli wars of 1948 and 1967,
    a. Jordan lost the West Bank and the city of East Jerusalem.
    b. Palestinian refugees fled to Syria.
    c. civil war broke out in Lebanon.
    d. Egypt gained control of the rich oil fields of the Sinai Peninsula.

17. _____ Agricultural production in both Iraq and Syria has been limited mainly by
    a. a lack of arable land.
    b. outdated farm equipment.
    c. few reliable sources of water.
    d. dependence on one cash crop.

18. _____ Oil-rich countries of the Arabian Peninsula have spent billions to create drinking and irrigation water from seawater
    a. through drip irrigation.
    b. by building dams and canals.
    c. through a process of desalination.
    d. by digging deep wells to tap underground springs.

19. _____ Unlike other countries on the Arabian Peninsula, Oman and Yemen
   a. are totally dependent on oil revenues.
   b. have increased economic opportunities for women.
   c. have changed little since ancient times.
   d. have broken with Islamic traditions.

20. _____ Turkey, Iran, and Cyprus are different from other Southwest Asian
   countries because they are not
   a. Muslim countries.
   b. Arab countries.
   c. oil-rich countries.
   d. modern industrial countries.

GRAPHIC STUDY

Directions: Use the circle graph to answer the following questions.
Write your answers on the lines provided.

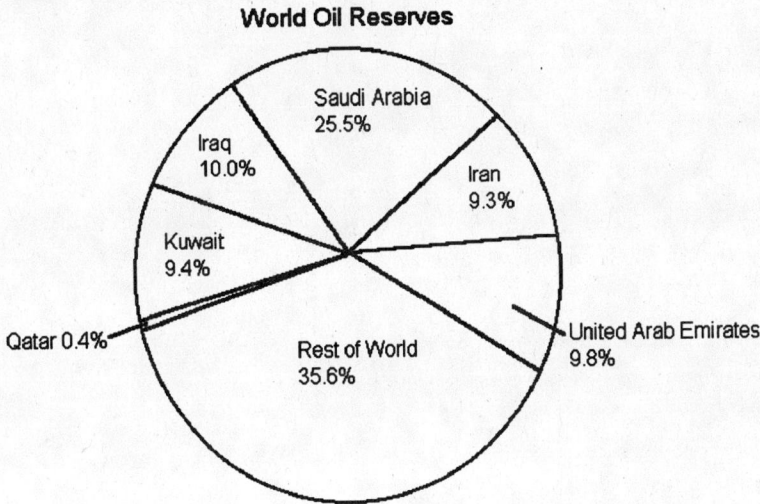

World Oil Reserves

Saudi Arabia
25.5%

Iraq
10.0%

Iran
9.3%

Kuwait
9.4%

Qatar 0.4%

Rest of World
35.6%

United Arab Emirates
9.8%

Total estimated proven reserves of oil (1990): 1,001,571,623 (1,000 bbl)

21. What does the whole circle represent?

   _____

22. What percentage of the world's proven oil reserves is located in the
   Persian Gulf nations? Which country in the Persian Gulf has the greatest
   share of oil reserves?

   _____

23. Based on the data in this graph, how would you describe the global
   distribution of oil?

   _____

SHORT ANSWER

C. Critical Thinking
Directions: Answer the following questions on the back of this paper or on a separate sheet of paper.

24. Synthesizing Information Southwest Asia is a region dominated by desert. Explain why some areas in this region are richer in vegetation and denser in population than others.

25. Identifying Assumptions During World War I, many groups made differing assumptions about the status of Palestine after the war. Identify the assumptions held by Jews, Arabs, Great Britain, and France and the agreements on which these assumptions were based.

26. Predicting Consequences What consequences might oil-rich countries on the Arabian Peninsula face when their oil reserves run out? Consider possible economic, social, and political consequences.

Answer Key   Unit 7

FILL-IN-THE-BLANK

1. ayatollahs

2. drip irrigation

3. falaj system

4. Hajj

5. monotheism

6. prophet

7. mosques

8. Zionists

9. anarchy

10. infrastructure

11. mandates

MULTIPLE CHOICE

12. a

13. c

14. b

15. d

16. a

17. b

18. c

19. c

20. b

GRAPHIC STUDY

21. world oil reserves

22. 64.4 percent; Saudi Arabia

23. uneven, with almost two thirds located in the Persian Gulf region

SHORT ANSWER

24. Some areas in the desert region are oases, created by underground springs that have surfaced. Oases may have enough water to support lush green plants, a small cluster of trees, or a small village or town. Rivers in the region deposit soil, making nearby lands fertile. Mountains also create pockets of fertile land in this arid region. Coastal lands in Syria, for example, receive enough rainfall for plants and crops to flourish. The most densely populated areas in the region are areas near reliable sources of water.

25. Both the Arabs and the Zionists assumed that Great Britain would give them Palestine as a homeland after World War I, but France and Great Britain assumed that they would continue to control most of the region. The Arabs based their assumption on Great Britain's promise to allow the creation of one large, independent Arab country. In exchange, the Arabs supported Great Britain in its fight against the Ottomans. France and Great Britain assumed that, based on the Sykes-Picot Agreement, the independent Arab state would be limited to what it is today—Saudi Arabia and Yemen—and that France would control Syria and Great Britain would control Palestine and Iraq. The Zionists based their assumption on the Balfour Declaration of 1917, in which the British government stated its support for the creation of a Jewish homeland in Palestine as long as the rights of Arabs were not violated.

26. If the countries on the Arabian peninsula have diversified their industries, the economic consequences would not be severe. Politically, without vast oil reserves, the Persian Gulf nations would lose their strong bargaining position in world affairs. Socially, many foreign workers would leave some of these countries where they often outnumber citizens. In turn, countries on the Arabian Peninsula might return to a more traditional culture.

Unit 8   Africa

MATCHING

A. Vocabulary
Directions: Match the descriptions with the terms. Write the correct
letter in each blank. You will not use all the terms.

a. deforestation
b. landlocked
c. land redistribution
d. apartheid
e. leaching
f. cataract
g. inland delta
h. strategic value
i. malnutrition
j. villagization
k. desertification
l. shifting agriculture
m. forage
n. refugee
o. mercenary
p. ancestor

1. _____ dissolving and washing away of nutrients contained in the soil

2. _____ practice of preparing and growing crops on a site for only a year
or two and then moving to another site

3. _____ without access to the ocean

4. _____ area of lakes, creeks, and swamps away from an ocean

5. _____ waterfall

6. _____ system under which South Africa's blacks were segregated

7. _____ food for grazing animals

8. _____ disease caused by not having a healthy diet

9. _____ act of forcing people to move into towns and to work on collective
farms

10. _____ person who leaves his or her home to escape danger or unfair
treatment

11. _____ government policy under which land is taken from those who have
plenty and given to those who have little or none

MULTIPLE CHOICE

B. Key Geographic Concepts and Skills
Directions: Write the letter of the correct ending or answer in the blank.

12. _____ Which of the following statements does not accurately describe the African rain forests?
    a. The rain forest has poor soil.
    b. The rain forest presented a barrier to European exploration.
    c. The rain forest provides habitats for many plant and animal species.
    d. The rain forest is a nonrenewable resource.

13. _____ Most of the people south of the Sahara live in
    a. large cities.   b. rural villages.
    c. the Sahel.   d. the Kalahari region.

14. _____ The Sahel is best described as
    a. the driest desert region in Africa.
    b. mostly savanna with a semi-arid climate.
    c. a transitional region between the Equator and rain forest to the south.
    d. a dense rain forest on Africa's western coast.

15. _____ All of the following characteristics describe one or more of the old Sahel empires—Ghana, Mali, and Songhai—except
    a. a center of Islamic learning.
    b. a thriving economy based on trade.
    c. a European colony.
    d. an intellectual center.

16. _____ The Sahel nations face all of the following challenges except
    a. desertification.
    b. developing their natural resources.
    c. a harsh environment.
    d. lack of foreign aid.

17. _____ The economies of the West African countries face all of the following problems except
    a. lower value of exports than imports.
    b. a heavy debt burden.
    c. unsuccessful agriculture.
    d. lack of natural resources.

18. _____ Zaire in Central Africa and Nigeria in West Africa are alike in that both countries
    a. have lower standards of living than other countries in their regions.
    b. are models of success for other African nations.
    c. have experienced civil strife since gaining independence.
    d. lack natural resources.

© Prentice-Hall, Inc.

19. _____ Which of the following statements about Kenya is not true?
a. The most fertile farmland in Kenya is located in the central highlands on either side of the Great Rift Valley.
b. After gaining independence from the British in 1963, Kenya experienced solid economic growth based mostly on agriculture.
c. Because of an emphasis on cash crops, Kenya has not been able to grow enough food to feed its people.
d. Kenya's population has been steadily declining since the 1980s.

20. _____ Which of the following did not contribute to the end of apartheid in South Africa?
a. South Africa's racial policies were criticized by the international community.
b. Many nations restricted their trade with South Africa because of its discrimination policies against blacks.
c. White South Africans generally supported apartheid.
d. A growing number of white South Africans began calling for an end to apartheid.

SHORT ANSWER

Directions: Number the statements below so that they form a coherent essay.

21. _____ As a result, countries often competed fiercely with one another to take over the richest areas of Africa.
_____ They needed raw materials for their factories and new markets in which to sell the goods they manufactured.
_____ In the 1800s, European nations were industrializing at a very rapid pace.
_____ One of the places where such raw materials and markets existed was Africa.

GRAPHIC STUDY

Directions: Use the map to answer the following questions. Write your answers on the lines provided.

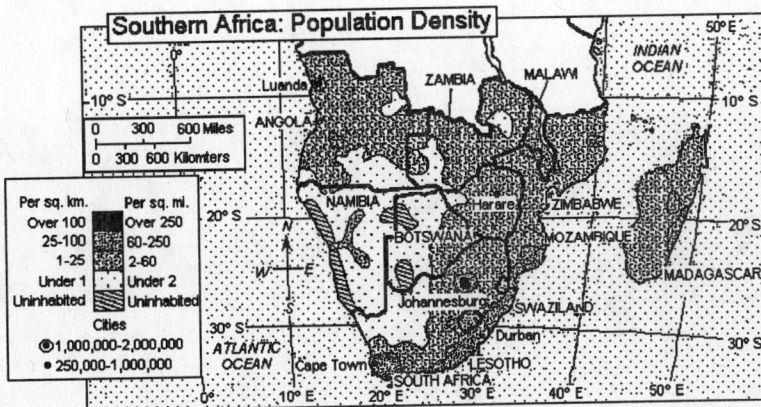
Southern Africa: Population Density

22. What part of southern Africa has the lowest population density? Why do you think this is so?

_____

23. Identify two areas of southern Africa that have population densities of 60-250 people per square mile (25-100 per sq. km.).

_____

SHORT ANSWER

C. Critical Thinking
Directions: Answer the following questions on the back of this paper or on a separate sheet of paper.

24. Synthesizing Information What parallel changes in the climate and vegetation patterns would you find as you traveled from the Equator toward the Sahara in the north and from the Equator toward the Kalahari in the south?

25. Perceiving Cause-and-Effect Relationships What was the link between trade and the development of the ancient African kingdom of Ghana?

Answer Key   Unit 8

MATCHING

1. e	2. l
3. b	4. g
5. f	6. d
7. m	8. i
9. j	10. n
11. c	

MULTIPLE CHOICE

12. d	13. b
14. b	15. c
16. d	17. d
18. c	19. d
20. c	

SHORT ANSWER

21. 4, 2, 1, 3

GRAPHIC STUDY

22. the southwestern part because the region is mainly desert and semi-arid land

23. Possible answers: the southeastern coast, the area around Cape Town, the east coast of Madagascar, southern Malawi

SHORT ANSWER

24. Around the Equator, the climate is hot and rainy and the vegetation is rain forest. In the areas just north and south of the rain forest, the climate has a dry season and the vegetation is grassland. These savanna regions become increasingly drier the farther they are from the rain forest. Areas to the north and south of these savannas are desert regions with little rainfall and only desert vegetation.

25. Because of its central location, the trade routes across the Sahel became a bridge between the Mediterranean coast and the rest of Africa. Merchants from the north brought salt to the Sahel region to trade. They sought ivory, slaves, and, most important of all, gold. The Sahel chiefs found that they could grow wealthy by taxing the traders passing through their kingdoms. The kingdom of Ghana was built around this trade.

Unit 9   South Asia

FILL-IN-THE-BLANK

A. Vocabulary
Directions: Complete each sentence by writing the correct term in the blank. You will not use all the terms.

malnutrition
buffer state
nonviolent resistance
boycott
deforestation
partition
purdah
alluvial plains
joint family system
subcontinent
cottage industries
hydroelectric power

1. The Indus, the Ganges, and the Brahmaputra rivers have formed rich _____ along their banks.

2. Overpopulation and natural disasters have led to _____ in Bangladesh.

3. Electricity produced by the movement of water is called _____.

4. In 1947, British and Indian leaders decided to _____ the subcontinent into two separate states.

5. People who produce goods in their own homes are engaged in _____.

6. The seven countries on the Indian _____ make up the area of the world known as South Asia.

7. The _____ of Sri Lanka, in which two thirds of its rain forest has disappeared, is caused by farming and development.

8. The sale of British cloth in India fell sharply as the result of the Indian _____ of that product.

9. Mohandas Gandhi used _____ as an effective weapon against oppression.

10. Afghanistan once served as a(n) _____ between Russia and British-controlled India.

MULTIPLE CHOICE

B. Key Geographic Concepts and Skills
Directions: Write the letter of the correct ending in the blank.

11. _____ All of the following statements accurately describe the monsoons
of South Asia except:
a. The winter monsoon brings dry air from mainland Asia to the
subcontinent.
b. Both winter and summer monsoons release heavy rains as they move
inland.
c. The summer monsoon often causes floods and landslides.
d. The Western Ghats prevent the monsoon rains from reaching India's
interior.

12. _____ The majority of South Asia's workers
a. depend on government jobs to earn a living.
b. belong to the middle class and work in service industries.
c. depend directly on the land for their livelihood and survival.
d. live in urban areas and are employed in manufacturing.

13. _____ Most of the people in South Asia practice Hinduism or
a. Buddhism.   b. Islam.
c. Christianity.   d. Sikhism.

14. _____ Because Hindus and Muslims could not agree on a form of government
for an independent India,
a. British and Indian leaders divided the subcontinent into the nations
of India and Pakistan.
b. Mohandas Gandhi led the Indian people in a massive boycott of British
textiles.
c. British and Indian leaders took steps to narrow the economic
differences between the two religious groups.
d. violence erupted between the Bengalis in the east and the
Urdu-speaking people in the west.

15. _____ Mass migrations followed the creation of India and Pakistan in
1947 when
a. Britain established Indian-run provinces.
b. India's textile industry disappeared.
c. Indian Hindus fled to Bangladesh.
d. Pakistan's Hindus fled to India and India's Muslims fled to Pakistan.

16. _____ West Pakistan and East Pakistan were divided by all of the
following except
a. 1,100 miles (1,770 km) of Indian territory.
b. ethnic and language differences.
c. economic and political differences.
d. religious differences.

© Prentice-Hall, Inc.

17. _____ A major change in India in recent years has been the
   a. decline of the middle class.
   b. return to agriculture and to traditional ways of life.
   c. growth of an urban middle class.
   d. disappearance of a wealthy class.

18. _____ All of the following statements about Pakistan are true except:
   a. Pakistan is a dry and rugged country.
   b. The Urdu language, spoken by a majority of Pakistan's people, helps
      to unite the country.
   c. Most of Pakistan's people live in farming villages in the Indus River
      basin.
   d. Temperatures in Pakistan are generally warm or hot.

19. _____ Nepal and Bhutan are located
   a. in the Himalayas.
   b. on the narrow coastal plain at the foot of the Eastern Ghats.
   c. on the northern edge of the Deccan Plateau.
   d. between the Khyber Pass and the Indus River.

GRAPHIC STUDY

Directions: Use the climate graph to answer the following questions.
Write your answers on the lines provided.

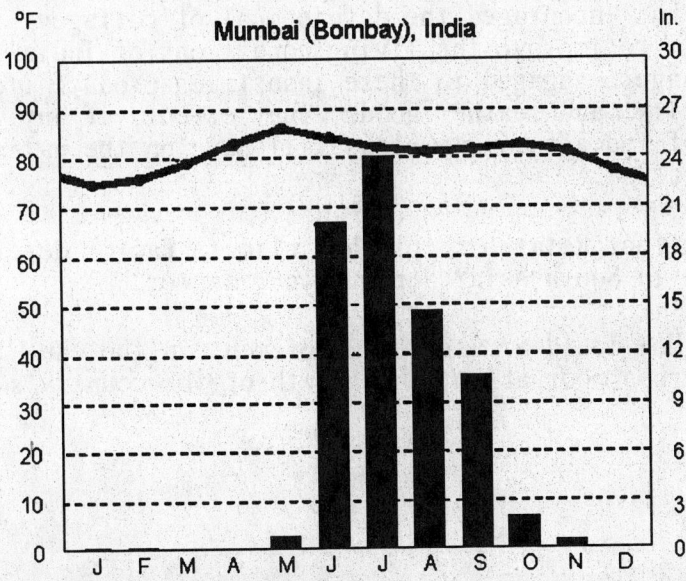

Mumbai (Bombay), India

Line graph shows average temperature.
Bar graph shows average precipitation.

20. What information is presented in the graph?

_____

21. How would you describe the average yearly temperature in Bombay?

_____

22. How many months of the year does Bombay receive less than three inches of rain?

_____

23. During which months does Bombay receive most of its rainfall? What climate factor produces Bombay's pattern of annual precipitation?

_____

SHORT ANSWER

C. Critical Thinking
Directions: Answer the following questions on the back of this paper or on a separate sheet of paper.

24. Predicting Consequences Read the following passage. Then, answer the question below. Two important developments have taken place in India in recent years. First, the production of consumer goods has risen as India's growing urban middle class has created a demand for products such as televisions, videocassette recorders, and cars. At the same time the Indian government has encouraged the development of cottage industries in an effort to improve the living conditions of India's rural population. Villagers engaged in these industries produce items such as textiles, jewelry, and leather goods. What effect, if any, do you think the growth of India's middle class will have on the nation's rural cottage industries?

25. Perceiving Cause-and-Effect Relationships What climate factor determines where most people live in South Asia? Support your answer.

26. Determining Relevance How would a massive improvement in the education of India's rural and urban poor affect the growth of the country's industries?

Answer Key   Unit 9

FILL-IN-THE-BLANK

1. alluvial plains

2. malnutrition

3. hydroelectric power

4. partition   5. cottage industries

6. subcontinent

7. deforestation

8. boycott   9. nonviolent resistance

10. buffer state

MULTIPLE CHOICE

11. b   12. c

13. b   14. a

15. d   16. d

17. c   18. b

19. a

GRAPHIC STUDY

20. average temperatures and precipitation in Bombay

21. warm, ranging from 75° to 86° F

22. 8 months

23. June, July, August, September; the summer monsoon

SHORT ANSWER

24. Continued growth of India's urban middle class
    might encourage the growth of the nation's
    cottage industries, as these industries could
    provide some of the products desired by the
    middle class, such as textiles and jewelry.

25. The availability of water determines where most people live in South Asia. Most South Asians, who work on small farms and grow their own food, depend on water for their livelihood and survival. The greatest population is concentrated in areas that receive abundant rainfall, such as the coastal regions and northeastern India and Bangladesh. Because most of Afghanistan and Pakistan are desert regions, most of the people in these countries live in river valleys.

26. Massive improvement in the education of India's rural and urban poor would promote the growth of the country's industries by providing the skilled workers necessary for such growth.

Unit 10   East Asia and the Pacific World

MATCHING

A. Vocabulary
Directions: Match the descriptions with the terms. Write the correct
letter in each blank. You will not use all the terms.

a. cyclone
b. typhoon
c. quotas
d. martial law
e. lagoon
f. tariffs
g. ice shelves
h. provisional
i. paddies
j. atoll
k. pack ice
l. seismographs
m. warlords
n. homogeneous

1. _____ type of law imposed on citizens during periods of strict military control

2. _____ sheets of frozen water extending over the ocean

3. _____ large, floating expanse of icebergs and ice mixed together

4. _____ regional leaders who maintain their own armies

5. _____ Australian term for a hurricane

6. _____ shallow body of water with an outlet to the ocean

7. _____ type of government that exists on a temporary basis

8. _____ machines that register movement in the earth's crust

9. _____ type of population in which people share a similar heritage

10. _____ fixed total quantities that are allowed or admitted

11. _____ wet lands on which rice is grown

MULTIPLE CHOICE

B. Key Geographic Concepts and Skills
Directions: Write the letter of the correct ending in the blank.

12. _____ The frequent occurrence of volcanic and seismic activity in East Asia is a result of the region's
    a. nearness to the Equator.
    b. mountainous terrain.
    c. location along the boundaries of tectonic plates.
    d. often violent summer weather.

13. _____ Compared to South Korea, North Korea has
    a. a greater abundance of mineral resources.
    b. a larger population.
    c. less mountainous terrain.
    d. a more developed economy.

14. _____ The rise of Japanese imperialism can be attributed to
    a. Japan's alliance with Nazi Germany during World War II.
    b. Japan's desire to emulate Western societies, particularly the United States.
    c. the overwhelming success of the Japanese economy.
    d. Japan's lack of natural resources, which fed its desire to conquer nations with valuable raw materials.

15. _____ The countries of Singapore, Malaysia, and Thailand are similar in that
    a. they were French colonies until the 1950s.
    b. their governments are controlled by Communists.
    c. their economies are primarily based on subsistence farming.
    d. all have successful economies.

16. _____ The economies of Vietnam, Cambodia, and Laos are in poor condition largely as a result of
    a. years of frequent and destructive volcanic activity.
    b. the defeat of French rule.
    c. their sole dependence on rice production as a source of national income.
    d. upheaval and destruction caused by years of war.

17. _____ All of the following statements accurately describe Australia except:
    a. Australia is the earth's flattest and driest continent.
    b. Australia's population is made up of European and Southeast Asian immigrants and their descendants.
    c. Most Australians live along the eastern and southeastern coasts.
    d. Australia is one of the most densely populated countries in the world.

18. _____ In the first half of the twentieth century, territorial claims to Antarctica were
a. pie-shaped wedges that met at the South Pole.
b. made only by the United States, Russia, Great Britain, and Norway.
c. heavily disputed because of the difficulty of setting boundaries.
d. abandoned because the continent appeared to be without significant resources.

19. _____ The high and low islands in the Pacific Island region differ in that the
a. high islands have a warm tropical climate and the low islands are mostly frigid and barren.
b. high islands are the tops of underwater mountains and the low islands are atolls.
c. high islands are dry and mountainous and the low islands support agriculture.
d. high islands are in the north and the low islands are in the south.

20. _____ The first Australians were the
a. Maori.
b. Melanesians.
c. Aborigines.
d. Europeans.

GRAPHIC STUDY

Directions: Use the graphs to answer the following questions. Write your answers on the lines provided.

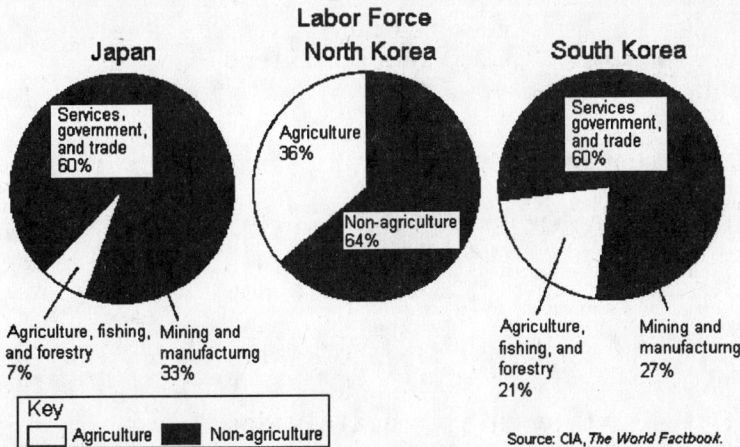

Labor Force

Japan
Services, government, and trade 60%
Agriculture, fishing, and forestry 7%
Mining and manufacturing 33%

North Korea
Agriculture 36%
Non-agriculture 64%

South Korea
Services government, and trade 60%
Agriculture, fishing, and forestry 21%
Mining and manufacturing 27%

Key
Agriculture   Non-agriculture

Source: CIA, *The World Factbook.*

21. Based on the information given in the graphs, which country is the most agricultural? Explain.

_____

22. Based on the information given in the graphs, which country would you expect to be the most developed? Explain.

SHORT ANSWER

C. Critical Thinking
Directions: Answer the following questions on the back of this paper or on a separate sheet of paper.

23. Drawing Inferences Based on what you have learned about East Asia, what can you infer about the effects of colonization and cultural divisions on a nation's success and prosperity? Support your answer.

24. Expressing Problems Clearly Explain the conflicts that exist between China and Taiwan and between China and Hong Kong.

25. Making Comparisons In what ways is the history of the Aborigines similar to that of the Native Americans?

Answer Key   Unit 10

MATCHING

1. d   2. g

3. k   4. m

5. a   6. e

7. h   8. l

9. n   10. c

11. i

MULTIPLE CHOICE

12. c   13. a

14. d   15. d

16. d   17. d

18. a   19. b

20. c

GRAPHIC STUDY

21. North Korea. It has the highest percentage of agricultural workers.

22. Japan. It has the highest percentage of workers in industry, manufacturing, and trade, and the lowest in agriculture.

SHORT ANSWER

23. Contributing to a nations' success and prosperity are cultural unity within a nation's boundaries and the absence of colonization by foreign powers. Both Thailand and Japan, neither of which has ever been controlled by foreign interests, have successful economies and strong national identities based on the homogeneity of their populations. On the other hand, countries with less successful economic development—such as Myanmar, Vietnam, and Cambodia—have suffered greatly from the effects of colonization and ethnic conflict.

24. Taiwan and Hong Kong each have a different relationship with China. The government of Taiwan was established by Chiang Kai-shek as a provisional government after Chiang's Nationalist forces were defeated by the Communists. Taiwan has become a successful industrialized nation, but it has very little contact with China. Hong Kong had been a British colony. Although Hong Kong and China have long been interdependent for trade and economic development, many of the residents of Hong Kong are fearful of the future.

25. Like the Native Americans, the Aborigines are the native people of a continent that was colonized by Europeans. In both countries, the native people were killed and driven from their land by colonists. Disease carried by Europeans decimated the native populations in both countries.

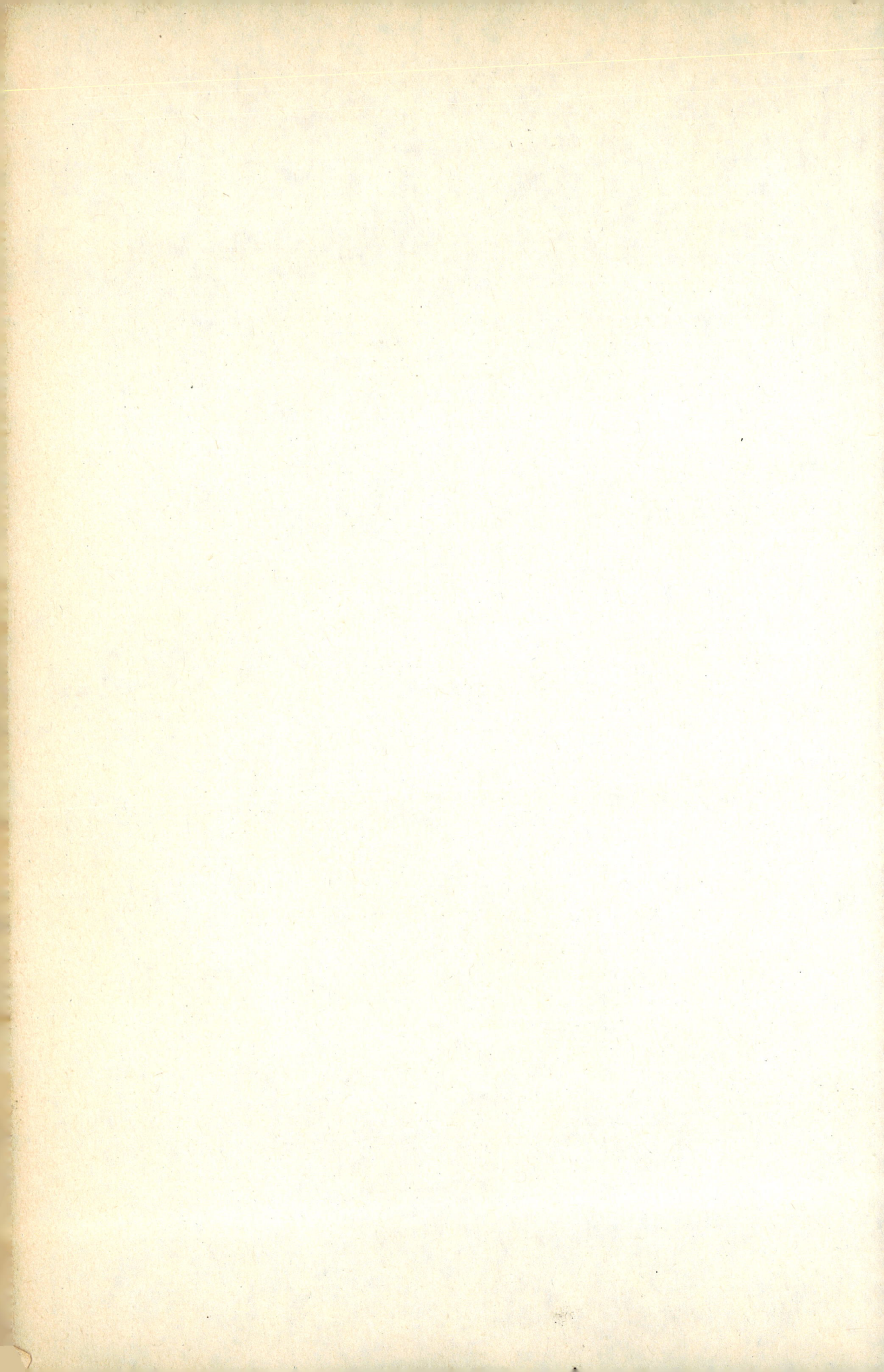